Women in Contemporary Culture
Roles and Identities in France and Spain

Edited by
Lesley Twomey

intellect™
Bristol, UK
Portland, OR, USA

First Published in Great Britain in Hardback in 2000 by
Intellect Books, PO Box 862, Bristol BS99 1DE, UK

First Published in USA in 2000 by
Intellect Books, ISBS, 5824 N.E. Hassalo St, Portland, Oregon 97213-3644, USA

Consulting Editor: Robin Beecroft
Copy Editor: Jeremy Lockyer

A catalogue record for this book is available from the British Library

ISBN 1-84150-040-2

Printed and bound in Great Britain by Cromwell Press, Wiltshire

Contents

Women and Politics

Women, Religion and Politics

Women and Work

Women and Feminisms

Women and their Writing

Contributors

Jean Burrell teaches French in the School of Languages at Oxford Brookes University, where she was Principal Lecturer until her recent (semi) retirement. In the second half of the 1990s she was part of a cross-disciplinary research team exploring the implementation of EU equal opportunities legislation in four member states. Her interest in women's studies also extends to literature.

Mercedes Carbayo-Abengózar is Senior Lecturer in Spanish at Nottingham Trent University. She was awarded the VIII Premio de Investigación Victoria Kent at the University of Malaga and has published her doctoral thesis as *Buscando un lugar entre mujeres: buceo en la España de Carmen Martín Gaite*. She has developed her research to publish on Spanish feminism and on the interface between language and women's identity in the Franco period.

Jacky Collins is Lecturer in Spanish Studies at the University of Northumbria at Newcastle. Her main area of research is lesbian cultures in contemporary Spain. She is contributor to Contemporary Spanish Cultural Studies by Barry Jordan and Rikki Morgan-Tamosun.

Sylvie Gambaudo is Lecturer in European Studies at the University of Durham, Stockton Campus. Her research focuses on the crisis of identity and the work of Julia Kristeva and she has published a series of articles exploring Kristevaís psychoanalytical theories.

Alison Holland is Senior Lecturer in French Studies at the University of Northumbria at Newcastle. Her Ph.D. thesis focuses on the textual strategies Simone de Beauvoir uses in her fiction and she has published a series of articles focusing on madness and writing practice. She is currently preparing a revised translation of *Les Belles Images*. In addition to her work on Simone de Beauvoir, her research interests include feminism in France and feminist theory.

Vanessa Knights teaches contemporary Hispanic literary and cultural studies and is also active in the Centre for Gender and Women's Studies at the University of Newcastle upon Tyne. She has published a monograph on the contemporary Spanish writer Rosa Montero, is co-author of *A History of Spanish Writing 1939-1990s* and has written on Spanish feminisms, contemporary Spanish women writers and science fiction. She is currently researching Latin American popular music.

Sheila Perry is Reader in French Studies at the University of Northumbria at Newcastle. Her research interests include television and politics in French, political communication and women and politics. She is the editor of a number of books about France including *Voices of France: Social, Political and Cultural Identity*; *Aspects of Contemporary France*; *The Media in France* and *Media Developments and Cultural Change*.

William Smith is Head of French Studies at the University of Northumbria at Newcastle. He first researched into aspects of the Catholic novel in France, with special reference to Henri Queffélec. In recent years, the focus of his research has shifted from the literary to the historical, in particular the interaction between the Catholic Church and the Vichy régime and the interface between the Church and the extreme Right in France.

Monica Threlfall is Senior Lecturer in Politics in the Department of European Studies, Loughborough University. She is editor of *Mapping the Women's Movement: Feminist Politics and Social Transformation in the North* (Verso 1996) and of *Consensus Politics in Spain: Insider Perspectives* (Intellect 2000). She has published widely on gender and politics in Spain and is currently preparing a co-authored book with Christine Cousins and Celia Valiente for Frank Cass & Co.

Lesley Twomey is Head of Spanish Studies at the University of Northumbria at Newcastle. She first researched on the theme of the Immaculate Conception in fifteenth-century poetry. Her research now focuses on misogynist writing, as well as the interface between the female author and female reader in conventual writing. She has developed her research interests to include contemporary women's writing and misogynist discourse in the modern Church.

Tables

Preface

Victoria Camps' intuition leads her to conclude that the twenty-first century will be the Century of Women, in which women are called to build on the achievements of their mothers and grandmothers. Alternatively, it might be more appropriate to coin the term 'Century of Women' to mark the century just gone, when a women's agenda was brought to the fore and when so many women, known and unknown, struggled to bring about legislative and institutional change. In either case, we cannot fail to see that we stand at an important moment for taking stock of what has gone before and for assessing what remains to be achieved. We can agree that the last century has brought formal equality, symbolized by universal suffrage and enshrined in Constitution and law. However, formal equality has been proved wanting: equal pay remains an issue, abortion may be on the statute books but still remains unacceptable to many sectors of society, whilst parity and the struggle to achieve it, has moved to the top of the agenda. This book celebrates the achievements of the past Century of Women and at the same time turns towards the new century. Whether that will also be a 'Century of Women' remains to be enacted and written. The future beckons with its opportunities and hopes of all that is to be consolidated and achieved.

This book has been brought about with support for research in terms of finances and time from the School of Modern Languages, University of Northumbria at Newcastle, for which I am very grateful. Without the support of the School, this volume would not have been possible. Its conception came from ideas generated at a research group in the School of Modern Languages which takes gender as its focus. The ideas generated by that collaborative venture eventually came to fruition in this volume.

Support has also generously been offered by the Association for Contemporary Iberian Studies whose allocation of small grants for publication of research in Iberian subjects provided another very valuable source of support for this publication. I am very grateful to the Association for their support for this project.

I wish to take this opportunity to thank colleagues in the School of Modern Languages, particularly Sheila Perry and Alison Holland for their support and helpful ideas. I would like to thank Sue Hart for her patient assistance in putting together the final text especially when those technical glitches came into force. Thanks also go to Enrique and Amelia for their care and support on my visits to the *Biblioteca (Discoteca) Nacional*. My family warrants special thanks, as always, for everything they do, especially when 'the going gets tough'. I can promise them I will be ready now to pick up my share of the double shift working day (*doble jornada*) – for a while at least.

> *This book is dedicated to the three generations of women in my life,*
> *Pearl, Kathryn and Becky*

Abbreviations for the political parties

(* indicates the party no longer exists)

Spain

AP*	*Alianza Popular*	Popular Alliance – (*now PP*)
PP	*Partido Popular*	Peoples' Party – (*Spanish centre right*)
PSOE	*Partido Socialista Obrero Español*	Spanish Socialist Party (*left*)
UCD*	*Unión de Centro Democrático*	Union of the Democratic Centre – (*centre right*)
CP*	*Coalición Popular*	Popular Coalition
PCE	*Partido Comunista Español*	Spanish Communist Party
CiU	*Convergència i Unió*	Convergence and Union – (*Catalan centre right*)
PNV	*Partido Nacional Vasco*	Basque National Party
EE	*Euskadiko Eskerra*	Basque Left
EA	*Euskadiko Alkartasuna*	Basque Solidarity
HB	*Herri Batasuna*	People's Unity – (*Basque separatist*)
BNG	*Bloque Nacional Gallego*	Galician National Alliance – (*Galician nationalist*)
IU	*Izquierda Unida*	United Left
CDS*	*Centro Democrático y Social*	Democratic and Social Centre
PDP*	*Partido Demócrata Popular*	People's Democratic Party
PSA	*Partido Socialista Andaluz*	Andalusian Socialist Party

France

FN	*Front National*	National Front
MN	*Mouvement National*	National Movement
PR	*Parti Républicain*	Republican Party
RPR	*Rassemblement Pour la République*	Rally for the Republic
UDF	*Union pour la démocratie*	Union for French Democracy
UDR	*Union des Démocrates pour la Republique*	Union of Democrats for the Republic

Introduction

Lesley K. Twomey

When they are constantly told that women in the past achieved nothing of any great or lasting value, it is in order to discourage them; what is being said is basically: be sensible, you will never achieve anything of real or lasting value so don't waste your time trying.

Simone de Beauvoir

The aim of this comparative study is to present a range of aspects of women's experience in order to exemplify how women construct their identities in the public sphere, as the new century begins. The book chooses to address a range of different aspects of women's lives and experiences, and to juxtapose or interweave them. In this way, the structure of the book could be seen as corresponding to the complexities of living in contemporary society, as women seek to come to terms with their roles as workers, as voters, as campaigners, as members of society with rights and expectations, as writers and as thinkers. To highlight issues which impact on women's roles and identities at the end of the 1990s and start of the new century, five interrelated themes have been identified as representative of that moment. Political behaviour and activism and features of the world of work take their place alongside those ideologies emanating from institutions which define the way women's roles and identities are conceived: the political parties and the Church. Women also define their own identities and roles through their feminist theorizing and their writing. These themes correspond broadly to those identified by Victoria Camps in her *El siglo de las mujeres*, where she identifies that politics, work, moral values along with education should be the objectives of a new feminism.[1]

In their introduction to *Culture and Gender in Nineteenth-century Spain*, Lou Charnou-Deutsch and Jo Labanyi point out the essentialist dangers inherent in theorizing about 'women' and their warning is timely to guard against addressing features of a presumed collective group, 'Spanish women' or 'French women'. In reality there are huge differences within each country, between lives in rural Spain and France and between lives unfolding against the backdrop of major metropoli like Madrid or Paris. Anny Brooksbank Jones in her *Women in Contemporary Spain*, cites the sociologist Luis Garrido, to show that there are even more complexities to be wrestled with. In fact, two biographies for Spanish women have to be posited: 'a traditional one, associated with women formed under Franco and a modern one, associated with those who have grown up during the transition and democracy periods.'[2] With all these complexities and caveats in mind, the intention of the book is not, then, to provide a definitive statement about women in France and in Spain, as though they were a homogenous category undifferentiated one from another by class, age or life experience, as though they could be defined through a series of common elements, but to set out examples of

3

current issues which affect a variety of groups of women and which correspond to a particular moment in contemporary culture: the end of the twentieth century and beginning of the twenty-first.

France has a long-established record in defending the democratic rights of its citizens, although as Sheila Perry and Sue Hart argue, those citizens are conceived as masculine subjects. Those rights are enshrined in those noble words 'Liberty, Equality and Fraternity'. Spain, on the other hand, is a fledgling democracy whose democratic Constitution dates from only 1978 and we might expect it to lag far behind its Pyrennean neighbour in implementing rights for all citizens. However, as Perry and Hart show, until January 2000, contrary to expectation, France's record on encouraging equality of representation in political life had been worse than Spain's, a latecomer to European democracy.

As Perry and Hart indicate, France had the lowest number of women MPs in all member states of the European Union in 1997, as opposed to Spain's creditable sixth position, following the elections of March 1996 when 22% of the elected deputies were women in the Lower Chamber. At the time of going to press, it remains to be seen what the Spanish elections of 12 March will bring for women candidates on the lists. Perry and Hart show how increasing the number of female candidates had proved virtually impossible against the backdrop of multiple office-holding at local, regional and national level and against a selection process which relies on perceived ability and individual personal profile as well as personal contacts rather than on objective criteria. They show how, by the enshrinement of parity within its Constitution, France has made a qualititative leap forward, and can congratulate itself on stealing a march on those non-Scandinavian EU countries who have yet to bring parity into effect. From now on, all French political parties will now be obliged to include a high quota of women candidates on electoral lists. For visible improvements to women's chances of being elected, as Perry and Hart note, France will have to wait until the next round of elections in 2001. Spain, in contrast, has opted to promote quotas of elected and electable women, although only in those parties which support positive action to redress the balance of an electorate with 51% women but only 18% representing them in Senate and Congress.[3] Monica Threlfall charts the progress of the Spanish Left in increasing the number of candidates at all levels of political representation. She explores how a traditionally male-dominated party like the Spanish Socialist Party came to adopt quotas for women candidates, setting these quotas initially at 25%, but later increasing them to 40%. In Spain, as opposed to France since January 2000, parties are not obliged to encourage female candidature. This means that, although the parties to the left of the political spectrum have made good progress in making sure that the number of women in the Spanish Parliament increases, parties to the right, like the party of Government, José María Aznar's People's Party, have not been willing to promote the inclusion of female candidates by means of a quota system and, indeed, have been opposed to so doing. The number of women candidates and MPs elected to represent right-wing parties now lags behind those representing left-wing parties, as Threlfall's detailed data reveals and this, both in terms of numbers of candidates and in terms of percentages of women making it through the system to the Congress of

Deputies. These two chapters provide an excellent counterpoint one to the other as they explore routes to changing the composition of national parliaments: France on the road to parity and Spain adopting the quota system.

Religion and politics are inextricably bound together in two chapters which explore women's issues from a traditionalist perspective. They both show how religious concepts, ideologies and moral dictates continue to impact on political life both in France and Spain. William Smith, in his consideration of the images of women central to integrist Catholic and right-wing parties examines the function of female icons, such as the Virgin Mary, Theresa of Lisieux or Joan of Arc, propagated by right-wing parties in France, in defining qualities appropriate to women. Smith argues that these icons impact on right-wing women's personal morality as well as on the nature of their political lives, regularly subordinate to their husband's. He shows in this way both how women in parties on the extreme Right are defined but also how they define themselves. His chapter, like Lesley Twomey's, explores the interface between religious concepts and political beliefs and draws, in the same way that she does on the concept of family values as a context for debate. Twomey's partner study shows how the Church has capitalized on modern media in order to put its anti-abortion message across. She also shows in which ways the Church has politicized its doctrine and mobilized the faithful in the context of a moral crusade to save the family. Debate on abortion in Spain has gone on for the best part of a century and is closely related to the Civil War in collective memory. The debate continues to be a live issue even in the current election campaign (March 2000). Both the Socialist Party and the United Left are manoevring the debate away from a widening of the existing abortion law to a new position. Their current position is that abortion should cease being a punishable offence at all under the Criminal Code. In political life, the abortion issue has the power to cause hackles to rise at the end of the 1990s and leads, as both Twomey and Smith show, to remarkably consistent images of feminists, pro-abortionists and other liberated women being propagated and decried in Catholic publications in both Spain and France.

Women's working lives are explored in two very different contexts by Jean Burrell and by Lesley Twomey. In the case of France, it is already well established that women are more likely to be unemployed than their male colleagues, more likely to be in low-paid jobs, more likely to be working part-time yet there have been considerable legislative advances, particularly those of the early 1980s.[4] In Spain, articles in a range of new laws, such as the Workers' Statute of 1980, have sought to ensure that there is no discrimination between male and female workers, despite this in the realm of paid employment is it still the case, at the end of the 1990s and at the start of the new century, that women are the 'strangers in Paradise'?[5] Burrell has undertaken empirical research amongst workers in the hotel trade and discovers that the prospects of female workers are worse than those of their male colleagues. She shows that women tend to be confined to certain feminized areas of work, such as housekeeping, whilst their presence amongst the elite professions, such as that of chef, is negligible. Twomey counterpoints an examination of the limiting factors on women managers in Spain with a contemporary novel, written by Lucía Etxebarría, in which the novelist constructs a plurality of identities, including professional, for her women characters. From a very different starting point, Twomey also points to the fact that women's presence in promoted posts is limited. She explores issues which sociological studies have shown to be important to women managers in present-day Spain and she examines how these contribute to a mythologization of work in the novel. Burrell explores women at work in rural France and her study uncovers very similar challenges to those facing women in the management sphere in Spain. From these very different perspectives, a similar picture emerges of differentiated pay, undervaluing of feminized sectors of employ and poor opportunities in the promotion stakes. It might be agreed that whilst primary human rights have in the main been achieved, that is to say those relating to politics and civil rights, it is in the second class of rights, those relating to economic and social rights that action is still required from the state. Although Victoria Camps (p.41) has pointed to this situation with regard to Spain, the two studies highlight how French women fare little better than their Spanish counterparts when it comes to workplace realities.

France has had a long tradition of contributing to the cutting edge of feminist theory, particularly, according to Toril Moi in her *Introduction to French Feminist Thought*, in psychoanalysis. Moi points out that French feminism has typically raised 'the question of sexual difference' and that in France, this has been carried out 'through the lens of French psychoanalytical or philosophical theory'.[6] No work including an approach to feminism could fail to address some aspect of the French contribution to feminist debate. Julia Kristeva is one of the so-called French theorists whose work is often grouped with that of Luce Irigaray and Hélène Cixous, all of whom began their writing in the 1970s. Kristeva's relationship with feminism, as with any other ideology, is problematic.[7] In *Desire in Language*, Kristeva indicates, 'I am quite dedicated to the feminist movement but I think, feminism, or any other movement, need not expect unconditional backing on the part of an intellectual woman' (p. 10). Sylvie Gambaudo turns her attention to an analysis of Kristeva's thinking, showing its development at the different stages of her career and addressing the principal concepts which inform Kristeva's methodology. She also presents an approach to Kristeva's later work, which has not yet been made available to an English readership through translation. In a complementary study of Spanish feminism, although her methodology is very different, Mercedes Carbayo-Abengózar charts the chameleon nature of feminism in Spain, focusing on the achievements and contributions of key female figures, often as little known within Spain as outside. She points the reader in the direction that Spanish feminism has taken since the early days of the century: she tracks Spanish feminism from its earliest appearances in the philanthropic ideals of the late nineteenth century, through its politico-legislative phase under the Republic. She points out the ongoing heritage of feminism in the Franco era, when women continued to press for reforms but from within the regime, and highlights feminism's current blossoming in university departments such as the Women's Investigation Centre in Barcelona set up in 1982 in the Faculty of Geography and History.[8] From the early days of the century to the last, she argues that Spanish feminism and education have been inextricably linked, with focus on training manifest even in the Franco era. In France, Women's Studies became part of University programmes from the early 1970s onwards. Spanish universities were aware of Women's Studies, although there were not the programmes of study available to students. In fact, the whole women's question had to be debated behind closed doors, given that it formed part of the opposition to the Franco regime.[9] Behind closed doors is a thread which runs through Jacky Collins' exploration of the lesbian contribution to the feminist organizations and other single issue associations. This leads her to evaluate the struggle for recognition of lesbian rights, now beginning to be achieved in some measure with reference to different models of family becoming incorporated into legislation with laws such as the law relating to tenancy agreements going onto the statute books. She points to greater visibility and acceptance of lesbian existence in the media and in literature, as well as in the economy but argues that lesbians still need to consolidate their achievements gained in the 1990s.

Within this exploration of how women see themselves in the public sphere, the work of female writers cannot be absent. Alison Holland and Vanessa Knights both approach the construction of female identity through textual study. Simone de Beauvoir never fails to be cited in any consideration of women's identity and her impact on the French Women's Movement has been much debated (Hughes, pp. 245-46). Her work, *The Second Sex*, is widely available in Spain and her words, 'One is not born a woman, one becomes one' have become standard in defining femininity as a social construct. Holland, whilst focus on *The Second Sex* is not her primary aim, sets out to examine the way in which Simone de Beauvoir's quest to show how femininity is constructed is continued in the context of fiction. The symbiotic relationship between text and female identity are explored by Holland as she argues that mental instability in Beauvoir's female protagonists is replicated in textual fragmentation. Vanessa Knights contrasts narrative technique and ways in which identity are constructed in the novels of two Spanish women writers. Carmen Martín Gaite was writing in the latter years of the Franco regime and Rosa Montero began her career at the point when democracy was being introduced in Spain. Both Martín Gaite and Montero can be considered as icons of the period when they wrote, although they are less well known outside their home country than Beauvoir. Rosa Montero has become emblematic for the new generation of women writers, writing as she has across the whole of the democratic period in Spain. Knights shows how Montero's early novel, *Crónica del desamor (Chronicle of Unlove)*, is not merely centred in autobiography but constructs the identity of the narrator whose decision to write the 'Chronicle of all the Anas' turns out to be the novel. Moreover, just as Beauvoir has an impact on present-day French women, so Montero's writing serves as a beacon for young women writers, like Lucia Etxebarría, who develop experimentation with form and narrative style.

The compilation of a book of this length has of necessity meant choices have had to be made and this will in turn imply that not all readers will find their interests satisfied. Some major aspects of women's identity are not included as a primary focus: women's experiences in the private sphere are not included at all or only where they impact on the roles and identities women adopt in the public sphere. Even with regard to the public sphere, there has had to be selectivity, and this has meant that important issues such as education appear only on a secondary plane. Within each of the major themes selected, the approach taken by the authors has been one of specificity rather than generalized overview. However, complementarity is an important feature of the book, enabling readers to draw their own comparative conclusions. In this way, in Beauvoir's words, the authors contribute 'something of value' to Women's Studies which will make it have been worthwhile trying.

The book contains bibliographies to each chapter, which include all the major works referred to in the chapter as well as some additional works to provide further reading on each theme. Newspaper articles are not included as a matter of course in the bibliography, unless they make an important contribution to an understanding of the particular topic of study. References to newspaper articles will be found in full in the endnotes to each chapter. Where several chapters are cited from an individual edited volume, chapters by individual authors are not cited in the bibliography. All references to French and Spanish sources appear in translation and since for reasons of length it has not proved possible to include original quotations in full, detailed references to the original are given to enable consultation.

References

1   Victoria Camps, *El siglo de las mujeres*, Feminismos, second edition (Madrid: Cátedra/Universitat de València/Instituto de la Mujer, 1998).

2   Anny Brooksbank Jones, *Women in Contemporary Spain* (Manchester: Manchester University Press, 1997), p. vii.

3   Figures from *El País*, http://www.elpais.es/p/d/20000308/espana/mujeres.htm.

4   Claire Laubier, *The Condition of Women in France 1945 to the Present* (London and New York: Routledge, 1990), pp. 113-15; Alex Hughes, 'Gender Issues', in *French Culture since 1945*, ed. by Malcolm Cook (London and New York: Longman, 1993), pp. 241-268, p. 243.

5   Paloma Alcalá, Oliva Blanco and Marián Lozano, 'Trabajo asalariado: extrañas en el paraíso', in *El largo camino hacia la igualdad: feminismo en España 1975-1995*, ed. by Oliva Blanco Coruja and Isabel Morant Deusa (Madrid: Instituto de la Mujer/Ministerio de Asuntos Sociales, 1995), pp. 77-98.

6   Toril Moi (ed.), *French Feminist Thought: A Reader* (Oxford: Blackwell, 1987), p. 4.

7   Toril Moi, *The Kristeva Reader* (Oxford: Blackwell, 1986), p. 9.

8   http://sr10.zoom.com/_XMCM/Duoda/pages/page1.html.

9   Inés Alberdi and María Antonia García de León, *Sociología de las mujeres españolas* (Madrid: Universidad Autónoma, 1996), p. 408.

1   Parity in French Politics

Sheila Perry and Sue Hart

As the French enter the new millennium, to what extent will they also be entering a totally new phase in politics, in which women will, at last, play a full and active role equal to that of men? The 1990s have seen a major campaign for legislative reform, destined to oblige political parties to ensure the equal access of men and women to electoral office by proposing an equal number of male and female candidates for election. A first major battle has been won, and in June 1999 the French Constitution was amended.[1] Given that for half a century, women have had the same political rights as men,[2] why has it been necessary to force the issue of parity by resorting to legislation? And what will be the effects of this move on women's participation and on French politics as a whole?

Positive Action
First of all, the necessity for some kind of positive action in favour of women was becoming glaringly obvious to all but the most traditional, misogynous elements of the extreme Right. The fact that theoretical equality in law had not translated itself into reality was evident from the shocking discrepancy between the number of women in the electorate, where they make up 53%, and their under-representation in the National Assembly, where they reached an all-time 'high' in 1997, at just over 10%. At best, at a rate of a 10% increase in fifty years, women could expect to achieve parity in another couple of centuries! In fact, however, this would be an optimistic estimate, as the past shows: in the intervening years, far from showing a slow but nevertheless sure progression, women's representation actually declined: from 6.7% in December 1946 to a mere 1.4% in September 1971, rising to 5.3% with the election of the Socialists in June 1981, to remain between 5 and 6% throughout the 1980s and early 1990s.[3] If there was a 'surge' in 1997, it was directly as a result of the adoption of a 30% quota system by the Socialist Party, and the fact that the Left won a clear majority in Parliament. There is absolutely no evidence to suggest that waiting for women's representation to increase 'naturally', alongside their increasing financial and social independence, would ever produce results.

The counter-argument to this is that it is enough for the law to provide equality of *access* and it is up to women to avail themselves of the opportunity presented. There are a number of implications here: that women themselves choose not to go into politics, that there are insufficient female candidates on which to draw, and that the legal situation is therefore perfectly adequate. However, studies have shown that these assumptions are not true. Christine Bard has illustrated, with examples from the 1930s, that women's civil and legal status often meant that their political activity was unorthodox if not outright subversive, but that in spite of constraints on their behaviour they sought to play an active role which goes counter to the argument that women are not interested in politics.[4]

Françoise Gaspard has pointed out that there has been no shortage of female candidates when they have been free to stand: in the 1993 parliamentary elections, there were as many women as men who stood for election on an independent ticket, and the imbalance between the sexes only occurred when political parties determined the nomination of candidates; similarly, when in 1996 the Socialist Party designated a number of constituencies to be reserved for female candidates at the forthcoming parliamentary elections, in a number of cases there were several women competing for the same nomination.[5] The fact that some of the most vociferous complaints regarding the imbalance between men and women came from women party militants – particularly on the Left – is also evidence of the fact that women who do want to enter politics are being obstructed and discouraged. More and more studies by women intellectuals, politicians and legal experts have gradually revealed the extent to which women's participation has been blocked by cultural, historical and institutional factors.[6] Blaming women for their own lack of interest simply does not hold water.

Gradually, therefore, resistance to positive action has been eroded, not least because the situation was becoming embarrassing for a nation which prides itself on being the birthplace of human rights. Until 1997, France came last of the fifteen nations of the European Union, equal only to Greece in the paucity of women in Parliament (an association cited, with characteristic chauvinism, with some horror),[7] and only crept into fourteenth place with the 1997 increase. It was in ninth position out of the nine EU states with a second chamber,[8] and even after the increase in 1997, moved only from seventy-second place on the world stage,[9] to seventy-first, trailing after countries such as Honduras, Uganda and Mongolia.[10] The phenomenon was being examined as a specifically French problem (*une exception française*), and a source of shame for the nation. It was also highly unpopular among the French electorate, who in numerous opinion polls expressed the desire to see change, through legislation if necessary.[11] Increasingly, political parties were finding that they needed to jump on the bandwagon of equality for women in politics, if they were not to lose massive support, not only from women (the majority of voters, let it not be forgotten) but also from men: the public at large was already disaffected with institutional politics, and abstention rates at elections had been hitting record levels since the 1980s, leading to a crisis in representation.[12]

However, it is one thing to recognize that change is necessary; but it is quite another to go for obligatory equality (parity), imposed by law, and to modify the Constitution in order to do so – especially when the need for change has been conceded somewhat reluctantly and for short-term electoral advantage (this has been particularly true of the Right, where conviction on the subject is less solidly anchored in the political culture, but the Left has also been slow to respond to women's demands in this area, fearing its effects on party support). So why have the French adopted such a radical position? The answer lies, paradoxically perhaps, in the extent to which the obstacles were stacked against women gaining power. At every level, social, cultural, historical and institutional, women found their path blocked, unconsciously as well as deliberately, so that nothing short of radical reform was going to solve the problem; and in fact, as we shall see, it is the very arguments used *against* positive action (the introduction of quotas, notably) which made anything short of parity impossible to get through the male-dominated institutions (in particular the Constitutional Council) and onto the statute books. Had the odds stacked against women been lower, women's demands might have been more modest.

Parity: The Republic Threatened

As it was, the battle for parity has been long and hard. Witness the article published in *Le Nouvel Observateur* as late as 14 January 1999, entitled 'Parité, la révolution qui divise', implying that it was the debate on parity which was threatening political stability, and hence problematic, rather than the lack of representation of women, and in which the authors were questioning whether Republicanism was not under threat from the pro-parity lobby. For the truth is, positive action in favour of women has been perceived as hitting at the very heart of French politics, threatening its most precious values, all that it stands for, and so threatening the very foundation of the regime! The expression of such apocalyptic fear made it possible for politicians to sympathize with women's demands, but argue that, alas, nothing could be done. . . The very life of the Republic was at stake – and women constituted the threat. Could there be any clearer diabolization of women, than this reworking of the myth of the Garden of Eden, whereby evil enters the world through a woman?

What could possibly justify such a view? Central to the notion of French Republicanism is that of 'universalism', that is, the theory that rights are universal, all citizens have equal rights, irrespective of social class, religion, education or gender. This was the major achievement of the French Revolution, to do away with a feudal system in which individuals were subjects of the monarch and possessed rights and privileges in accordance with the social class into which they were born. Now, it is clear that equal rights are a fundamental tenet of any modern democracy. But where the debate has taken a particular turn in France is in the belief advanced by certain legal experts and politicians, that this universalism could only be protected as long as citizens remained undifferentiated. Because they have rights *regardless of gender*, then it is dangerous, if those rights are not to be threatened, to lobby for women *because they are women*, as such action differentiates between citizens. Differentiation has been equated with division: the point of universalism is that it applies to everyone; once distinctions are made on the grounds of sex, then that indivisibility has been broken, and so there is no basis for universal human rights. Worse, what is there to stop other groups – ethnic or religious groups, for example – from also claiming representation in Parliament in proportion to their representation in the population as a whole? And with all different groups and communities vying for position (a phenomenon called '*communautarisme*') the 'one and indivisible Republic', in which all French children are taught to believe, would no longer exist.[13]

Such is the argument of the camp which became known as the 'Universalists'. Within this group figures Elisabeth Badinter, a writer who has been prominent in the debate as a woman arguing against parity in the name of feminism. She endorses all the arguments set out above, and also sees in the pro-parity movement a dangerous return to essentialism, i.e. the notion that women are different from men *in essence*, biologically, from birth – the very notion, she argues, which has been used over the centuries to constrain women to the private sphere and exclude them from the public, reserved for men. She sees it as retrogressive to argue that men and women are different; progress for

11

women in society has been made, she says, by showing that so-called masculine characteristics are shared by women, and vice versa:

> It's by recognizing that masculine and feminine virtues belong to both sexes that we progress towards equality. Humanity is not dual in nature. Each man and each woman is a repository for the whole of humanity.[14]

In short, the universalists have argued that positive action in favour of women constitutes a threat to the Republic, and would be to the detriment of women themselves.

The pro-parity group has argued persuasively against all of these assertions. First of all, the Revolution and all subsequent regimes until after the Second World War gave civil and political rights only to men, and so universalism was not at all neutral towards gender, as the anti-parity lobby has suggested. This was put succinctly by Gisèle Halimi, lawyer and former MP, when she wrote: 'The universal is, above all, masculine' (Halimi, p. 171). What is more, she claims, the sacrosanct Revolution and its *Déclaration des droits de l'Homme et du citoyen* fully intended it to be this way:

> Some historians [...] argue that the Rights of Man = Rights of Men and of Women. That the citizen referred to in the masculine in all these sacred texts is also the female citizen, but that circumstances and lack of social progress have not allowed women to claim their equal rights. This is a load of rubbish. Reread the texts. The citizen is clearly a male citizen.
>
> (Halimi, pp. 99-100)

and she goes on to cite examples from the texts in question, which clearly illustrate slippage from use of the term *Homme* (with a capital, to designate humankind), towards *homme* (lower case, to designate a male member of the species) – not least the fact that it is specified in Article 4 of the 1793 Constitution that citizenship is conferred on any man '[who] marries a Frenchwoman'. She points out what she calls the 'the savage irrationality' of an article which enables a French woman to confer on to someone else – a man, by definition – a right which she herself is denied! (Halimi, p. 100). Universalism is, therefore, a false myth: it claims that rights are universal while reserving them for men. Indeed, it is *because* it claims that these rights, designated for men, are shared by women, that women are unable to obtain them: 'The contradiction between the principle and its application is primarily a result of the denial that there is a difference between the sexes' (Halimi, p. 99). It is necessary to recognize that the human race is both masculine and feminine so that the rights accorded to men can also be extended to women. In other words, the introduction of parity is the only way to make universalism become reality. Universalism as it stands, without parity, claims to make no distinction between men and women but in fact assimilates women to men: 'Parity alone can take this unilateral identification of one sex with another and replace it with real equality between the sexes', writes the specialist in law, Francine Demichel.[15] Far from threatening Republican ideals, therefore, parity is the means by which they can be properly realized, and France can become a true democracy, not a 'a one-legged democracy',[16] as it has been so far. It is in this context that parity has become a viable proposition for legal reform, whereas quotas had been hotly contested: parity can be claimed in the name of equality; on what basis can one require 25% or 30% representation?

It is this distinction between quotas and parity which has also helped the pro-parity lobby to argue against the threat of *communautarisme*, the fear that the introduction of positive action in favour of women would open the floodgates to religious or ethnic groups likewise claiming proportional representation. 'Parity is not a 50% quota', wrote another jurist, Eliane Vogel Polsky, 'We're demanding parity on the grounds that we have equal status, and not on the grounds that we represent a minority.'[17] Parity is not simply a large quota, designed to match women's (roughly) equal representation in the population to men, but a right, claimed because women have equal status. This makes a distinction between women and other groups, who may lay claim to representation on the basis of difference or in proportion to their (minority) status within society. Gender is not to be seen as a category like any other (ethnicity, religion, age, etc.) as it is the only distinction which exists in roughly equal proportions throughout the human race. It is interesting that the proponents of parity have had thus to separate themselves from the multiculturalists, a development which reveals a specifically French conception of the nation state. Arguing against parity, Robert Badinter (husband to Elisabeth, and former Justice Minister and President of the Constitutional Council) evoked two opposing conceptions of democracy:

> One is a democracy in which citizens see themselves first as members of a community, and all the communities come together to build up the nation. The other concept, which to me seems more genuinely Republican, and in line with what the founding fathers intended, is that of the French nation, of all French citizens, whatever their origins, their sex, their cultural affinities, their religion or their race.[18]

Other than the fact they have removed gender from the final list of attributes of the French citizen, the pro-parity campaigners have rallied round this second definition, seen as more specifically French.

However, in spite of the special status accorded to gender over other kinds of human distinctiveness, the parity lobby has had to stress that the human race is not indistinguishable, but mixed, made up of two sexes – so to what extent is it true, as Elisabeth Badinter has warned, that in order to promote positive action women have had to sacrifice the progress made on male and female identity and argue that women are essentially different from men? Some militants have indeed used such an argument, and French women politicians almost invariably claim to behave differently from men in their approach to politics.[19] Quite possibly, some of these differences are exaggerated and spring from an inculcated belief, rather than empirical evidence. Nicole Belloubet-Frier has conducted research which shows that women politicians do not behave or speak differently from their male counterparts.[20] It would be easy to cite examples of women who are as ambitious, aggressive, and devious as men, characteristics which are generally considered to be 'masculine'. Any kind of generalization which presents all men as the same, and all women as different from men, and like each other, regardless of social class, education, background, etc. would be on very shaky ground. But if, as women politicians assert, they tend, *on the whole*, to be more pragmatic than men, to be less inclined to practise *la langue de bois*,[21] and to see politics more as an opportunity to get things done and change society, than as a talking shop designed solely for self-advancement, there is nothing to say that such differences are biological rather than socio-culturally determined. Boys and girls are not taught the same skills in school or at home. It is possible to argue that men and women are socio-culturally different and avoid the pitfalls of essentialism which sees them as different from birth. When Elisabeth Badinter cites Simone de Beauvoir's famous phrase 'One is not born a woman, one becomes one' to argue that feminism can be advanced only if differences between men and women are minimized (or even denied), she is giving undue attention to the first part of the phrase over the second. Yes, Simone de Beauvoir put the nail in the coffin of biological determinism ('On ne naît pas femme') but she did not deny socio-cultural differences ('on le devient'). Beauvoir's insights have enabled women to resist certain kinds of patriarchal conditioning, and to determine more for themselves what 'being a woman' might mean, as a result of which considerable progress has been made in women's status and identity in French society since the publication of *Le Deuxième Sexe*, but it would be naïve to think that differentiation between the sexes has ceased to occur, or that gender roles are not still perceived and presented in patriarchal stereotypes.[22] It is on the basis of that which is common in their socio-cultural history that French women can claim the right to power in the name of their difference from men. And who knows whether, once men and women work more closely together, the old distinctions between masculine and feminine might not be overcome?

> Men and women may, for philosphical or tactical reasons, defend parity by arguing that there is an ontological (essential) difference between men and women. They have every right to do this if they so choose. Our fight for parity is based on a different notion, that of sexual equality based on difference, difference which we neither glorify nor deny, but which is surpassed, recognized so as to be eliminated anywhere it produces inequalities.[23]

It is when they are assigned to different spheres (the public for men, the private for women) that men and women are different; once they come together, their differences diminish.

Politics: A Male Preserve

It is in the current context of a differentiated socio-cultural heritage for men and women that politics can be such a difficult world for women to enter. In France, as in other Western countries, politics has functioned for so long as a male preserve that it is hardly surprising that it carries all the marks of traditional 'masculine' culture. It is, but for a few isolated individuals, essentially a male club. Such segregation almost invariably leads to the accentuation of those characteristics which differentiate the group from those excluded from it. So when women enter it (for the boundaries of this milieu are fluid, and women are not expressly forbidden to enter) they are immediately made to feel that they are intruders, and do not belong. Françoise Giroud, the first Minister for Women (1974-76) put it thus: 'It's as if a woman had gone into the changing room after a football match. Oh, they don't like it!'[24] Many women politicians testify to the outrageously sexist comments to which they are subject.[25] These are part and parcel of this traditionally all-male environment, a sign that men feel sufficiently secure 'among themselves' to throw out quips destined to amuse the immediate male entourage (speaking of women in terms they would use if genuinely alone), while also making the woman in question feel as uncomfortable as possible for daring to enter the charmed circle. The idea that politics is an essentially 'masculine' activity is deeply-rooted, as can be seen from the fact that Lionel Jospin, forcing the Socialists to accept quotas of women candidates for the forthcoming parliamentary elections, rather incongruously called upon his party to 'Show they were men!'[26]

The 'male club' mentality is not exclusive to France but exists in other countries where men are in such a massive majority in politics. However, in France, it is compounded by other factors. Because the French language is gendered, this has given rise to a whole series of images and metaphors which make women's relations to politics problematic. For example, *la France, la République*, in the feminine, is symbolized by a woman, Marianne, which led Georges Pompidou to announce on the death of General De Gaulle: 'General De Gaulle is dead. France is a widow.'[27] In other words, the relationship between politician and nation was likened to that of husband and wife, so that women entering politics were effectively 'changing sides', as it were, trying to play the husband's role. It is as though through politics a woman has to be de-feminized. Indeed, until very recently, there was no feminine term for any of the political offices that women might hold – and this in a language in which there are no gender-neutral nouns![28] The same double standard applies to men and women in relation to their sexuality. Sexual relations are seen as valorizing for men (for whom they are interpreted as conquests), and devalorizing for women (seen as wives or harlots), and this ambivalent attitude is applied also to politicians. Opinion polls show that the French electorate are likely to view male politicians no less favourably – and maybe even more! – if it is found that they have extra-marital sexual partners – unlike in Britain and the US, where such revelations are used to force the politician to resign. However, women politicians have to be very careful to have only one partner (though cohabitation is accepted as readily as marriage), if they are not to be surrounded by scandal. This reinforces a situation in which men can use sexual innuendo to their advantage, at the expense of their female counterparts. There is one way, and one way only, to break down the 'male club' mentality in French politics, and that is to increase the proportion of women sufficiently so that it no longer functions as a male club. The weight of cultural tradition and sexual stereotypes, which work to the advantage of men and to the disadvantage of women, is another argument in favour of reform on a large scale, and has reinforced the case for parity.

For the fact is, that while men continue to hold the power, they will continue to refuse to relinquish it. After all, women really do constitute a threat to them, in so far as there are a finite number of positions to be filled, and increasing the proportion of women has to be done at the expense of the men who currently hold those positions. What is more, the institutions and systems in place enable men to retain their advantageous position. There are two ways by which one can accede to office in France: by election, or by appointment. Government appointments are made officially by the Prime Minister (though when Prime

Minister and President are from the same political party or side of the spectrum, it is usually the latter who decides), and the person appointed does not have to be an elected MP (indeed, any such person has to give up his or her parliamentary seat in favour of a substitute, or *suppléant*). This has been a route through which a number of women have come to politics: for example, Simone Veil, famous for having made abortion legal in France, was appointed Minister of Health in 1974, at the age of 47, by Jacques Chirac (under Valéry Giscard d'Estaing), without ever having been engaged in politics before – and she is certain she was chosen because she was a woman.[29] A number of women have become MPs as *suppléantes* for a man called to Government, or deceased: Nicole Ameline, when called to Government in 1995, was an MP as a replacement for the late Michel d'Ornano; 20% of *députées* used this route between 1945 and 1993.[30] Often, women have replaced their husbands.

While this can be a fertile route for women to follow, it is a notoriously precarious one. It means that women are directly dependent on male patronage, which can be withdrawn as quickly as it has been given, the most notorious example being the Juppé Governments of 1995. The first Government appointed by Alain Juppé, with twelve women out of forty-three ministers, set an all-time record for women's participation (28%). Six months later, the second Juppé Government was announced and with it, the dismissal of eight of the twelve women. It is a prime example of the way in which women can be called upon when it is seen to be in the interests of the men in power (the first Government was set up with maximum media coverage) and dispensed with for the same reasons. This 'instrumentalization' of women's participation does little to legitimize their position: it is referred to as the *fait du prince*, redolent of pre-Revolutionary days when the Salic Law prevented women from acceding to the throne, and royal and feudal lords had absolute power over their vassals. In that sense, the term *Juppettes* to refer to these women was far more demeaning, because it contained a greater grain of truth, than the equally frivolous expression *Blair's Babes*, used to refer to the influx of women into the British Parliament on the election of Tony Blair's Labour Party to power in 1997.

This process also does little, in the long term, for women's political careers: indeed, as Simone Veil has pointed out, the freedom to choose ministers from what is called 'civil society', as opposed to political circles, actually prevents party militants from attaining higher office, as noted by Adler (p. 179). Françoise Gaspard has studied the 'political capital' of all the members of the first Juppé Government and shown that the women had only meagre power and support, compared to men, all of whom had several other influential positions, and 'local areas of support which national politicians have to reckon with'.[31] Women, in comparison, are not a force to be reckoned with, and so are dispensable; in addition, it is more difficult for those who lose their posts to find an alternative position in politics. Men have the full support of the party machine behind them, or hold other positions simultaneously which they can use to rebuild their power base. This system, whereby one person holds several posts on the local and national scene, is known as the *cumul des mandats*, and it is, as Françoise Gaspard has shown in some detail in the article from which the above quotation was taken, the way in which men network and build their careers. Women not only find it more difficult to enter politics, but also more difficult to stay. This is true of parliamentary as well as ministerial posts: by 1997, only seven women had been MPs for fifteen years or more. Madeleine Dienesch held the record for women, at twenty-five years. Of those elected in 1993, only one, Louise Moreau, was embarking on a fifth term (she started her sixth in 1997), whereas there were fifty-six men in the same position. Some men had held office over ten times, and Jacques Chaban-Delmas was on his fourteenth term.[32]

The system of *cumul des mandats* also blocks new entrants. If one person holds several posts, there are obviously fewer posts to go around. Despite the law of 1985 limiting the number of offices which can be held simultaneously to two, it is still possible to be a minister and President of the General Council, like François Bayrou, or a minister and President of the Regional Council like Jean-Claude Gaudin, or even Prime Minister and mayor of a large town such as Bordeaux, like Alain Juppé between 1995 and 1997. If the town is small enough, three posts can be held, as two other offices can be combined with being a mayor of a town of fewer than 20,000 inhabitants or a deputy mayor of a town of up to 100,000 inhabitants. This has led some to argue that the *cumul des mandats* should be further curtailed to make room for women (it was a secondary recommendation of the *Observatoire de la parité* set up in October 1995 to look into the question of parity[33]), and legislation to that effect is currently in its third reading in Parliament.[34] However, as a measure in isolation it will not necessarily help women, as there are plenty of men waiting to take up any positions thereby liberated (indeed, it is not specifically for women that the measure is being debated).

Such a limitation would, however, reduce the power base that any one individual can acquire. This should also help to open up the system to newcomers (male as well as female). At present, the status quo is reinforced by the phenomenon known as the *prime au notable* – i.e. when a position becomes available, priority is given to the most well-known person with the greatest power base. There is logic in this. In a system in which voters choose one candidate (*scrutin uninominal*), as is the case for parliamentary elections, for example, it is often argued that the person who is most widely known is most likely to win. On the same basis, priority is often given to the sitting candidate (a practice known as the *prime au sortant*). The fact that these tendencies work less frequently when women are involved is proof that the argument is sometimes an alibi for other motivations (helping a friend, returning a service rendered, keeping women out) but whatever the 'real' reason(s) behind a particular nomination, the fact is that it is a self-perpetuating system which is an obstacle to women, as indeed to all newcomers.

Because women have difficulties in being selected as candidates, some have argued for a list system for all elections, as women have, on the whole, fared somewhat better where lists are used, as in the European elections. (It was the abolition of the list system for parliamentary elections, at the start of the Fifth Republic in 1958, which caused women's participation to plummet.[35]) However, it has also been demonstrated that the list system, *per se*, is not sufficient to guarantee that more women attain office. For this to happen, women have to figure in a high enough position on the list, and this is often not the case: for example in 1985, the Socialist Party's Central Committee simply crossed many women off the lists and put Edwige Avice and Yvette Roudy, both ministers at the time, in impossible positions near the bottom of the list for Paris.[36] Women had a fairer place on the lists in 1994, because their representation had become an electoral issue, with the result that the Socialists, under Michel Rocard, placed men and women alternately on the list. Five other parties also adopted parity (or near-parity): the Trotskyist Lutte Ouvrière, the Communist Party, Mouvement des Citoyens, the Greens, and a list led by C. Cotton.[37] However, as the Socialists did badly in these elections, and the other parties have only a minor following, this did not lead to the anticipated increase in the number of women elected – and women were blamed for the poor result.[38]

The electoral system is, therefore, only a secondary issue. Whatever the type of election, the ultimate, decisive factor which proves an obstacle to women is the fact that the choice of candidates is controlled by male-dominated political parties, and that political parties do little to advance the cause of women – on the contrary. Although women make up 40% of party membership, on average, they constitute a very small percentage of the higher echelons: in 1977, the Socialist Party adopted a quota of 15% in its hierarchy![39] This is significant because it is at party headquarters that candidates are chosen, and, as Françoise Gaspard has pointed out, 'To be elected, one has first to be a candidate'.[40] This same author has also described in graphic detail the lack of a democratic voting system within parties whereby either leaders or electoral candidates can be chosen.[41] Nomination of the party leaders takes place either behind closed doors or by acclamation, the product of secret arrangements made by party 'heavyweights', who are in positions of power because of their personal charisma, and the *cumul des mandats* has made them into forces to be reckoned with. They are capable of surrounding themselves with a sufficient number of cronies who claim to have the same political ideals whilst really having the same electoral interests.[42] They weigh each other up, fight over the allocation of political power and negotiate the distribution of influential positions discreetly, between themselves. Prior to the election of Michèle Alliot-Marie to the presidency of the RPR in November 1999, none of the party leaders was appointed as the result of an open election, and, except for some minor parties, all were men.[43]

In such circumstances, the interest of the party is synonymous with men's self-interest: men can pursue political careers while purporting to serve 'the cause'. In the name of that same cause women can be asked to step down in favour of a man, presumed to have better chances of winning. Véronique Neiertz recounts how she and Elisabeth Guigou were evicted from the top of their respective lists by the Socialist Party, in favour of men, in a deal done between two *courants* (as these groupings around a leading figure are called) led by Michel Rocard and Laurent Fabius.[44] The culture of *prime au sortant, prime au notable* and *cumul des mandats* can be used to justify the procedure, but even a relatively unknown man is often presumed to be a safer bet than a woman, considered a handicap unless she has been tried and tested. It is interesting that women's inexperience is frequently cited as a problem: Jacques Chirac, addressing the *Conseil national des femmes françaises* in April 1995, commented on the difficulties which occur when attempting to find enough competent women to act as ministers, and went on patronizingly to inform his audience that 'Make no mistake about it, being a Government minister is a job, and not just anybody can improvise anything they like'.[45] Rarely, if ever, is it suggested that men need to gain experience in more menial tasks before holding a post of responsibility. So, not only are women not given safe seats, which men reserve for themselves, neither are they trusted to win marginal ones – unless they are so marginal as to be lost causes.

Colette Chaigneau (RPR) recounts how she fought a left-wing majority of 60% to win a seat on the *Conseil Général* in the Department of Maine-et-Loire in 1982 – when she succeeded, she heard men saying, 'Oh, if only we'd known, we would have gone for it!'[46] That women like Colette Chaigneau have succeeded, by sheer dint of effort and determination, in turning such situations to their advantage should not mask the fact that through the party system, men protect their own interests at women's expense. As Janine Mossuz-Lavau has put it: '[Political parties] are male coteries which function in a closed circle, reproducing themselves in identical form. They are not prepared to take a place from a man to give it to a woman.'[47] In fact, according to Françoise Gaspard, in 1993: 'When the candidates were selected, the more chances a party had of winning seats, the fewer women it chose.'[48]

Meanwhile, the party heavyweights have persistently done what they could to discourage women's movements from promoting a higher female profile within political party ranks.[49] Their task was made the easier because of the widely-accepted universalist ideology, making women concerned that a specifically feminine organization might marginalize them and constrain them to issues which are seen as specifically feminine. This has been compounded by a certain view of feminism which has prevailed in France. It has been argued, even by figures such as Françoise Giroud, that there was no need for feminism *à l'anglo-saxonne*, by which she meant a strident, anti-male militancy, because of the superior relations which men and women supposedly enjoy in France in comparison with countries such as Britain and the US.[50] Without entering into the debate as to whether such assertions can be substantiated, it is clear that the effects of such a belief can be far-reaching. On the one hand, as Alison Holland has argued, even if it is true, it has made no substantive difference to French women, who enjoy no better social, economic or legal rights than their foreign European counterparts.[51] On the other hand, one can easily see how such a belief might make militant feminism seem out of place, and un-French. It implies there is a problem, when French culture suggests there is not. Indeed, women who militate for their rights can once again be accused of threatening something which they have been taught to believe constitutes French superiority! As a result of these combined factors, French women have not always had the networks, or the solidarity, which enabled women in other countries to campaign for political rights. It was parity which provided the motivating factor to bring women together from all sides of the political spectrum, to argue their case.[52] It was parity which gave them the arguments they could use confidently, without fear of eliciting the accusation that they were harpies or viragoes.

In a way, men fell victim to their own intransigence and blatant cynical abuse of their power. In 1982, Gisèle Halimi, as MP for the Isère Department, campaigned to introduce a quota of women candidates for the forthcoming municipal elections.[53] Settling for a figure of 25% in order to get a broad consensus, she framed the bill in the negative: 'Electoral lists must not include more than 75% of candidates of the same sex.' This was designed to be egalitarian in its approach to men and women, rather than simply to discriminate in favour of women, and was also a concession, as Gisèle Halimi's group *Choisir* had once presented all-female lists in the 1978 parliamentary elections;[54] with the new law, this would no longer be possible. The wording was designed primarily to meet the

Republican requirement of universalism, as it treated men and women in exactly the same way. The vote was carried by 475 to 8 and the law definitively adopted on 21 October 1982. Definitively, that is, until it was annulled by the Constitutional Council on the grounds that it divided citizens into categories.

We have discussed the issue of categories and shown how the proponents of parity have argued that gender is not a category like any other and so should be exempt from sanction by the Constitutional Council. However, not prepared to take the risk of failing once again to convince the Council's members, the lobbyists have successfully campaigned to have the Constitution amended. There are those who had argued that it should not be necessary to revise the Constitution, which states in its preamble that equality between men and women is guaranteed, the word guarantee being interpreted as, 'Obligation to translate theoretical freedom into concrete rights'.[55] However, the purpose behind revising the Constitution has been to put any legislation in favour of parity out of reach of the Constitutional Council. For even if the arguments were won, the experience of 1982 has shown that the Council cannot be trusted.

For, as Gisèle Halimi has explained, not only were the Council's arguments spurious, but it in fact had no legal right even to consider the article on quotas, let alone annul it![56] It is curious, to say the least, that the guardians of the Constitution should act so blatantly in infringement of the rules governing their remit. And then, having ridden roughshod over the laws of the Republic, they accuse women of threatening Republicanism! Of course, the Constitutional Council is composed entirely of old men – average age 76 years old– and is typical in this respect of the lack of renewal of the political system that the introduction of parity is designed to cure (Halimi, p. 117). Moreover, the 1990s' parity debate had clearly had no impact on the Constitutional Council – in January 1999 the Council approved the law reforming regional elections and Regional Councils, minus the article stipulating that lists of candidates should have equal numbers of men and women. This article was annulled on the grounds that it distinguished between candidates according to sex.[57]

Parity is, therefore, now embedded in the Constitution – at the time of writing (January 2000), it has yet to be enshrined in law. And there is the rub. For in order to gain a broad consensus, and to ensure the safe passage of the Constitutional amendment through the male-dominated institutions, the wording of the text has been diluted. In its final version, the law simply *favours* equal access for men and women, whereas the original intention was that it should *determine* their access. The element of obligation has clearly been weakened, and major electoral reform – necessary to guarantee parity in elections not operated under a list system – has been jettisoned. As a result, parity is only certain to exist for the European, regional and municipal elections (the latter where there are 2,000 or more inhabitants), and for the election of senators in those departments with five or more representatives.[58] For most of these, this will be parity *of candidacy,* since only in the European and senatorial elections are male and female candidates to figure in strict alternation, while for the rest, parity only has to apply to candidates in groups of six, so that the actual results could diverge from strict parity. For the other elections: town councils with fewer than 2,000 inhabitants, the majority of senators, General Councils and the National Assembly, however, even parity of candidacy is not obligatory. For elections to the National Assembly, the latest proposal is for a sliding scale of financial penalties to be incurred by parties presenting a gender imbalance of more than 2%. This is on one level a slight improvement on the proposal originally adopted by the cabinet in December 1999, whereby financial incentives were to be offered to parties who presented 40% of women candidates – 40% is a large quota, but it is not parity!, and a 2% gap between the proportions of male to female candidates comes closer to the target of 50-50. In addition, the substitution of a penalty for those who fail to comply with the legal requirement to move towards parity is preferable to a reward for those who succeed – the idea of 'buying' votes for women was distasteful to many – and the funds released in this way can be used to advance the cause of parity. However, the amounts involved are relatively small: even a party presenting all-male candidates, incurring the highest penalty, would lose only a quarter of the State reimbursement of its expenses for which it would normally qualify. Some parties may simply choose to dispense with the funding. Furthermore, the emphasis is once again placed on candidacies, not results: it is left to the discretion of parties to choose where to place male and female candidates: if, as in the past, women are selected for unwinnable seats, the party incurs no penalties. In the absence of State funding for some elections to General Councils (cantonal elections in which there are fewer than 9,000 inhabitants), these have had to be excluded from the legislation altogether, as there would be no way of enforcing parity. In other words, *quantitative* parity remains a target, rather than a certainty, and *qualitative* parity still has to be fought for. Perhaps unsurprisingly, it is the positions which carry most political prestige which are the ones women will find it hardest to obtain. And this is not to mention those offices with even greater clout – Government minister, leader of the General or Regional Council – which are either direct appointments from above or elected indirectly.

Increasing Female Representation

However, although much remains to be done to ensure parity, this should not mask the fact that there will be some improvements in women's participation in elected political institutions. In 1997, the Socialist Party, with a quota of only 30% of women candidates – which it failed to achieve anyway – still helped to increase the proportion of women in the National Assembly to its highest level so far, and this has gone some way towards enabling the constitutional amendment in favour of parity. What the compromise means is that parity still remains a goal rather than reality – albeit a slightly less distant goal. Thus in spite of the radical approach adopted – legislative reform to impose parity on recalcitrant male-dominated institutions – the effect will be more gradual and incremental, and less immediate, than originally envisaged.[59]

A major milestone has nonetheless been passed: the Constitutional Council's power to obstruct legislation in favour of parity has been cut off at source, and with it go all the theoretical arguments about the so-called gender-neutrality of citizenship. Attention can at last be focussed on the practicalities of implementation. The new millennium does not offer a political revolution for women, but it offers major reform and exciting new opportunities.

Will this affect French politics in the wider sense? There are two aspects to consider here: the effects of this on policy issues (will French women adopt a 'women's agenda'?) and its consequences for French political culture. Women's increased numbers should help to improve the way in which women politicians are treated by their male counterparts, as we have argued above, but will it change attitudes among the wider public? This will depend not only on the degree to which parity is implemented, but also on whether it leads to a greater *visibility* of women politicians through the media. If this happens, politics will no longer be seen as a purely masculine enterprise, and girls and young women might more readily consider it a viable career. So the important issue is whether women's increased participation will effect a change in media attitudes and practice.

Initially, of course, the influx of women into political institutions will be in the spotlight of media news coverage. Insofar as the focus will be on this as an exceptional event, each woman elected will carry the burden of representing all women. Only once women's participation ceases to be the centre of attention can it be said that true equality with men has been reached. For politics, a significant indicator of women's integration will not, therefore, be news coverage of them, but their role in political debate programmes, which generally call not on new politicians, but on well established ones, whose notoriety they thus reinforce and legitimize. Media professionals have always argued that the paucity of women participating in televised political debates, for example, springs from their low participation in political office. In a previous study, we have shown that numerically, women have indeed participated in political debate programmes on French television in much the same proportions, if not indeed in slightly higher percentages, than they figure in political institutions.[60] Although it is easy to demonstrate that programme makers missed many opportunities to give women a higher profile, this does suggest that broadcasts do at least reflect the gender composition of political institutions, and when more women hold political office, more are interviewed on television. In the present scenario, however, their increased participation is not envisaged in those areas which guarantee television access. Interviewers call most readily upon Government ministers, party leaders, leaders of parliamentary party groups, and mayors for their debate programmes. None of these positions is directly targetted by the legislation on parity. In order to have greater access to airtime as a result of their increased participation, women would need to take on more of these positions of responsibility. In the meantime, they will be more visible through images of Parliament shown on the news, a passive presence which they will be able to make more active as they take on specific roles in parliamentary commissions and as *rapporteurs* (responsible for presenting new legislation to Parliament).

It is difficult to say to what extent women's increased participation will change the image of women politicians presented by the media. A number of studies have shown the myths and symbols through which women are portrayed, both positively and negatively.[61] These stereotypes – Joan of Arc, Marianne – are so embedded in broader French culture that it is totally implausible that they should cease to be used, but the sheer numbers of women may mean that it will be much more difficult to portray all women in the same terms and to generalize quite so much. Women have already begun to break free from the supposedly 'feminine' areas of interest in which they had been constrained (health, social affairs, education) and occupy posts previously considered too 'heavy' for them: for example, Elisabeth Guigou is the first woman to have become Minister of Justice, in 1997.

They have gradually also occupied higher rank: Martine Aubry (Employment and Solidarity) and Elisabeth Guigou are respectively in second and third place in the hierarchy of Lionel Jospin's Government. As women in higher numbers begin to undertake a wider variety of roles, these developments could cease to be noteworthy. This will take some time, however. Initially, many appointments and responsibilities will be symbolically charged (as they are now), as women will have to prove they are competent and not elected or appointed just because they are women.

It is unlikely that the question of how women manage to reconcile public and private responsibilities will cease to be raised. During the 1995 presidential election campaign, Martine Aubry was the only female politician out of ten on the programme *La France en direct,* broadcast by France 2, and the only one to be asked whether her daughter missed her when she was out campaigning. It is more probable that if women have a higher media profile, the reconciliation of work and family will become a more frequently debated issue. This question will probably also continue to be reserved for women. In its report in 1998, the *Observatoire de la parité* proposed as an accompanying measure to the introduction of parity that the subject be discussed and a new *statut de l'élu* devised (a kind of 'elected person's charter' setting out roles and responsibilities, with a view to reconciling political office with family commitments), but although this was intended to apply to men as well as women, the distribution of household tasks between French couples still leaves working women with a double shift (*double journée*). Like part-time work, the *statut de l'élu*, if adopted, will be seen as a measure 'for women'. It will take a wider socio-cultural shift for that to change.[62]

Maybe women themselves, if they do manage to get elected to Parliament in greater numbers, will be in a position to engineer such a shift. This brings us back to the question of the extent to which women are likely to propose and vote for different kinds of policies than those put forward by men, which once again raises the issue of difference. Given women's different socio-cultural heritage and experience, it is possible to envisage that a higher proportion of women will bring to French politics more qualities which are traditionally defined as 'feminine'. At the same time, however, women will be socialized into an existing, largely male group which has established modes of operation, and in spite of their numbers, they will be in the weaker position (having to prove their worth) in the company of men convinced they are there by right (and perhaps feeling that their place has been usurped). The degree to which Parliament or local Government will become more mixed in terms of the values which are traditionally defined as either male or female will depend on the outcome of that power struggle, which in turn will depend on the desire, and the ability, of women to establish a 'women's' agenda. To a certain degree, this will depend on the legitimacy they feel parity gives them (they are there by right, but also because of their gender rather than because of their political nous) and on the extent to which they want to differentiate themselves from men. Different women will obviously have different opinions on any of these questions and it is impossible to say at this stage whether a majority view will emerge. That parity should also bring about a 'cultural revolution' was, however, an aspiration expressed with some enthusiasm by those debating the legislation before Parliament in January 2000.

If women do have a different socio-cultural heritage from men, then its prime feature must be the responsibility they take for childcare and domestic duties. If French women want to bring about greater socio-cultural change, it would be in the area of the reconciliation of the nation's economy and family life, for both men and women, that this could be done. With the reduction of the working week on the current Government agenda, and the policy of *natalisme* (promoting a higher birthrate) making childcare a national issue in France, French women may stand a better chance of effecting such change than, say, their British counterparts, where economic pressure is extending working hours and women are expected to content themselves with part-time work to enable them to continue to carry the domestic burden. However, the battle over the working week is proving a difficult one, and it is by no means certain French women will be any more successful against economic forces than British women. Nor, indeed, is it certain that they would want to be.

And, after all, why should they be? Women politicians do not *have* to make a difference to the nature of politics for parity to be justified. In response to the question as to whether parity will improve French politics, Gisèle Halimi rightfully objects:

> Here we are, called upon to prove that parity is infallible, that it will keep promises it hasn't made, that it will make democracy a citizens' paradise, etc. In other words, we're being told we have to produce results. Which was never the case, don't forget, for political systems based almost exclusively on men's decision-making – for if it had been, all those in positions of responsibility would have been dismissed long ago. And forever: not just with a change of party in power at election time. [...] Parity as we see it has this in its favour: justice.
>
> (Halimi, p. 196)

Anything short of parity is a 'a transgression of the principle of "popular sovereignty", whereby half the population have to obey laws they have not voted for'.[63] Parity is the only true democracy. It can be justified on the grounds of equality between men and women – whatever its consequences. French women have now set out on their journey towards it, and for that reason alone, France will be a more democratic country in the new millennium than it was in the old.

References

1   The following phrases have been added to Articles 3 and 4 respectively of the Constitution: 'La loi favorise l'égal accès des femmes et des hommes aux mandats et fonctions.' (The law favours the equal access of men and women to electoral office), and 'Ils contribuent à la mise en oeuvre du principe énoncé au dernier alinéa de l'article 3 dans les conditions déterminées par la loi.' (They [political parties] help to implement the principle expressed in the last line of Article 3 in conditions determined by law), J.O. No. 157, 9 July 1999, p. 10175.

2   According to the 1944 ordinance (decree having the power of law), 'les femmes sont électrices et éligibles dans les mêmes conditions que les hommes'. (Women can vote and stand for election in the same conditions as men.)

3   For a full table of statistics from 1945 to 1993, see Jane Jensen and Mariette Sineau, *Mitterrand et les Françaises. Un rendez-vous manqué* (Paris: Presses de Science Po, 1995). Reproduced in Françoise Gaspard, *Les Femmes dans la prise de décision en France et en Europe* (Paris: L'Harmattan, 1997), pp. 104-105.

4   Christine Bard, 'Les femmes et le pouvoir politique dans la France de l'entre-deux guerres', in *Les Femmes et la politique*, ed. by Armelle Le Bras-Chopard and Janine Mossuz-Lavau (Paris: L'Harmattan, 1997), pp. 41-54, p. 50. As Siân Reynolds had already illustrated, there are many forms of action which can be described as 'political' and women's exclusion from mainstream politics meant that their energies were channelled elsewhere. See Siân Reynolds, *Alternative Politics: Women and Public Life in France between the Wars* (Stirling, Scotland: Stirling French Publications, 1993). Similar accounts have been made of women's activities in the nineteenth century: see, for example, Patricia Latour, Monique Houssin, and Madia Tovar, *Femmes et citoyennes. Du droit de vote à l'exercice du pouvoir* (Paris: Editions de l'Atelier, 1995).

5   Françoise Gaspard, 'Système politique et rareté des femmes élues. Spécificités françaises?', in Le Bras-Chopard and Mossuz-Lavau (eds), pp. 108 and 105.

6   In particular, the publication of a book co-authored by Françoise Gaspard, historian and political scientist but also a practising politician, marked a turning point in the debate on women's representation. See Françoise Gaspard, Claude Servan-Schreiber, and Anne Le Gall, *Au pouvoir citoyennes. Liberté, égalité, parité* (Paris: Seuil, 1992).

7   *L'Express*, 6 June 1996.

8   Ibid.

9   Mariette Sineau, 'Les femmes politiques sous la Ve République' in *Pouvoirs*, 82, special issue on *Femmes en politique* (1997), 45-57, p. 52.

10 Gisèle Halimi, *La Nouvelle Cause des femmes* (Paris: Seuil, 1997), p. 52.

11 Gisèle Halimi has reproduced a number of polls on the subject in the appendices to her book, pp. 225-26.

12 For a list of abstention rates for the period, see Sheila Perry, 'Politique spectacle, politique débâcle?', in *La Société française*, ed. by Máire Cross (Newcastle upon Tyne: Newcastle Polytechnic, 1991), pp. 72-85. A number of French journals produced special issues debating the crisis: for example, *Regards sur l'actualité*, 164 (September-October 1990); *Débat*, 70 (May-August 1992).

13 For a fuller outline of the various strands of universalism and its main proponents, see Mariette Sineau, 'La parité française: un contre-modèle de l'égalité républicaine?' in Le Bras-Chopard and Mossuz-Lavau (eds), pp. 121-42, p. 121.

14 Elisabeth Badinter, 'Un remède pire que le mal', *Le Nouvel Observateur*, 14 January 1999, p. 43.

15 Cited by Sineau, 'La parité française', p. 128.

16 A phrase used by Prime Minister Alain Juppé in his speech to the National Assembly on 11 March 1997, during the debate on women in politics. Cited by Sineau, 'La parité française', p. 138.

17 Cited by Sineau, 'La parité française', p. 125.

18 Interview in *Le Figaro*, 9 March 1995, quoted by Sineau, 'La parité française', note 5, pp. 121-22.

19 See in particular the testimonies in Laure Adler, *Les Femmes politiques* (Paris: Seuil, 1993) and Régine Saint-Criq and Nathalie Prévost, *Vol au-dessus d'un nid de machos* (Paris: Albin Michel, 1993), also Elisabeth Guigou's book recounting her own experiences in politics: *Etre femme en politique* (Paris: Plon, 1997).

20 Nicole Belloubet-Frier, 'Sont-elles différentes?' in *Pouvoirs*, 82, special issue *Femmes en politique* (1997), 59-75, p. 65. In particular, she takes Elisabeth Guigou to task for some of the assertions in her book (see previous note) and substantiates her case with an analysis of parliamentary questions in January 1997. One might take issue with the research methods adopted (parliamentary questions are a very narrow part of a politician's activity, so it is dangerous to generalise from such a specific example) but the study has the merit of raising the question of the extent to which assertions regarding male and female behaviour can be substantiated.

21 This is the term commonly used to refer to empty rhetoric, devoid of practical content or meaning.

22 See, as one example among many, Béatrice Damamme-Gilbert's article on advertising, in which she shows

that even though modern advertising is culturally and artistically innovative, it remains traditional in its portrayal of gender. Béatrice Damamme-Gilbert, 'French Magazine Advertising: New Forms of Dialogue'; in *Media Developments and Cultural Change*, ed. by Sheila Perry and Pamela M. Moores (Newcastle-upon-Tyne: University of Northumbria at Newcastle, 1999), pp. 47-61.

23   Françoise Gaspard, 'La parité, pourquoi pas?' in *Pouvoirs*, 82, special issue on *Femmes en politique* (1997), 115-25, p. 124.

24   On the literary television programme, *Apostrophes*, broadcast by Antenne 2, 18 February 1987.

25   A number of books giving personal testimonies have been published, and all cite examples of such comments: see, for example, Elisabeth Schemla, *Edith Cresson, la femme piégée* (Paris: Flammarion, 1993), pp. 50, 118; Adler, pp. 193, 203, 204. See also Gaspard, 'La parité', p. 124.

26   Cited by Gaspard, 'Système politique', p. 100.

27   On national radio and television, on 10 November 1970.

28   As Marina Yaguello has pointed out, this lack is ideological, not linguistic. The French language is based on the binary structure masculine/feminine, so that 'Tout masculin appelle un féminin', and French children play games in which they invent corresponding couples. Moreover, words like *ministre*, ending in mute e, are normally epicenes, that is words which can be either masculine or feminine depending on the person denoted (like *enfant*). The refusal to say *Mme la Ministre* is sociological, not linguistic. (See Marina Yaguello, *Les Mots et les femmes, essai d'approche socio-linguistique de la condition féminine* (Paris: Payot, 1978). Refusal to use feminine forms led to all sorts of circumlocutions when Edith Cresson became Prime Minister (1991-92), for example, as she was 'la première femme Premier Ministre'. The formula *la ministre* is now widely, though not universally used; *député* is, however, still more common than *députée* except in feminist texts.

29   Cited by Adler, pp. 170-71.

30   Françoise Gaspard, 'Les Françaises en politique au lendemain des élections législatives de 1997', *French Politics and Society*, 15: 4 (Fall 1997), 1-11, p. 5.

31   Gaspard, 'Système politique' in Le Bras-Chopard and Mossuz-Lavau (eds), pp. 115-17.

32   Gaspard, 'Les Françaises en politique', p. 6.

33   See Halimi, p. 67.

34   January 2000. Once adopted, this will mean that certain dual functions will cease to be legal: for example, a Government minister will no longer be able to become mayor or president of a General or Regional Council.

35   Gaspard, 'Les Françaises en politique', p. 2.

36   *L'Express*, 11 October 1985. To add to the irony, Yvette Roudy was Minister for Women's Rights!

37   Janine Mossuz-Lavau, 'Les Françaises et la politique: de la citoyenneté à la parité', *Regards sur l'actualité*, (December 1997), pp. 3-14, p. 11.

38   Gaspard, 'Les Françaises en politique', p. 7.

39   Mossuz-Lavau, 'Les Françaises et la politique', p. 10.

40   Gaspard, 'Les Françaises en politique', p. 2.

41   This and the following are from Gaspard, 'Système politique' in Le Bras-Chopard and Mossuz-Lavau (eds), pp. 100-102.

42   This is compounded by the presidential regime, which makes men vie to become *présidentiables*, that is potential presidential candidates, for which a certain degree of notoriety on the national level is needed.

43   A couple of minor parties are led by women: Les Verts by Dominique Voynet, and Lutte Ouvrière by Arlette Laguiller (the one woman to have been a candidate in all three presidential elections since 1981). Lionel Jospin was made the official Socialist Party presidential candidate in 1995 by open election – when the candidate designated by common acclaim, Jacques Delors, declined to stand.

44 Saint-Criq and Prévost, pp. 48-49.

45 Quoted in Catherine Rambert, *La Présidente* (Paris: Editions N°1, 1997), p. 21.

46 Saint-Criq and Prévost, pp. 41-42.

47 Mossuz-Lavau, 'Les Françaises et la politique', p. 9.

48 Gaspard, 'Les Françaises en politique', p. 2.

49 Mossuz-Lavau, 'Les Françaises et la politique', p. 9.

50 This view was expressed in the political programme *A armes égales*, in a debate on the theme *Faut-il décoloniser la femme?*, broadcast by Antenne 2 on 17 November 1970. It has been developed by Mona Ozouf in her book *Les Mots et les femmes. Essai sur la singularité française* (Paris: Fayard, 1995).

51 Alison Holland, 'Women', in *Aspects of Modern and Contemporary France*, ed. by Sheila Perry (London and New York: Routledge, 1997), pp. 137-52.

52 On 27 January 1993, a *Réseau Femmes pour la parité* was created, and published a manifesto in favour of parity in *Le Monde* on 10 November 1993, signed by 577 men and women, in almost equal numbers (577 being the number of seats in the National Assembly). After Alain Juppé's Government reshuffle at the end of 1995, a group of women politicians from all parties formed a *Mouvement pour la parité*, and on 6 June 1996 published a *Manifeste des dix pour la parité* in *L'Express*.

53 This story is recounted by Halimi in Chapter 7 of her book, pp. 107-21, and its legal implications discussed in Chapter 8, pp. 123-37. She was following in the footsteps of Monique Pelletier, who had tried and failed in 1980, blocked by the Constitutional Council. Adler, p. 184.

54 Unsuccessfully, as it happens. 'It was at the time of tactical voting, and voting for us was not seen as tactically useful', Halimi, p. 118.

55 Gisèle Halimi, in *Le Monde Diplomatique*, October 1994.

56 The Council can only consider a text which has been referred to it and only consider those articles called into question in the referral (and with such a massive vote in favour of the article on quotas, this was not – could not – be the case).

57 There was one faint glimmer of progress – distinction on the grounds of sex was declared contrary to fundamental law 'en l'état actuel des normes constitutionnelles' (as constitutional law currently stands), showing that the Constitutional Council recognized its anti-parity days were numbered. *Libération*, 16-17 January 1999.

58 These and the following details are taken from the text adopted by the National Assembly on 25-26 January 2000, obtained from the National Assembly's website: http://www.assemblee-nationale.fr.

59 The first elections affected will be the municipal elections in March 2001, followed by elections to the Senate (September 2001), to the National Assembly (2002), regional and European elections (2004).

60 Sheila Perry, 'French Television and Women Politicians' in *Women and Representation*, ed. by Judith Still and Diana Knight (Nottingham: Nottingham University Press, 1995), pp. 21-42.

61 As well as our own, cited above, see Jane Freedman, *Femmes politiques: mythes et symboles* (Paris: L'Harmattan, 1997); Pamela M. Moores, 'Women in the Presidential Race, Arlette Laguiller and Dominique Voynet, 1995', *Women in French Studies*, (Winter 1997), pp. 281-92; Diana Holmes, 'The Madonna and the Dragon: The Representation of Women Politicians in the French Press'; *Modern and Contemporary France*, 33 (April 1988), 10-16; the chapter by William B. Smith in this book.

62 Indeed, in its second report (September 1999), even the *Observatoire de la parité* refers to the *statut de l'élu* as an issue specially designed for women.

63 Evelyne Pisier and Eleni Varikas, 'Femmes, République, et démocratie', in *Pouvoirs*, 82, special issue on *Femmes en politique* (1997), 127-43, p. 136.

Bibliography

Adler, Laure, *Les Femmes politiques* (Paris: Seuil, 1993).

Bard, Christine, 'Les femmes et le pouvoir politique dans la France de l'entre-deux guerres', in *Les Femmes et la politique*, ed. by Armelle Le Bras-Chopard and Janine Mossuz-Lavau (Paris: L'Harmattan, 1997), pp. 41-54.

Damamme-Gilbert, Béatrice, 'French Magazine Advertising: New Forms of Dialogue', in *Media Developments and Cultural Change*, ed. by Sheila Perry and Pamela M. Moores (Newcastle-upon-Tyne: University of Northumbria at Newcastle, 1999), pp. 47-61.

Débat, 70 (May-August 1992).

Freedman, Jane, *Femmes politiques: mythes et symboles* (Paris: L'Harmattan, 1997).

Gaspard, Françoise, *Les Femmes dans la prise de décision en France et en Europe* (Paris: L'Harmattan, 1997).

————, Claude Servan-Schreiber and Anne Le Gall, *Au pouvoir citoyennes. Liberté, égalité, parité* (Paris: Seuil, 1992).

————, 'Les Françaises en politique au lendemain des élections législatives de 1997', *French Politics and Society*, 15: 4 (Fall 1997), 1-11.

Guigou, Elisabeth, *Etre femme en politique* (Paris: Plon, 1997).

Halimi, Gisèle, *Femmes: moitié de la terre, moitié du pouvoir. Plaidoyer pour une démocratie paritaire* (Paris: Gallimard, 1994).

————, *La Nouvelle Cause des femmes* (Paris: Seuil, 1997).

Holland, Alison, 'Women' in *Aspects of Modern and Contemporary France*, ed. by Sheila Perry (London and New York: Routledge, 1997), pp. 137-52.

Holmes, Diana, 'The Madonna and the Dragon: The Representation of Women Politicians in the French Press', *Modern and Contemporary France*, 33 (April 1988), 10-16.

Jensen, Jane and Mariette Sineau, *Mitterrand et les Françaises. Un rendez-vous manqué* (Paris: Presses de Science Po, 1995).

Latour, Patricia, Monique Houssin and Madia Tovar, *Femmes et citoyennes. Du droit de vote à l'exercice du pouvoir* (Paris: Editions de l'Atelier, 1995).

Le Bras-Chopard, Armelle and Janine Mossuz-Lavau (eds), *Les Femmes et la politique* (Paris: L'Harmattan, 1997).

Moores, Pamela M., 'Women in the Presidential Race, Arlette Laguiller and Dominique Voynet, 1995', *Women in French Studies* (Winter 1997), 281-92.

Mossuz-Lavau, Janine, *Femmes/Hommes. Pour la parité* (Paris: Presses de la FNSP, 1998).

————, 'Les Françaises et la politique: de la citoyenneté à la parité', *Regards sur l'actualité* (December 1997), 3-14.

Ozouf, Mona, *Les Mots et les femmes. Essai sur la singularité française* (Paris: Fayard, 1995).

Perry, Sheila, 'French Television and Women Politicians', in *Women and Representation*, ed. by Judith Still and Diana Knight (Nottingham: Nottingham University Press, 1995), pp. 21-42.

————,'Politique spectacle, politique débâcle?', in *La Société française*, ed. by Máire Cross (Newcastle-upon-Tyne: Newcastle Polytechnic, 1991), pp. 72-85.

Pouvoirs, 82 (1997), special issue on *Femmes en politique*.

Rambert, Catherine, *La Présidente* (Paris: Editions N°1, 1997).

Regards sur l'actualité, 164 (September-October 1990).

Reynolds, Siân, *Alternative Politics: Women and Public Life in France between the Wars* (Stirling, Scotland: Stirling French Publications, 1993).

Roudy, Yvette, *Mais de quoi ont-ils peur? Un vent de misogynie souffle sur la politique* (Paris: Albin Michel, 1995).

Saint-Criq, Régine and Nathalie Prévost, *Vol au-dessus d'un nid de machos* (Paris: Albin Michel, 1993).

Schemla, Elisabeth, *Edith Cresson, la femme piégée* (Paris: Flammarion, 1993).

Yaguello, Marina, *Les Mots et les femmes, essai d'approche socio-linguistique de la condition féminine* (Paris: Payot, 1978).

2   Women and Political Participation

Monica Threlfall

When North-American feminists such as Jean Bethke Elshtain developed the concept of public man, private woman, which became a dominant paradigm for analysing women's relationship to politics, little did they know how familiar a concept it already was in Spanish culture, both high and low.[1] Not only were traditional bars everywhere adorned with a mass-produced decorative tile, all graphically illustrated, bearing the excruciating aphorism: 'La mujer, en casa, y con la pata quebrada' (Woman – indoors and with a broken leg), but high culture too had long engaged with the concept. The most distinguished of Spain's pioneering feminists, the first woman to hold a public post, Concepción Arenal (1820-93), who also happened to be Spain's first serious criminologist, first scientific sociologist, and first person to write a treatise on international law, had examined the idea of separate spheres and found them appropriate. Writing in 1861, she thought women should want nothing of political rights or participation and should refuse the vote, because politics was an arbitrary, intolerant world riddled with faults and vices. The law was such an ass in her view that there was nothing to be gained from women taking on any responsibility for it. But she made a clear distinction between the desirable and the flawed parts of the male sphere, and wanted women to take part in education, have a profession and a useful activity outside the home. By the 1880s, she was criticizing the ideal of the housebound wife, contained as a recluse in her private sphere, because of her restraining influence on her menfolk as well as on the spread of progressive liberal ideas through society. Arenal ended up agreeing with Susan B. Anthony and Elizabeth Cady Stanton on the positive effect women's political participation would have.[2]

It was not until after the proclamation of the Second Republic in 1931 that the first women were allowed into formal politics on the basis of a passive suffrage. With only three women elected to Parliament, the fight for the right to vote was launched. Clara Campoamor's determination and eloquence in the *Cortes,* together with Socialist support, were responsible for achieving women's suffrage before the end of the year.[3] Spain thus became the first of Europe's Latin countries to grant women the vote, fourteen years before France or Italy. These three women had remarkably distinguished careers.[4] Victoria Kent, as head of the prison service, Federica Montseny, as Minister of Health and Dolores Ibárruri, the Communist leader, all became distinguished figures of the Republican and Civil War period.

But, during the military dictatorship (1939-75), women once more became conspicuous by their absence from public affairs. The woman of the 'new' Spain was to bear a remarkable resemblance to the woman of the *ancien régime*. During its first eight legislative periods the unelected, rubber-stamping National Assembly only ever had two female members (*procuradoras*) and by the time of its abolition in 1977 it had no more than ten. Franco never appointed a woman cabinet minister. Over nearly four decades only one woman achieved national prominence as a politician and that was Pilar Primo de Rivera, the sister of the murdered fascist leader José Antonio.[5] To cap it all, she was head of the *Sección Femenina* (Feminine Section) of the fascist *Falange* (later remodelled as the official state party, the 'National Movement'), which extolled women's subordination to men and their confinement to the home as a virtue to be obligatorily inculcated into all Spanish women who were called up to do a six-month stint of 'social service' to the fatherland.[6]

Whatever their differences on other matters, both the monarchists and the national-syndicalists agreed that a woman's place was in the home.[7] Francoism widely and effectively implemented its own version of Nazism's *Kirche, Kinder and Küche* philosophy. As their contribution to the public sphere, women only needed to provide their heroic warrior returning from the political front with his well-earned solace, *el reposo del guerrero*, and this was their main input to public affairs. Women's restricted environment was backed up by law until 1961, after which they became entitled to the same rights as men in political, professional and employment activities, with the exception of the law and the armed forces, but the stereotype lived on.[8]

At the beginning of the transition, little information existed upon which predictions of women's political behaviour could be based. Neither the recent nor the more distant past had given women much political experience, and few of them had gained sufficient fame to be remembered by the public.[9] The organized women's movement only began to grow during International Women's Year (1975). On the eve of democracy, it had not yet succeeded in spreading to most parts of the country and still involved a rather small minority of women. A powerful feminine stereotype mitigated any assertiveness on the part of women in public affairs. Women were considered silent bystanders of the unfolding process. Yet a few months into the transition, a national survey showed that a majority of women favoured democracy and believed that it was better for everyone to take an interest in politics and to take on political responsibilities. However, just under one quarter of all women thought authority and decision-making could be entrusted to a single 'eminent man'. The survey also showed that women understood the implications of democracy, associating it with equality of rights, freedom of expression and social justice.[10] They also displayed considerable consistency between thought and action: over 60% were intending to vote and less than 20% said they would abstain (Metra/Seis, p. 47). Undertaken just before democratic reform actually started, the survey showed that women had a positive attitude towards participation in the decision-making process.

For the first elections, the stereotype of the conservative housebound woman was so strong that the democratic parties, particularly those on the left wing, expected them to stay home on polling day too, or if not, to vote for the Centre and Centre Right.[11] Electoral turnout and abstention rates, still considered a good indicator of the popular legitimacy of the political system, tell us something about women's responses. The evidence for Spain points to persistent differences in voter turnout between the sexes, but within a record of generally high turnout rates.[12] Women tended to decide whether to vote at a later point in the campaign than men (often in the last two weeks). There was also more 'last minute' abstention by women who had intended to vote, mainly due to practical difficulties, such as illness and household responsibilities. Still evidence of lower levels of participation was insufficient to confirm any thesis about the political passivity attributed to women, since the size of the gender gap in turnout remained small. Thus, the first of many stereotypes was shattered.

This chapter will focus on the development of women's participation in decision-making spheres of two types of institution: democratic parties and elective public office. For reasons of space and the wealth of material on these matters available to researchers, this article will not be in a position to deal with the equally rewarding spheres of gender politics: voluntary activism, advocacy and defence of women's rights, equality policy-making, voting behaviour or political attitudes and culture. This chapter traces the rise of women's public presence, comparing parties and tiers of decision-making and power. It is able to focus in some depth on the relationship between internal party politics and gender parity of representation because of the extent to which the PSOE has been involved in the issues and the continuous gender monitoring it has undertaken, as well as its willingness to make public and to publish the data that other parties do not gather or consider to be 'internal affairs'.

A further problem is the regional question. Given Spain's socio-economic and political diversity and its well-developed devolved Government structures, a regionally-based analysis would seem to offer a way of avoiding the pitfalls inherent in discussing women as a homogeneous group across the nation. Yet a preliminary survey conducted during the research for this article revealed that the question was far too complex for clear characteristics or trends to become evident at a superficial level. In addition, the seventeen Autonomous Communities are of themselves enormously diverse: the small ones consist of one province with a single large town and the large ones contain widely contrasting socio-economic and geographical characteristics. It would not be wise to postulate (without an in-depth investigation), that women did consistently better, or suffered particular constraints in any particular region or province. Party members, it appears, are a self-selected elite which is not necessarily representative of its locality. Moreover, nationwide parties have something of a homogenizing effect where the participation of women is concerned, diffusing their values, policies and practice.

The chapter's main analytical concern is to use available empirical data to examine whether women participating in institutional politics only find a space to operate at the margins or in the lower echelons of power. It will assess whether the Spanish case illustrates or belies this commonly-held view. In its conclusions, it emphasizes the decisive impact that the adoption of a quota of women candidates and of gender parity made on the PSOE and other parties, and asks how far women's progress is, paradoxically, a case of strong top-down political leadership and even of 'enlightened elitism'.

Women and Party Membership
Membership of a party and activism within its ranks are, strictly speaking, voluntary

acts. Yet, through their policies, democratic parties can and do have an influence on the composition of their membership. The gender composition of Spanish parties is the result both of citizens' choices and of the endeavours of parties to attract them. There is a gendered nature to those choices: party affiliation has not been taken up equally by both sexes. In Spain, men predominated to such an extent that women in most parties comprised only a fraction of the membership until the late 1980s. Early figures were poorly recorded by the parties, as seen in Table 1.

In the early stage of democracy the parties reported a considerable upsurge in affiliation, but the question of how many female members they had enlisted was dismissed. 'We don't discriminate' was a frequent reply, 'in this party everybody is treated the same'. By the time of the 1979 election campaign, they had been badgered into giving an estimate of the proportion of women members, and by 1982 the PSOE and PCE had computerized their membership records, but the AP and UCD were still relying on guesstimates (Table 1). These early patterns of female affiliation had striking features. First, the lowest percentage belonged to the PSOE (9%) – though once the PCE had made a proper count its female component dropped to a similar proportion (11%). Secondly, guesstimates by parties of the Right and Centre were higher than the real figure of the Left, though in a briefing given to me by the PP at the time it turned out that becoming a member was easy for women: their husbands could sign on their wives as supporters! Membership in the PP was more of a social affair in which both spouses participated, whereas in the left-wing parties membership involved an individual proposal and acceptance procedure designed to weed out affiliations considered undesirable. In other words, *gatekeeping styles* had a significant impact on the figures. Thirdly, women had a stronger presence in the ranks of the far Left. It seems that politically active women were polarized between the Centre Right and Right on the one hand, and the far Left on the other. The PSOE displayed the anomaly

Party	1978/9 %	1982 %	1984 %	1989 %	1991 %
AP (Right)	–	35	33	-	30
PDP (Right)			28		
UCD / CDS	25	30	5	-	19.6
PSOE	10–15	9* (July)	12	17.8	21.1
PCE	30	11*	12	17.6	-
PTE (non-parliamentary Left)	25	Dissolved	-	-	-
ORT (non-parliamentary Left)	35	Dissolved	-	-	-
MC–OIC (non-parliamentary Left)	40–45	Dissolved	-	-	-
LCR (non-parliamentary Left)	30	–	-	-	-
EE (Basque Left)	-	-	39	-	-
Total	-	-	21	-	-

Sources: 1979, 1982: Estimates given by each party, except those marked with an asterisk which come from a database. Absolute figures were not available.
1984: IDES, *Las españolas ante la política* (Madrid: Instituto de la Mujer, 1988), pp. 60-61.
1989 and 1991: *La mujer en cifras: Una década, 1982-1992* (Madrid: Instituto de la Mujer/Ministerio de Asuntos Sociales, 1994), p. 64.

Table 1. Women party members 1978–91.

of receiving most votes from women while having the least members, a situation which gave it an enormous opportunity it was to start to exploit rather belatedly in the latter part of the 1980s.

Women in the PSOE

In the first decade of return to democracy, the presence of women in the party that was to win a landslide victory with 48% of the vote in 1982 and govern for over thirteen years was almost derisory. Other European Socialist parties, even in Catholic or southern European countries, had at least twice the proportion of women members at the time.[13] The marked increase in popularity of the PSOE, the extension of its public activity and street presence, the forums provided by its positions of power in municipal and regional administrations were expected to stimulate a growth in affiliation by a broad spectrum of people, including women. Yet the 1977 wave of affiliations soon petered out, leaving membership fluctuating at around 100,000 in 1981. Members in the first period of democracy were 91% male, unduly old (only 5% of members were aged between eighteen and twenty-five, and 43% were over fifty). The party itself was worried that if they did not act soon to attract different members, the risk of 'an excessive ageing of the party' would be considerable (*Perfil*, p. 9). It acted to stem this trend.

Political success and better organization were to set the PSOE on a lasting new course from 1982, with a steady, lasting, year-on-year increase in membership and in women's presence to reach 388,000 in 1998, with 103,000 women. At the same time, the proportion of women rose without hiccup from 10% in 1982 to 26.5% in 1998.[14] Regular internal elections depending on entitlement to vote and the presence of a Secretariat for the Participation of Women in each regional and many provincial PSOE organizations mean that membership figures are carefully watched over but may not be regularly culled to remove non-renewals. Unlike quotas for public posts no-one can enforce a quota of members and it is notable that the party is still well over 70% male.

In the early years, the gender gap in affiliation was outdone by the gender gap in political leadership and public office. Women were under-represented at these upper levels even in relation to their low affiliation rates. A complex mechanism of political discrimination operated against the selection of women for such positions, as demonstrated by a study showing that women affiliates were younger, better educated, in employment, often as professionals (*Perfil*, p. 6) and tended not to be dormant members.[15] PSOE women were therefore more highly qualified than the average party member, over half of the PSOE members being manual workers (*Perfil*, p. 15). All these factors suggested that the proportion of women with political responsibilities should have been higher than the proportion of women rank-and-file members. Yet it was not. Only 26% of women party members had ever held any post of 'political responsibility' – most of them at a modest level such as the Branch Committee, as opposed to 35% of men (*Perfil*, p. 6). The party leadership consisted of a Federal (Spain-wide) Committee, on which only three women sat or 2.8% of the total[16] and a Federal Executive Commission where there were three women out of 24 members or 12.5%, a much higher proportion; though when the Executive was divided into two tiers of responsibility only one woman was left at the top. The figure of 12% was the same in 1985-86 (IDES, p. 61).

All this was to change by the turn of the millennium, to such an extent that women were now over-represented in public and internal posts in relation to their presence among the membership. The party had moved from the argument that leaders should reflect the composition of the party (which they never did anyway, being on the whole composed of working classes and led by professional middle classes), to the belief that they should reflect wider society. Two key party conferences marked the two stages of an internal reform, a notable feminist victory, which brought women to many positions of leadership in the party: first the quota of 25% was approved at the XXXI Conference in 1988 and then parity democracy with a minimum of 40% for both sexes was taken up at the XXXIV Conference in 1997.

The full story of how an overwhelmingly male party was persuaded to take these drastic measures is still to be written.[17] Its impact was remarkable and by no means superficial, as it was implemented throughout the party at every level: a greater women's presence was engendered in the provincial and regional and emigration party structures as well. Within a year after the XXXIV Conference decision, all the twenty-one regional party federations moved to raise the percentage of women in their leadership (Regional Executive Committees) and reached 34% or more, with ten out of twenty-one reaching the full target in one go. Only Castilla-La Mancha lagged behind with 32%, but the national average reached 37%, a respectable implementation rate over such a short period.[18]

What was the political salience of women's greater presence in the PSOE? Much has been written about how women tend to be given the 'soft' portfolios or areas of responsibility. In this the PSOE is no exception. In fact 58% of the above-mentioned regional leaderships is currently composed of women without any portfolio at all, having been brought in as 'junior' members (*vocales*). Of those with a portfolio, the largest number, so predictably, have the Participation of Women brief, followed by Social Welfare, Environment, Social Movements, Political Education, Education, Culture and Youth, the full roll-call of feminized areas of interest. A very similar pattern repeats itself at provincial level, where the number of women in the Provincial Executives has risen to 39% from 25% before the historic decision. Again, this is a large, sudden rise, but women are concentrated in exactly the same areas.

Top Posts in the PSOE

As for top posts in the PSOE, an interesting pattern is developing since the 1997 adoption of gender parity. At the Federal Executive Committee level, the XXXIV Conference implemented its policy immediately in the elections held the very day after the decision was adopted: fourteen women out of thirty-three members, which is over 42%. But they are mostly (79%) in the lower tier of posts without a portfolio or specific policy responsibility. Only three are federal spokespersons: on Social Movements, Social Welfare and Participation of Women – typically feminized posts, although Social Welfare was quite a major policy area, commanding a whole ministry in the previous

PSOE Government. There is no woman in the top PSOE leadership posts of President, Secretary-General, Deputy Secretary-General, or Organization Secretary.

At regional level, among the eighty-four very top posts in the PSOE's twenty-one regional and nationality federations (four each), there are now ten women (12%), spread across the country as follows: three Regional Party Presidents (Madrid, Cantabria, Baleares); two Regional Secretaries-General (Murcia, America); two Regional Deputy Secretaries-General (Castilla-La Mancha, Navarra); and three Regional Organization Secretaries (Extremadura, La Rioja, Europe).[19]

At the provincial level, thirteen women have reached one of the four most powerful posts in thirty provincial party organizations (11%). These are distributed as follows: six Provincial Presidents (Cordoba, Huesca, Teruel, Ciudad Real, Guadalajara, Toledo); two Provincial Secretaries-General (Seville, Cáceres); three Provincial Deputy Secretaries-General (Almería, Toledo, Soria); and two Organization Secretaries (Alava, Cáceres).

Table 2 highlights the overall gender distribution of power in the PSOE. The picture obtained on female leadership in the PSOE is revealing. On the one hand, posts in column (a) are governed by the binding decision on parity of the XXXIV Conference, the supreme organ of the party, and this would explain the similarity in the proportion of women. There is a lag at the regional level, but it is mostly explained by the two regions which held their Conferences before the parity decision not including as many women. Columns (b), (c) and (d) are a better reflection of spontaneous party dynamics within the 40% 'constraint' and here the pattern is clear: women are still quota-fillers in the lowest tier of leadership in all three levels. Nevertheless, the three levels present similarities, so there is no case here for saying that the *further* from the centre of power, the more women there are. In fact, regional and provincial party structures are also power centres in their own right, controlling decisions in several important spheres: on the one hand elections, policies and public management of regional Governments, of city councils in provincial capitals, and of mayors of smaller towns and villages; and on the other hand the sphere of internal party politics and policy through the delegates to Conference and to the Federal Committee which is mandated to oversee the Federal Executive between the triennial Conferences.

	(a) % of all posts	(b) 4 posts with most power	(c) Upper tier	(d) Lower tier
Federal Executive Commission	14 of 33 42 %	0	3 21%	11 79%
Regional and Nationality Executive Commissions	232 of 626 37%	10 of 84 12%	98 42%	134 58%
Provincial Executive Commissions	386 of 988 39%	13 of 120 * 16%	145 38%	241 62%

* 120 = 4 x only 30 provincial organizations. Cataluña, Galicia, País Valenciano, Canarias and Baleares are excluded because party structures are different (smaller units) and the data is not available.
Source: Own calculations on the basis of data in Secretaría de Participación de la Mujer, table 9, p. 39.

Table 2. Women in leadership positions in the PSOE in 1998.

These power centres are, evidently, more reluctant to hand over 40% of real power, as opposed to just posts, to women. Nevertheless, for women with little political experience who get to stand for a leadership position relatively soon after becoming active in the party, having no portfolio in the lower tier, or a stereotyped portfolio she enjoys can be viewed as an opportunity for political training experience. More importantly, the PSOE system may offer women a less brutal experience than the one they might well have had if there had been no quota and they had had to battle their way in against male gatekeepers and their biases. For the time being, marginal power with future prospects appears to be the price of women's sudden inclusion and surge towards parity.

Women in Public Office

Parliaments everywhere are under a certain pressure to increase their proportion of women in the name of equity and balanced gender representation but parties are responsible for delivering the women members to Parliament. The job of the top party leaders in this process is not as straightforward as it seems. They do not have full control of the process of selecting candidates to stand, and the electorate's choices, given the eternal secrecy of the ballot, can be both hard to predict and volatile over time. In the Spanish case, the decentralized, federal nature of the PSOE, the province-based list system and the d'Hondt seat allocation method all intervene in the process of adding to the uncertainty. For this reason, feminists in Spain have tended to draw as much attention to the candidate lists in the run-up to elections as to the outcome in Parliament. During election campaigns a competitive situation is created between the parties, with the gender composition of the lists generating media comment. Over time the debate has become more sophisticated, distinguishing between run-of-the-mill candidates, candidates likely to win a seat, and candidate lists headed by women. Candidate lists are the nexus between internal party life and public life, and reflect the gender balance in power within the party as the top provincial party leaders often head the list or share its peak with a heavyweight candidate adopted from outside the constituency.[20]

Candidates to Parliament

Simple aggregates of women candidates provide the data that goes back furthest in time. A long-range comparison is constructed in Table 3. It reveals a marked contrast between the first ten years of elections, in which progress was slow, and the last decade in which a substantial leap forward was taken by all parties after the adoption of quotas in the PSOE and IU. The proportion of candidates is well over the quota, which can be viewed as positive, but this table should be read in relation to Tables 4 and 5 and actually indicates that when it comes to filling up the electoral slates with candidates who have no hope of getting elected (a party tends to field candidates for all possible seats), there is no objection to their being women. They are there to conduct the less glamorous parts of the campaign in the remoter villages and to gain a political training *vis-à-vis* their parties and the public. Table 3 also shows that, whereas the Right

Party lists	1977	%	1979	%	1982	%	1986	%	1996	%
AP/CD/PP (Right) (1)	49	9.3	54	11.9	48	8.4	51	14.3	91	25
UCD (Centre Right)	33	6.2	36	7.1	45	8.1	-	-	-	
CDS (Centre)	-	-	-	-	56	10.0	48	13.6	-	
PSOE	50	10.7	44	8.7	46	8.2	48	13.6	129	35.4
PCE /IU (Left)	60	14.3	54	10.8	54	9.7	38	10.7	133	36.5
Other new Left parties	-	-	454	25.1	-	-	555	31.2	-	-
PNV (Basque nationalist)	2	6.0	2	5.7	4	12.1	4	15.4	9	37.5
CiU (Catalonia)	6	8.7	5	8.9	4	6.8	n/a	n/a	11	24.4
EE (Basque Left)	7	12.0	3	10.7	6	18.2	} *	} *	-	-
HB (Basque separatist)	-	-	3	8.6	3	9.1	} 7	}16.7	-	-
PSA (Andalusia)	-	-	9	10.7	-	-			-	-
Far Right and other rightists (2)	13	8.5	57	12.2	-	-	88	20	-	-
Total	690	11.6	1226	16.4	1080	16.4	1092	21.8	373 (of 5 parties)	33.3 (of 5 parties)

(1) In 1977, Alianza Popular; in 1979, Coalición Democrática; in 1982-89, Alianza Popular (including the Partido Demócrata Popular led by Oscar Alzaga); from 1986, Partido Popular.
(2) In 1977, Alianza Nacional 18 de julio and Fuerza Nueva; in 1979, Unión Nacional, led by Blas Piñar; in 1986 right-wing parties are not given separate mention.

* In 1986 all Basque nationalists other than PNV.

Sources: 1977: Dirección General de Desarrollo Comunitario, *Mujer y 16 de junio*, pp. 84-85 and 106-107.
1979 and 1982: own calculations based on *Boletín Oficial del Estado*, 3 February 1979 and 2 October 1982.
1982: data from *Situación social de la mujer en España* (Madrid: Instituto de la Mujer/Ministerio de Cultura, 1983), p. 17.
1986: data from *La mujer en España: Política* (Madrid: Instituto de la Mujer/Ministerio de Asuntos Sociales, n.d.), pp. 48-49.
1996: Federación de Mujeres Progresistas, *Políticas sobre igualdad de oportunidades para la mujer* (Press dossier for the 1996 general election, 1996)

Table 3. Women candidates on elections lists for Congress.

and the Left were neck-and-neck in the first decade, the Left was outdoing the Right in the 1990s.

Candidates likely to Win

There was a time when it was considered a sign of progress to find any women on electoral lists. Today analysts make the difference between candidates 'to win' (*para salir*) and candidates 'to make up the numbers' (*de relleno*). The indicator of likely candidates to win is based on whether they occupy a place on the list which did get a seat in the previous election, on the supposition there will be no swings, as seen in Table 4. This is not quite the 'safe' seat of British elections but the likely seat of the PR-list system. In 1989, the PSOE fielded thirty-three (17.5%) likely female deputies, AP ten (9.5%) 'likelies', CiU one (5.5%), HB one (20%), EE one (50%) and the rest, e.g. PNV, no likely women deputies.[21] Regionalist parties are the worst offenders when it come to

37

not putting up any women who are likely to win (p. 115), whereas the Basque Left parties are the best.

By 1996 there was a marked increase in women candidates' chances of being allocated to a place with a possibility of winning a seat. All in all they had almost doubled in number, from forty-six to eighty-four. The increase was even more marked in the PP than the PSOE, because in the first three elections the presence of women on the top half of the lists had actually been diminishing from 28% to 25% to 20% The rise was also notable in the smaller Left and regional parties. Overall, the PSOE remained, at 33%, the party to give most women a fair chance (see Table 4).

With regard to the Senate, the PSOE also had the best record in 1996:[22] it fielded thirty-four candidates with a chance of winning out of fifty-six, while the PP fielded sixteen likely winners out of twenty-seven women; the IU none; CiU one out of one and the PNV two out of five (Federación de Mujeres Progresistas, *Políticas*, 1996). Of course there was no security of obtaining a seat, but both men and women had a chance of winning, 61% for women and 63% for men, if there were no swings.

Leading Candidates

As mentioned, occupying the top places of a candidate list is an indicator of being in a leadership position in the constituency party. Therefore, leading candidates give a better indication of what is internal politics in a party than of the socio-economic environment in which they are standing. In 1989, it was still the case that the parties that were led by women at constituency level were mostly the radical ones. The parliamentary parties had few women constituency list leaders, as Table 5 shows.

In 1989 the PP fielded the highest number of woman-headed lists, six out of fifty-two constituencies. The IU followed with five, the PSOE with three, and the CDS with one. That made only fifteen women electoral list leaders out of a potential two hundred and eight (fifty-two constituencies multiplied by four nationwide parties) or 7.2%. Though by 1996 this had grown for the three nationwide parliamentary parties to twenty (12.8%) the obvious conclusion was that top constituency-level parliamentary

	1989 No. of women	% of candidates	1996 No. of Women	% of candidates
PSOE	33	17.9	52	32.7
PP	10	9.5	22	15.6
IU	0	0	5	27.7
CiU (Catalan)	1	5.5	4	23.5
PNV (Basque)	0	0	1	20.0
HB (Basque)	1	20	0	-
EE (Basque)	1	50	0	-
Total/Average	46	-	84	24.7

Sources: 1989: Barbadillo, Juste Ortega and Ramírez, p. 110.
1996: Federación de Mujeres Progresistas, *Políticas sobre igualdad de oportunidades para la mujer* (Press dossier for the 1996 general election, 1996).
2000: Secretaría de Participación de la Mujer, 31 January 2000; *El País*, 30 January 2000, p. 29.

Table 4. Women candidates likely to be elected to Congress.

Party	1989	1996
PSOE	3	8
PP	6	7
IU	5	5
CiU	0	0
PNV (Basque)	0	0
EE (Basque)	2	-
BNG (Galician)	1	-
CDS	1	-

Source: 1989: Barbadillo, Juste Ortega and Ramírez, Table 5, pp. 130 and 132.
1996: Federación de Mujeres Progresistas, *Políticas sobre igualdad de oportunidades para la mujer* (Press dossier for the 1996 general election, 1996).

Table 5. Women heading constituency candidate lists.

party leadership was still not a woman's job in the late 1990s. One reason put forward is that large nationwide parties feel obliged to offer a discourse which is progressive and reflects women's desire to participate in politics, but when it comes to top seats, they hold back from giving them to women, as if they had a certain lack of confidence in women's leadership ability (Barbadillo, Juste Ortega and Ramírez, p. 129). Nevertheless, the following years were to see a steady rise. And in 2000, a significant leap occurred because by then the whole issue of gender parity had been taken on board.

Women Elected to Parliament
There has been an equally notable change in the presence of women in Parliament from the first decade of democracy to the second. In the first, few women's voices were heard inside the Congress of Deputies or in the Senate. From 1977 to 1979 only twenty-two women or 6% of all deputies shared with 332 men the crucial task of amending and approving the new Constitution, and even fewer participated in the key phase of law-making that followed it. In fact, until the mid-1980s, the situation was deteriorating. Matters were no better in the Senate: in the first four elections the number of women senators only crept up from 3% to 5%.

The change started in 1986 with the Conservatives' effort to catch up with the PSOE. Then in 1989 the PSOE for the first time managed to obtain a critical mass of thirty-four women, two-thirds of all women deputies in the Congress. The Conservatives took another leap forward in 1993 and the PSOE did so again in 1996. Despite losing the election, it retained well over half all women deputies during the last legislature of the millennium. Other parties of the Left such as the IU and the Basque nationalist Left have followed suit, while the Centre Right has lagged, so that nearly two-thirds of congresswomen belong to progressive or radical groups. The outgoing Parliament's seventy-seven women, 22% of the total, is a healthy achievement that is unlikely to be jeopardized at the March 2000 elections if the PSOE pushes forward with its gender parity policy, though it is unclear what the other parties will do (see Table 6).

Parliamentary group	1977-79 No.	%	1979-82 No.	%	1982-86 No.	%	1986-9 No.	%	1989-93 No.	%	1993-6 No.	%	1996-2000 No.	%
AP/CP/PP	1	6.3	1	11	2	1.9	8 *6	7.6 *7.5	10	9.3	21.0	14.9	22 *29	14.1 *18.7
UCD/CDS	7	4.2	10 11	6 6.6	0	–	–	–	–	–	–	–	–	–
PSOE *	10 *11	8.5 *9.3	5 *6	4 *5	18	8.9	13	7.1	34	19.4	28	17.6	39 *44	27.6 *31.2
PCE/IU	3	15	2	8.7	–	–	–	–	2	11.8	4	22.2	7 *5	33.3 31.3
CiU (Catalan)	–	–	1	12.5	1	9.1	1	5.6	1	5.6	1	5.9	4	25
PNV (Basque) EA (Basque)	–	–	–	–	2	25	–	–	–	–	–	–	1 1	20 100
HB (Basque)	–	–	–	–	–	–	1	20			1	50	2	100
Mixed Group	–	–	–	–	–	–	PDP 2	PDP 5	4	28.6	ERC 1	ERC 100	–	–
Total in Congress	21 *22	6 *6.3	20 *21	5.7 *6	18 *22	5.1 *6.3	23 25	6.5	51	14.6	56	16	77 *87	22 *25

*Where two figures are given, the first number is that arising from the election and the bottom one at the end of the legislature. New women deputies came in after the resignation (or death) of a male deputy because they had been the second candidate on the party's list.

Sources: 1977: José Ignacio Cases, Lourdes López Nieto, Miguel Ángel Ruiz de Azúa and Francisco Vanaclocha, *Mujer y 15 de junio* (Madrid: Ministerio de Cultura, 1978);
1979-82: J. de Esteban and L. López Guerra (eds), *Las elecciones legislativas del 1 de marzo de 1979* (Madrid: Centro de Investigaciones Sociológicas, 1979).
1982-86 and 1986-89: *La mujer en cifras: Una década 1982-1992* (Madrid: Instituto de la Mujer/Ministerio de Asuntos Sociales, 1994), p. 58; *La mujer en España: Política* (Madrid: Instituto de la Mujer/Ministerio de Asuntos Sociales,n.d.), p. 45.
1993-96: Ministry of Social Affairs press release, 7 March 1996.
1996-2000: Servicio de Información del Congreso de los Diputados, 7 February 2000.

Table 6. Women in the Congress of Deputies as a percentage of party group.

In comparative terms, Spanish women's share of legislative power in the Lower House was below the European average until the second half of the 1980s, though their position was, ever since the return to democracy, slightly better than in Britain and France. This suggests that the adoption of the electoral system of the 'reinforced' proportional representation with the d'Hondt method of seat allocation was more favourable to women than the single member plurality system would have been, even in the early years of low awareness of the issue and before quotas. By the 1990s, women's parliamentary participation was well above the average, coming sixth from the top in the EU and nineteenth from the top in the world classification.[23]

It has been harder for women to gain access to the Upper House even though it captures far less of the political limelight than the Lower. Their presence in the Senate was steadily around three percentage points lower than in the Congress.[24] The percentage rose to 12.5% in 1993-96 and to 15% in 1996, considerably behind Congress's 22%. Again, this probably reflects the fact that the system for the Senate is a single mixed list of candidates from all parties and those with the most votes get the seats. Voters have to choose a person from a party, rather than a party with a set of people. Individual reputation counts for more in the Senate, and this seems to disadvantage women. It may also indicate that the electorate is agreeable to voting for a party list that contains many women, especially if it is headed by a man as most are, but less agreeable to singling out women candidates for support. This is a hypothesis that needs further investigation, for it may signal that the parties aiming at gender parity are ahead of the electorate in their understanding of the issue. There is no 1990s European model for this, as Upper Houses can be found with both lower and higher proportions of women. The European average is brought down by the British House of Lords' heavy preponderance of men.[25]

Regional and Local Assemblies

While there is no room for a full analysis of the presence of women in the regional and local tiers of legislative power, it is interesting to observe that, as far as the PSOE's office-holders are concerned, there was a considerable lag in women's presence in comparison with the Spanish Congress and the European Parliament, but the regional tier performed better than the Senate. This becomes apparent in Table 7.

Viewed in this way, it appears that one explanation of the differences is that the institutions with less prestige and in some respects less power (from the practitioner's point of view) are the ones with a lesser presence of women. Outside Spain, the European Parliament is not considered to have been particularly powerful, yet dealing with 'Europe' involves a wider, more complex set of concerns than dealing with regional affairs, even if the power to implement and make changes through the European Parliament is not as great as in domestic politics. It is not clear whether the hierarchy of power-sharing observed in Table 7 is due to the party at the respective level displaying varying levels of commitment to increasing women's share of power when it comes to fielding the candidates, or whether it is the electorate's choices that intervened, or again whether the political decisions of PSOE women activists have had a hand in creating this hierarchy.

Cabinet Appointments

In Spain, Prime Ministers appoint the cabinet of their choice without having to limit themselves to MPs. The cabinet is not subject to the quota or parity rule. Nevertheless, the sheer visibility of ministers puts some pressure on Prime Ministers to appoint women. The Socialist Government's first two cabinets were totally male in spite of the precedent set by the UCD's 1981 appointment of Soledad Becerril as the first woman cabinet minister since the Republican Government. But after the 25% quota was won in 1988, Rosa Conde and Matilde Fernández joined the cabinet, as Minister for the

European Parliament	1994	36 %
Congress of Deputies	1996	31%
Autonomous Community deputies*	1994-7	26%
Senate	1996	22%
Local councillors	1995	17%

Source: Own elaboration from data in Secretaría de Participación de la Mujer, *La participación de las mujeres en el PSOE y en las instituciones públicas* (Madrid: PSOE, 1998). Years chosen to be post-25% quota but pre-40% parity.
* Elections held in different years, though mostly in 1995.

Table 7. Women in PSOE-held elected posts, by institution.

Presidency and for Social Affairs respectively. After winning again in 1993, González put three women in charge of the Ministries of Social Affairs (Cristina Alberdi), Culture (Carmen Alborch) and Health (Ángeles Amador). PP upped the ante with four women: Esperanza Aguirre in charge of Education, Isabel Tocino at Environment, Margarita Mariscal at Justice and Loyola de Palacio at Agriculture, until she was demoted in time to gain a seat in the European Parliament elections in 1999. They have had a mixed press, sometimes overtly sexist, sometimes enthusiastic and admiring, but mercifully free from scurrilous obsession with personality and private life.

Women and Institutional Power: Key Turning Points

In the first decade of democracy, heralded as a great period of change, women accompanied the change, but were minor protagonists in it. By the second decade, they were much more forceful actors in the political system at the institutional level. The surge in their presence coincided with the PSOE's leftist turn on social policy in its last seven years in power, without the link between the two being explicit.

The beginning of the shift can be traced back to the political debate in the PSOE which culminated in the acceptance of minimum quotas of 25% of women in party-controlled public posts in January 1988. This is not to say it was a popular decision. In fact it was quite the opposite. The issue of women's representation has been fiercely argued in the PSOE since the late 1970s, with slow and irregular progress being made. But feminist members had lobbied party structures hard and the XXXI Party Conference finally approved the motion. The debate reflected the wider discussion in the Socialist International, of which the PSOE has long been an active member, where Socialist International Women had been pressing for quotas too.[26]

The effectiveness of the quota mechanism for bringing more women into public life is without doubt in Spain.[27] It had an immediate effect. At the very first parliamentary elections held after the quota was agreed, there was an astonishing 89% and 116% rise in the number of women elected to the national and regional Parliaments, respectively.[28] The PP did not adopt a quota, but the leftist United Left did. While the number of women given political responsibilities by the PP has risen, the change has been nowhere as marked as it has in the parties operating a quota. Discussions at the PP's latest Party Conference indicate an awareness of the issue of the gender balance in participation, for one of the documents discussed states: 'It is necessary to transfer to party structures the social reality which surrounds us, seeking a real balance between men and women, so that the party may be a reflection of society'.[29] But José María Aznar, party leader and Prime Minister since 1996, made no reference to women's participation in his closing speech, during which he repeatedly addressed his audience as '*Amigos*', the masculine form of friends.[30]

The quota debate had been accompanied in Europe by a parallel discussion on parity democracy, defended particularly in France but taken up by the Socialist International in 1988 (SIW, p. 7). It was endorsed as a general feminist claim at the European Summit of Women in Power held in Athens in 1992, which agreed that no more than 60% nor less than 40% of either sex should be represented anywhere in politics. By 1994 the Socialist International Council was asking all its members to increase their women candidates by a minimum of 10% in every election, with the goal of reaching 50: 50 gender parity by 2000 (SIW, p. 7). In Spain, parity democracy was incorporated into a wider claim to gender-sharing (of household tasks, work and power) made by a range of feminists and submitted by the Federation of Progressive Women to the PSOE's XXXIV Federal Conference in June 1997. Sharing power, they argued, should lead to changing the laws on elections and on parties and to implementing parity in professional bodies, trades unions, and workers' councils.[31] It was circulated as an appendix to the outgoing Federal Executive's political analysis framework document (*Ponencia Marco*) with Felipe González's personal backing. The Party Conference decision has been carried forward. In November 1999, Joaquín Almunia, the PSOE leader and prime ministerial candidate for the March 2000 elections, announced his intention to see the electoral law amended to ensure all parties fielded a minimum of 40% from either sex as parliamentary candidates.[32] The Andalusian Socialist leader Manuel Chaves promised that after the next regional elections, his new Government would have no less than 50% of women.[33]

Conclusion

We are familiar with the notion that if women in politics are a minority, women in real power are almost a rarity, and that there are two simple complementary equations: 'The further from power, the more women' and 'The closer to power, the fewer women'.

There are grounds for thinking that in Spain this must be radically rethought. As the evidence in this article shows, the 'more power = fewer women' equation only works in certain circumstances. One might have expected that the Senate, the lower-ranking chamber whose role is criticized for ineffectiveness, would have been more permeable to women, yet this has not been the case. The closer the Conservatives came to winning power, the more women were elected. The PSOE's Federal Executive has implemented the quota more exactly than the lower tiers of the party. The Autonomous Assemblies and local politics do not provide a more accessible forum for women politicians.

Some of the explanation lies with the quota system itself. It has had what could be called a 'homogenizing' effect, bringing the gender balance at each level and each area increasingly into line with a decision first adopted at the centre. The issue this raises is how far has the centre enjoyed sufficient independence of power to adopt radical new policies and to enforce them throughout the party. Have women benefited from top-down pressure in a party which is, albeit decentralized, nevertheless politically led from the centre? Is this a case of enlightened elitism? Yet another part of the explanation also lies with women's agency, their choices and the resources of education, personality and networks that they can draw on, which would need extensive further examination.

The reconsideration of the question of women's access to power can start with this interesting paradox for Spain. The party which gained access to the greatest number of public posts since the return to elections in Spain, effectively offering its candidates the likelihood of an income, a lifestyle and a career, the PSOE, was also very predominantly a male party. Such a party is bound to have strongly motivated male gatekeepers. Yet it is the very party that has led a great opening up of politics to women. Though aided in this endeavour by the general expansion of its popularity and power, there can be no doubt that the PSOE also closed off some, if not many, of these new opportunities to the men-in-waiting and passed them to women instead.

Some of the reasons for this lie with the party's apparent belief that fielding women is popular with the electorate and that putting public administration in the hands of women is a safe step. Women politicians are now profitable assets, no longer embellishments. For instance, Cristina Almeida thought parties were beginning to appreciate women's ways of governing, which were 'different and efficient', while Rosa Aguilar, IU's candidate for mayor in Cordoba, said there came a point when the parties began to think that because women in public posts seemed to go down well with the public, when it came to an election, fielding a woman candidate might just swing it for the party.[34]

It is the sheer speed of the transformation which most people agree on. As Cristina Alberdi said when she was Minister for Social Affairs, where equality is concerned, Spain has progressed as much in twenty years as other countries have in forty.[35] A decade and a half ago, Spanish women were asked whether they thought that by the year 2000 there would be more or fewer women in public office. A full 83% of them went for the optimistic answer and only 2% were pessimistic enough to think there would be fewer. This confidence has been well rewarded. Perhaps the respondents would not have predicted that Spain would figure so highly in the international league tables of female political representation as it did at the turn of the millennium.

References

1   Jean Bethke Elshtain, *Public Man, Private Woman: Women in Sociological and Political Thought* (Princeton: Princeton University Press, 1981).

2   Concepción Arenal, *La emancipación de la mujer en España*, selected writings, ed. by Mauro Armiño (Madrid: Ediciones Jucar, 1974).

3   See Clara Campoamor, *El voto femenino y yo* (Barcelona, Ediciones laSal, 1981; first published 1936).

4   See Esperanza García Mendez, *La actuación de la mujer en las Cortes de la II^a República*, second edition (Madrid: Ministerio de Cultura, 1979).

5   See Paul Preston, 'Pilar Primo de Rivera: El fascismo y los arreglos florales' in Paul Preston, *Las tres Españas del 36* (Barcelona: Plaza y Janés, 1999), pp. 153-92.

6   See María Teresa Gallego Méndez, *Mujer, Falange y franquismo* (Madrid: Taurus, 1983).

7   Geraldine M. Scanlon, *La polémica feminista en la España contemporánea* (Madrid: Siglo XXI, 1976), p. 320.

8   The law of 22 July 1961 maintained restrictions on the right to a career in law and the armed forces. See María del Rosario Ruiz Franco, 'Nuevos horizontes para las mujeres de los años 60: la ley de 22 de julio de 1961' in *Arenal*, 2: 2 (1995), July-December, 247-68.

9   Only 17 of the twentieth century's 100 top Spanish women were political figures. See *La Actualidad Española*, 1335, 21 January 1978, cited in María Antonia García de León, *Las elites femeninas españolas* (Madrid: Queimada Ediciones, 1982), p. 56.

10   Metra/Seis, *La mujer española y la política: Informe de un estudio de opinión y actitudes políticas de la mujer española en edad de votar* (Madrid: Presidencia de Gobierno, 1976), pp. 20-22.

11 This had been observed in numerous studies of other countries; see the authoritative volumes of the time, Joni Lovenduski and Jill Hills (eds), *The Politics of the Second Electorate* (London: Routledge and Kegan Paul, 1981) and Vicky Randall, *Women and Politics* (London and Basingstoke: MacMillan, 1982).

12 Respondents' answers tend to be inaccurate on turnout: either both sexes exaggerate their turn-out to the same extent (and the *gap* remains accurate), or one or the other exaggerates more and the gap recorded is distorted. Evidence from José Ignacio Cases, Lourdes López Nieto, Miguel Ángel Ruiz de Azúa and Francisco Vanaclocha, *Mujer y 15 de junio* (Madrid: Ministerio de Cultura, 1978), p. 152; Emopública survey, No. 1259, April 1979; and Centro de Investigaciones Sociológicas, Survey, No. E 1327, November 1982.

13 Grupo Federal de Estudios Sociológicos, *Perfil del militante socialista* (Madrid: Boletín PSOE March 1981), p. 8; and Janine Mossuz-Lavau and Mariette Sineau, 'France', in Lovenduski and Hills, p. 118. The figure for the PS in France was 22%, in the Italian PSI it was nearly 17% in the north and nearly 14% in the south at the time. Further references to this text will be in the form *Perfil*.

14 Secretaría de Participación de la Mujer, *La participación de las mujeres en el PSOE y en las instituciones públicas* (Madrid: PSOE, 1998), pp. 52-53.

15 This is the opinion of the PSOE Women's caucus, *Socialism and Women* (*Mujer y Socialismo*).

16 Information provided by the Organization Secretariat for 1982.

17 Part of the PSOE feminists' strategy is related in Monica Threlfall, 'State Feminism or Party Feminism?', *European Journal of Women's Studies*, 5: 1998/1 (1997), pp. 69-93.

18 Secretaría de Participación de la Mujer, p. 37, Table 7. Two regions, Catalonia with 29% of women and Galicia with 25.5%, had held their Conferences before the Federal Party Conference, an indication of what a difference the decision made.

19 Own calculation from data in Table 9 of Secretaría de Participación de la Mujer, *La participación*, p. 39.

20 Briefing by Isabel Martínez Lozano, given at the PSOE Secretariat for the Participation of Women, 26 January 2000.

21 Barbadillo Grian, Juste Ortega and Ramírez Mayoral, 'La mujer en el congreso de los diputados: Análisis de su participación en las candidaturas electorales de 1989', *REIS*, 52/90 (1990), 101-35, p. 110, Table 2.

22 This indicator is not available for earlier Senate elections.

23 Inter-parliamentary Union figures in European Commission, *Women of Europe*, Newsletter No.87, July/August 1999.

24 Government of Spain, *Report to the IV UN World Conference on Women, Beijing 1995* (Madrid: Ministry of Social Affairs, 1994) pp. 50-51.

25 European Parliament data for 1993.

26 Socialist International Women (SIW), *A Quota for Women: Promoting Gender Equality*, leaflet (1995).

27 María Teresa Gallego Méndez, 'Women's Political Engagement in Spain', in *Women and Politics Worldwide*, ed. by Barbara Nelson and Najma Chowdhury (New Haven: Yale University Press, 1994), pp. 660-73; Eva Martínez-Hernández and Arantxa Elizondo, 'Women in Politics: Are they really Concerned about Equality? An Essay on the Basque Political System', *European Journal of Women's Studies*, 4: 4 (1997), 451-72, p. 455; Barbadillo, Juste Ortega and Ramírez Mayoral, pp. 101-35; Federación de Mujeres Progresistas, 1996.

28 Calculations on the basis of data in *La mujer en cifras: Una decada, 1982-1992* (Madrid: Instituto de la Mujer/Ministerio de Asuntos Sociales, 1994), p. 60.

29 E. Zaplana, 'La España de las oportunidades', presentation given at XIII Congreso Nacional del Partido Popular, in Partido Popular, *Documentos políticos*, enero 1999, p. 103.

30 José María Aznar, 'Discurso de clausura' in Partido Popular, *Documentos políticos,* January 1999, pp. 207-31.
31 Text of the Proposal for a Resolution to the XXXIV Congress by Federación de Mujeres Progresistas, Part 3.
32 'Almunia propone cambiar la ley electoral para que las mujeres ocupen el 40% de las candidaturas', *El País,* 7 November 1999, p. 24.
33 'Chaves promete que su próximo gobierno será femenino al 50%', *El País,* 7 November 1999, p. 24.
34 *El País Semanal,* 6 June 1999, p. 55.
35 *Diario 16,* 25 March 1996, p. 1.

Bibliography

Arenal, Concepción, *La emancipación de la mujer en España,* selected writings, ed. by Mauro Armiño (Madrid: Ediciones Jucar, 1974).
Barbadillo Grian, Patricia, María Gracia Juste Ortega and Ana Ramírez Mayoral, 'La mujer en el congreso de los diputados: Análisis de su participación en las candidaturas electorales de 1989', *REIS,* 52/90 (1990), pp. 101-35.
Bethke Elshtain, Jean, *Public Man, Private Woman: Women in Sociological and Political Thought* (Princeton: Princeton University Press, 1981).
Campoamor, Clara, *El voto femenino y yo* (Barcelona: Ediciones laSal, 1981, first published 1936).
Cases, José Ignacio, Lourdes López Nieto, Miguel Ángel Ruiz de Azúa and Francisco Vanaclocha, *Mujer y 15 de junio* (Madrid: Ministerio de Cultura, 1978).
European Commission, *Women of Europe Newsletter,* No.87, July/August 1999.
Gallego Méndez, María Teresa, *Mujer, Falange y franquismo* (Madrid: Taurus, 1983).
————, 'Women's Political Engagement in Spain', in *Women and Politics Worldwide,* ed. by Barbara Nelson and Najma Chowdhury (New Haven: Yale University Press, 1994), pp. 660-73.
García de León, María Antonia, *Las elites femeninas españolas* (Madrid: Queimada Ediciones, 1982).
García Mendez, Esperanza, *La actuación de la mujer en las Cortes de la IIa República,* second edition (Madrid: Ministerio de Cultura, 1979).
Grupo Federal de Estudios Sociológicos, *Perfil del militante socialista* (Madrid: Boletín PSOE, 1981).
IDES, *Las españolas ante la política* (Madrid: Instituto de la Mujer, 1988).
Instituto de la Mujer, *La mujer en cifras: Una década, 1982-1992* (Madrid: Instituto de la Mujer/Ministerio de Asuntos Sociales, 1994).
López Nieto, L., *Alianza Popular: Estructura y evolución electoral* (Madrid: C.I.S., 1988).
Lovenduski, Joni and Jill Hills (eds), *The Politics of the Second Electorate* (London: Routledge and Kegan Paul, 1981).
Marin, K., 'Ellas se las juegan', *El País Semanal,* 6 June 1999, pp. 44-58.
Martínez-Hernández, Eva and Arantxa Elizondo, 'Women in Politics: Are they really Concerned about Equality? An Essay on the Basque Political System', *European Journal of Women's Studies,* 4: 4 (1997), 451-72.
Partido Popular, *Documentos políticos* (Madrid: Partido Popular, 1999).
Preston, Paul, 'Pilar Primo de Rivera: el fascismo y los arreglos florales', in *Las tres Españas del 36,* ed. by Paul Preston (Barcelona: Plaza y Janés, 1999).
Randall, Vicky, *Women and Politics* (London: Macmillan, 1982).
Scanlon, Geraldine M., *La polémica feminista en la España contemporánea* (Madrid: Siglo XXI, 1976).
Secretaría de Participación de la Mujer, *La participación de las mujeres en el PSOE y en las instituciones públicas* (Madrid: PSOE, 1998).
Socialist International Women, *A Quota for Women: Promoting Gender Equality,* leaflet (1995).
Threlfall, Monica, 'Presencia de la mujer en las elecciones legislativas', *Zona Abierta,* 19 (1979), 56-70.
————, 'State Feminism or Party Feminism?', *European Journal of Women's Studies,* 5: 1998/1 (1997), pp. 69-93.

3 The Image and Role of Women Promoted by the Extreme Right and Catholic Integrists in Contemporary France

William B. Smith

One of the key words in the lexicon of the French extreme Right is 'difference'. Jean-Marie Le Pen has frequently reiterated his belief in the difference between races and has explicitly extended that notion to one of a hierarchy (for he also believes in the inequality of races) which has as its logical outcome the segregation and exclusion, the submission and dependency of the 'lesser' (i.e. non-European and particularly non-autochthonous French) races living in France. The vision of the Front National (FN) is the total antithesis of a multicultural society based on 'Liberty, Equality, Fraternity'. It is rather a society of domination by the white race and particularly, as we shall see, by the white male because the role of the female is perceived as essentially subordinate. The metaphor of 'family' has been exploited constantly within the organization of the FN itself with its authoritarian hierarchy presided over by the patriarch Le Pen whose position was challenged at the end of 1998 by Bruno Mégret. 'Divorce' on the right wing then ensued and familial imagery gave way to vituperative abuse. Traditional and integrist Catholics (for whom notions of hierarchy and authority are necessary and welcome for the preservation of an unchanging faith) have been drawn to the FN because it has become, in their eyes, the defender of a society based on three pillars: God, the natural order and tradition.[1] The emancipation of women has served only to destabilize this society and a traditionalist reading of the Scriptures buttresses this view.

The parish bulletin of the integrist church of Saint Nicolas-du-Chardonnet (January 1990) reminded women of their role, citing St Paul's first letter to the Corinthians: 'The head of every man is Christ, the head of a woman is her husband [...] for man was not made from woman, but woman from man. Neither was man created for woman, but woman for man.' The natural order is invoked to sustain the difference between male and female: woman's role is to be a wife and mother, to procreate and to educate her children, so as to fulfil her biological destiny. Le Pen evokes tradition in virtually every speech: he regularly cites Mary and Joan of Arc as icons for modern woman and his ideal society is the pre-Revolutionary one with its sense of hierarchy, male domination, harmony and order, all of which is threatened by modern decadence and the rise of feminism which he regards as responsible for the decline of the family and the widespread recourse to contraception and abortion.

The Icons
The Virgin Mary

Catholic and Orthodox Christianity have made of Mary, the mother of Jesus, a figure of immense veneration and an exemplar for Christians. She is the 'Virgin Mother', the 'Mother of God', 'ever virgin', 'immaculate', 'assumed into Heaven'. In addition, she has achieved immense cultural importance: in feasts, devotional services, in pilgrimages to Marian shrines such as Lourdes, Medjugorje, Fatima. She is a universal theme in the Arts: there are countless paintings of the Mother and Child, the Coronation of the Virgin, the Annunciation, the Visit with Elizabeth, Mary at the foot of the Cross. However, by the nineteenth century, the Catholic Church, in honouring Mary, had come to celebrate a particular and rather narrow vision of goodness, a femininity of idealized virtue, of chastity, humility, gentleness. It was as if the Church had been unable to cope with femininity: Woman was Eve, temptress and whore, and only Mary, pure virgin and perfect mother, had escaped the curse of Eve. Over the course of the last two centuries, Marian piety, the hymns to Mary, for example, characterize the world as dark and evil, society as hostile and humans, particularly women, as steeped in sin and oppressed by enemies who hate the goodness and piety represented by Mary and the Church. The FN, and particularly Le Pen, presses Mary into service as a symbol of female commitment to resist what it sees as the decadence of contemporary France, a decadence characterized by feminism, abortion, contraception and promiscuity. Mary becomes the champion and exemplar of the French wife and mother under threat in her traditional role.

Similarly, for integrist Lefebvrist Catholics, Mary will emerge: 'victorious over disloyalty, vice and materialism', she will 'crush the head of the serpent', she is the only one capable of 'overcoming the forces of evil united under the direction of those secret societies which dominate our lives today, degrading the human person [...] destroying the family'.[2] Mary is made the model of the traditionalist conception of woman's role, the paradigm of the wife and mother in a world which is seen to be torn apart by a Manichean conflict between good and evil.

To take such a universally iconic figure as Mary and make her a protagonist in a right-wing political and religious campaign in French society is not only absurdly reductionist but is also knowingly and wilfully to deform the mainstream Catholic view of Mary, as it has evolved since the Second Vatican Council.[3] From the Bible, little is known of her. She appears infrequently in the Gospels but she is depicted by Luke as the prototypical Christian disciple: she is the believer who submits herself unreservedly to God's will. She is the champion of the poor against the wealthy, of the humble against the powerful. Biblical scholars are generally agreed that the hymn of Mary,[4] the Magnificat, was not composed by her but rather by Luke himself, who drew on many Old Testament sources (e.g. 1 Samuel 2) to compose what he saw as the defining statement of Christianity, described by Charles Maurras, a main protagonist in the Action Française movement and the voice of the right-wing Catholic middle classes, as well as former supporter of the Vichy regime, as 'the most revolutionary in history':

He has shown the power of his arm,
he has routed the proud of heart.
He has pulled down princes from their thrones
and exalted the lowly.
The hungry he has filled with good things, the
rich sent empty away.

(Luke 1: 51-53)

The Right also falls into the trap of attributing to Mary the characteristics of the caricatural 'Jewish mother': inexhaustibly emotionally generous, forever consoling and rewarding her children, devoting herself entirely to their emotional and material well-being, the immensely well-meaning but ultimately damaging figure in her children's lives, who by denying them autonomy, denies them also maturity.

This is the mother of the 'Holy Family type', the housewife and mother confined to the home, extolled by the Right, and modelled on the nineteenth-century French middle classes. The figure depicted in Luke's Gospel is quite different: this was a woman who spent the last three years of Jesus' life wandering the roads of Galilee with him and who, when he died, was homeless and had to be entrusted to the care of his disciples. It is a woman who gave her twelve-year-old son such autonomy that he disappeared for thirty-six hours on the way home from Jerusalem (Luke 2: 41-50) before she realized he was missing and when she was reunited with him, accepted his explanation without question: 'Why were you looking for me? Did you not know that I must be busy with my Father's affairs?' (Luke 1: 49).[5] The Right's virulent attacks against single mothers (as subversive of 'family values') appear to totally miss the point that Mary, as a fifteen-year-old girl, was asked to bear a child of whom her intended husband Joseph was not the progenitor. Two thousand years on, Christians perceive this acceptance as the supreme example of obedience to the will of God: 'Let what you said be done to me' (Luke 1: 38). At the time, however, the perception was not the same: adulterous women and single mothers were roundly condemned and even stoned in Jewish society. By being obedient to God's will, Mary laid herself open to the censure of her own society, a censure which the political and religious Right is only too ready to heap on the heads of contemporary French single mothers.

It is characteristic of the Right, especially traditionalist Catholics, to refer to Mary not by her name but by pious titles or epithets: 'Our Lady', 'The Holy Virgin', 'The Virgin Mother', 'The Immaculate One'. This serves also to further distance Mary and to mask what should be seen as her humanity.

Joan of Arc

Le Pen uses French history on a very selective basis to define and reinforce his concept of French identity and nationhood. The paradigmatic models on which he builds his mythical France are selected to justify his own ideological positions of exclusion, difference and hierarchy. Figures who embody consensus and acceptance of difference such as Saint Louis and Henry IV are scarcely mentioned. Joan of Arc on the other hand is the object of an FN rally or pilgrimage which occurs every year around 1 May.

49

The fact that Joan is a saint of the Catholic Church serves also to reinforce the links between the FN and traditionalist Catholics. She symbolizes resistance to foreign invasion and the preservation of national independence at the cost of her own life. Her life and martyrdom are distorted by Le Pen so that she becomes the emblematic figure who encapsulates the ideology of the FN: France for the French, the defence of the country against foreign aggression, identified by Le Pen as *maghrébin* immigration, European integration and the plots fomented against France by an international Jewish financial conspiracy.

By using 1 May for his demonstration, Le Pen succeeds in confusing and amalgamating the historical figure (martyred by the English in 1431), contemporary political issues and 1 May which is Labour Day. The FN celebrates the virginity, the purity of intention and the pathos associated with the martyrdom of a nineteen-year-old woman. But she is also depicted, both in Le Pen's speeches and by the young woman selected every year to dress up in chain mail and ride on horseback to represent her, as an essentially androgynous figure where the perceived male characteristics of strength and resistance predominate. This allows Le Pen to depict himself as her successor in late twentieth-century France.

Le Pen uses this May Day demonstration each year to deliver a major speech and his technique is unvarying: he starts with a purportedly historical anecdote about Joan of Arc and then creates a parallel with contemporary France. The 1998 speech delivered in the Place de l'Opéra in Paris after the homage to the saint's statue in the Rue de Rivoli was extensively reported in the extreme right-wing press and followed this pattern.

National Hebdo (720, 7-13 May 1998) devoted extensive coverage to the speech under the headline 'From Joan of Arc to the FN, a mystique of Freedom'. The initial invocation of Joan of Arc followed the established pattern:

> ...a young girl rooted both in the land and in heaven, given as her mission in times of adversity to save a France in danger, because of violence and betrayal, of being absorbed into a foreign entity and thus of losing her sovereignty, her independence, her language, her identity. But is it possible to compare the great predators of the fifteenth century, Isabeau of Bavaria, Bedford, Cauchon with the manikins who run the European Union? Or the infamous Treaty of Troyes with the unspeakable Treaty of Maastricht?
>
> What was it all about almost six hundred years ago? It was about handing over France to the King of England with the connivance of the University of Paris, the Church of France and the plotters amongst the nobility. What is it all about today? It is about losing the unity, the independence and inalienable sovereignty of France in a so-called European entity, the geographical and political boundaries of which are unknown, with the complicity of those whose sacred mission it is to defend France.

Joan of Arc was thus conscripted yet again into opposition to the single European currency before being made a champion of integrist Catholicism: she would have opposed 'the obliteration and adulteration of religious dogmas' (*National Hebdo*, 7-13 May 1998).

The main thrust of the speech was anti-European. High unemployment and North African immigration were seen as results of European integration, but his audience was urged not to give up hope:

> Since Joan remains forever the eternal, mystical embodiment of France and since, what she did, she did with the help of heaven, let us not despair...

In an article entitled 'With Joan for France', *L'Action Française Hebdo* (2508, 7-20 May 1998), paraphrased rather than reported Le Pen's speech and gave its own gloss to a number of the points mentioned in *National Hebdo*. It took the reference to the Treaty of Troyes and Isabeau of Bavaria and drew an elaborate parallel between the twentieth-century European Union based in Brussels and what it described as the purely mercantile aspirations of the fifteenth-century English and Burgundians who traded in what is now the Flemish area of Belgium round Brussels. Joan is thus enlisted in the extreme Right's hostility to Europe. Joan is said to have lived in a time of decadence and religious confusion. Her century parallels the twentieth where the Catholic Church has allowed itself to be led into error and whose weakness is allowing the spread of Islam in France. French Church leaders are accused of cowardice and compared to Bishop Cauchon who condemned Joan to be burnt at the stake.

Joan of Arc, the Maid of Orleans, is the principal female icon of the political extreme Right and another very important figure for traditionalist Catholics. In the picture which they paint of her, she has merely become a convenient symbol on which to hang an ultra-nationalist political agenda: 'secularism and globalization are not invincible. Joan demonstrated that as early as 1429' (*Action Française Hebdo*, 2508)

Saint Theresa of the Child Jesus

Saint Theresa of the Child Jesus (1873-97), also known as Saint Theresa of Lisieux, was a nun who died of tuberculosis having entered her Carmelite monastery with special permission from the Vatican at the early age of 15. She was canonized in 1925. Her method of sanctification was based on the search for childhood simplicity and in her spiritual autobiography, *The History of a Soul*, she elaborated the doctrine of spiritual childhood. Theresa is the object of particular devotion by the integrist Catholic counter-reformation movement led by Fr Georges de Nantes. De Nantes was suspended *a divinis* by his local bishop (of Troyes) in 1966 and thus banned from saying mass or exercising any other function within the Catholic Church because of his repeated, virulent criticism of the reforms enacted by the Second Vatican Council. He has ignored this ban and attracted some two hundred 'Phalangists' as they refer to themselves, (women and men), to his community houses at Saint Parres-lès-Vaudes (Aube) and has also founded a house in Quebec. De Nantes is a prolific writer and his monthly bulletin, entitled *The Catholic Counter Reformation in the XXth Century* (CRC), has a circulation of more than 13,000 copies (published both in English and French). His movement has, as we shall see, all the characteristics of a sect and has been designated as such by the French civil authorities who have denied the *CRC* the taxation concessions normally attributed to religious organizations. The bishop of

Troyes condemned the *CRC* (August 1996) as an anti-Semitic sect of the extreme Right and de Nantes' own writings bear this out: he considers the French Revolution of 1789 to be the incarnation of original sin; he was a supporter of French Algeria and of the use of torture there by French troops; he adulates Salazar and Franco and frequently writes articles extolling Pétain and Vichy. He even has a good word to say for Hitler and the Third Reich:

> You must not forget that Hitler's Germany sought to rid the world of the Bolshevik scourge (and also of the other scourge which I think it wiser not to name, but you can guess which one I mean), and which is all too visible today as it returns in force to dominate the world alongside Bolshevism.

(CRC, 105, [May 1976])

What, then, are the qualities which de Nantes perceives in Saint Theresa's life which may provide support for his ideas and his movement? His writings on Theresa were summarized in a thirty-four page article in *CRC* (301, September 1997) by a member of his Phalangist community, Mother Godelieve of the Eucharist, who refers to de Nantes throughout the article as 'Our Father' when she cites him directly.

Theresa was born into a middle-class family in north-eastern France which was both Catholic and monarchist. In Catholic circles at that time (when the Third Republic was creating a secular state (in which the Church would no longer have a privileged position), there was a strong sense of being besieged by what was termed 'the world', that is to say, everything which was not Church, by a society which was born of the Revolution, hence of sin, and which denied God. Theresa's mother died when she was four and her dominant, patriarchal father (who was subsequently to become insane) ensured that the child grew up in an atmosphere of rigid piety. Theresa chronicles two episodes in her life when she claimed to have been possessed by the devil, perhaps the result of a hyper-scrupulous nature falling short of the high spiritual standards which she set herself. Once inside the Carmelite monastery, she demonstrated the characteristics of docility and self-abnegation which had been inculcated into her in her early childhood. Writing of her prioress, she says: 'The good God allowed her, without her knowing, to be very severe; I could never meet her without kissing the ground' (*CRC*, 301, p. 11). De Nantes' quoted comment on this action is illuminating when we will see how he behaves within his Phalangist community: 'There are words of gold! exclaims our Father' (*CRC*, 301, p. 22). When she fell ill with tuberculosis and intestinal gangrene, she rejoiced that she was not given any painkillers by her prioress for 'the salvation of France, and of the world, can only be obtained at the price of undergoing suffering' (*CRC*, 301, p. 22). Before her illness had fully developed, she composed and acted the main part in a dramatic production within the monastery entitled *The Mission of Joan of Arc*. The timing of this production was very significant. Pope Leo XIII introduced the beatification cause for Joan of Arc on 27 January 1894 and this play was produced just six days beforehand. The author of the article draws a parallel between the two saints:

he [de Nantes] was very impressed to discover in Theresa of Lisieux a reincarnation, as it were, of Joan. He does not hesitate to assert that God wanted it so at the very period when the great forces of Antichrist were being mobilized for the final battle against France and against the Church [...] Saint Theresa transposes the lamentable state of France, once occupied by the English, divided and rebellious to her king and the Pope, into the current life of her day. In Theresa's day, France was under the control of a Masonic and persecuting Republic.

(*CRC*, 301, p. 22)

So, Theresa of Lisieux, alongside Joan of Arc, is pressed into service to support an extreme right-wing monarchist agenda and to serve as a role model for female members of de Nantes' sect.

The word sect is used advisedly because the Phalangist communities, unlike genuine religious communities which strive to foster the personal growth of their members, share characteristics with those sects which have come to light recently in North America, Guyana and Switzerland where the outcome has been suicide. The characteristics which these groups share with de Nantes' Phalangist communities are the following:

- A sect is usually dominated by an all-powerful guru seen as the uniquely inspired prophet and saviour, whose teachings and writings alone are true. No other authority is tolerated.
- The sect has all the truth. It presents itself as having a new message of salvation for all the world. This gives a total meaning to its members' lives and an intense motivation to proselytize and recruit.
- For those in the sect, society is divided into the good and the bad, the saved and the damned. Strong walls of fear are created making it difficult to question anything. They are cut off from family, friends and all other social institutions.
- Members are obliged to sacrifice their personal conscience, freedom and critical capacity to the group.
- Anguished, fragile, lonely people are attracted and seduced into the group. The togetherness, security and powerful goals of the group transmit a good feeling and relieve the anguish and pain of loneliness, worthlessness, meaninglessness and lack of direction. This makes it almost impossible to leave without going through even greater anguish and the apparent risk of emptiness, loneliness and inner death.[6]

These characteristics all apply to the *CRC* and Theresa's history lends authority to de Nantes' rule: for example, she cut herself off from her sister who was also a Carmelite nun: 'It is better that I do without you because we are not at home now' (*CRC*, 301, p. 11).

Children, as young as seven years old, are sent by their parents to summer camps run by the *CRC* where they are indoctrinated. Intimidation and guilt are two of the means used to shape future Phalangists. A girl, aged twelve, who had attended three such camps, spoke of her experiences:

The camp begins with an examination of conscience, we are told we are all liars. We make a list of damning sins, which we would never have thought of [...] Clothes were judged to be indecent if they were a bit tight or a bit short. I used to cry at some of the readings because they were unhealthy. [7]

Another girl, aged fourteen, has been prevented from seeing her father, 'her satanic progenitor' by the sect which manipulates the mother and the grandmother who are totally under the influence of de Nantes. Nor are young Phalangists allowed to marry without the permission of the leader:

I cannot conceive of a young Phalangist getting married without telling me, asking my view, getting my permission. A young woman comes to me and begs me to find her a husband, she goes around the young men of the CRC. She says that she despises them all, she doesn't want any of them. That takes me aback; a young woman like that, I can't be bothered with her. Young women today are crazy with arrogance.

Georges de Nantes is the most extreme case of abusive, patriarchal authority. His religion has little to do with Christianity; it is a perversion of Catholicism intended to serve an extreme right-wing political agenda where women have no role other than to obey orders and serve.

Familial and Sexual Issues

When dealing with sexual and familial issues, three fundamental principles govern the stance of both the political and religious Right:[8]

- Natural and divine law gives man and woman different hierarchical and complementary functions.
- Virility and femininity are natural characteristics which must be respected and valued.
- The family is the basic cell of society and the model for other institutions.

These principles permeate the writings of the religious Right on these issues:

If you aren't resigned to the collapse of France, you have to be aware that the family is at the centre of the political agenda [...] The weakening of the family has direct consequences: decadence, disorder and demographic decline.

(*Permanences*, August 1987)

The family is where fundamental order is based in the authority of the father [...] The Church vests this authority with a sacred character, for authority, even civil authority, is exercised in the name of God. Authority, whether it be of a monarch or a father, is sacred.

(*Fideliter*, September-October 1988)

A structured society is built like a pyramid [...] Families form the base of the social
pyramid [...] The family is the most natural of the natural groupings and, in the family,
nature grants to the father the headship of the family and hence authority.

(Lecture et Tradition, 132, February 1988, ch. 4)

Le Pen echoes the preoccupation of the most extreme Catholic organizations
concerning the place of women in society: their role is essentially that of housewife and
mother. For men, work is one of the key values, vital for personal development; but for
women, work is presented as a constraint which endangers her child: 'What is the use
of going out and earning a second salary, if you have to pay for that by your child
becoming a drug addict, for example? Is it worth it?' 'Nowadays, many women are
obliged to go out to work in a factory or an office not because work is a source of
personal development for them but because their household needs a second salary.'
The creation of a 'maternal salary', paid by the State, would allow mothers to make a
choice without financial constraint.[9] Natalist preoccupations and a substantial
allowance or salary paid to a parent (in practice the mother) to stay at home and look
after her child or children have been among the key policies of the FN since its
foundation and are supported enthusiastically by even the 'neo-pagan' Mégretist
faction:

> Abortion, except for therapeutic reasons, should be made illegal. A 'parental salary'
> should be paid to a mother who chooses to stay at home to look after the children.
> Preferential mortgages should be made available to French married couples and the
> income tax system should be reformed to penalize couples living in concubinage.[10]

There is a strong consistency of views between the religious and political extreme Right
on familial and sexual issues and both movements point to what they see as the same
malign influences which are weakening the moral fibre of the French and destroying
family life.

Homosexual practices and proselytism are condemned out of hand. Homosexuality
is seen to be a breach of a fundamental principle: the distinction between virility and
femininity, and is seen as the 'feminization' of the male. For the religious Right,
homosexuality is unnatural, a deviancy which is contrary to natural law. The *Catechism
of the Catholic Church*, whilst condemning homosexual acts as 'intrinsically disordered'
(para. 2357), nonetheless urges Catholics to behave towards homosexuals with 'respect,
compassion and delicacy' and condemns 'unfair discrimination' against them (para.
2358). The extreme Right is more vehement in its condemnation. *Présent* speaks of the
'confusion of the sexes' or their 'inversion'. It sees in unisex clothing a sign of
decadence because it blurs the distinction between the sexes and threatens the
differentiation between the sexes established by natural and divine law. For Le Pen,
homosexuality is 'a biological and social anomaly', which constitutes a real threat to
French society.[11] Homosexual AIDS victims have, for Le Pen, brought the disease upon
themselves by their disordered behaviour. Their disease is perceived by him as a
punishment for their having infringed the natural law. They constitute a danger to

society because of their promiscuity and should be locked away in *sidatoria* (the French acronym for AIDS is SIDA), just as victims of tuberculosis were isolated in sanatoria in former times.

The other major malign influence as far as the extreme Right is concerned is feminism which has transformed a complementary relationship into one of conflict and division. For Le Pen:

> Feminist demands are an essentially revolutionary development, which seeks to bring about conflict and destructive opposition. It is a conflict between social classes, races, peoples, sexes, ages [...] I believe that we are dealing with a revolutionary dialectic fostered by Marxists and of which some naïve women are making themselves the unwitting allies.[12]

For the National Association of French Mothers, 'the so-called "women's liberation movement" [...] seeks to reduce women to slavery by forcing them to work' and they see it as their vocation to fight 'so that French mothers [...] may resume this natural role as educators of their children'.[13] Women can only find fulfilment in motherhood. They should devote themselves to bringing up their children and live in respect of their husbands. This way they will achieve real fulfilment as opposed to feminists who are often depicted as having little about them which is feminine. The feminist is:

> hard, embittered, narrow and asexual. She sags like a withered flower. She is the anti-mother. She thought she was taking charge of her own destiny but she has been subjugated and we know that subjugated species only reproduce with difficulty. She has fallen into the trap of perversion.[14]

Feminists are held to be mainly responsible for the proliferation of abortion and for the widespread use of contraception. The Right invariably champions the rights of the foetus over the rights of women and never speaks of the foetus or the embryo, always of 'the child' or 'the little one'. The issue is not just a moral one, it has strong political overtones too: France is depicted as being in the throes of a demographic crisis where the indigenous population risks being overrun by Islamic immigrants whose birthrate is markedly higher. Le Pen is quite explicit:

> The fall in the birthrate is a phenomenon with fatal consequences [...] The drop in the number of births resulting from a Malthusianism born of globalization, of laws against nature, has not only brought about the elimination of many children but also the malfunctioning of the individual and collective mechanisms which ensure the perpetuation of the species.[15]

> For a number of years now we have not replaced our older generations and this in spite of the contribution of immigrant families, who, as is well known, profoundly alter the homogeneity of our people when they are injected into our nation in large doses.[16]

The new *Catechism of the Catholic Church*, published in 1992, which reaffirms moral absolutes, particularly in sexual matters, and rejects any sort of situation ethics, condemns both artificial contraception (para. 2368) and abortion (para. 2270). The attitude of most mainstream French Catholics towards the contraception prohibition is arguably one of indifference: they will continue to consult their own consciences in the matter and regard this as a private affair outside the jurisdiction of the Church. Many would accept the need for abortion for therapeutic reasons or in cases of rape but would be uneasy about what they would see as abortion on demand for social reasons. The various militant anti-abortion groups in France: *Trêve de Dieu* (Truce of God), *SOS Tout Petits* (SOS Tiny Tots), *Laissez-les vivre* (Let Them Live), *Mère de Miséricorde* (Mother of Mercy) are all rooted in the right wing, with its roots in integrist Catholicism and the Charismatic movement. Their interpretation of Christianity is an essentially fundamentalist one which arises out of their Manichean view of the world opposing good and evil, spirit and body and leads them to reject any sexual activity which is not potentially procreative. They go further than the Catechism in their rejection of even natural forms of birth control, which they argue leads inevitably to an acceptance of abortion. They oppose sex education, which they see as an invitation to young people to vice and depravity. One of the most militant proponents of direct action against abortion clinics is Dr Xavier Dor, a retired gynaecologist, who is both a member of the FN and of the congregation of St. Nicolas-du-Chardonnet and who has been arrested on a number of occasions for leading commando-style raids on abortion clinics to disrupt their activities. Dor opposes abortion in all circumstances. He believes that it is a crime even when an unwanted pregnancy results from a rape or an incestuous relationship. For a man with a scientific and medical background, he makes the astonishing assertion that if a woman resists rape, her body is so traumatized that she incurs no risk of becoming pregnant. If she resists insufficiently or allows it to happen, then she can become pregnant and she bears moral responsibility for her pregnancy.[17] Hard-line opponents of abortion use language which makes parallels between abortion and the Holocaust (the existence of which, ironically, a number of them deny or minimize as a 'historical detail'), using terms like 'sent to their death' and equating the 'morning-after' pill with Zylclon B. Pilgrimages have been organized to Auschwitz to commemorate aborted foetuses rather than the victims of the Holocaust.

A major flashpoint in the struggle of the French far Right to defend the traditional model of the family occurred when the Socialist Government introduced into the National Assembly on 9 October 1998 a bill to give legal recognition to couples living together, whether hetero- or homosexual, in order to regularize their situation in terms of taxation and inheritance. Unlike marriage, the *Pacte Civil de Solidarité* (*le PACS*) would not imply any obligation of fidelity, might be broken unilaterally and would confer no adoption or artificial insemination rights. It is an attempt by the French Government to acknowledge and regularize the reality of French society today where homosexual couples live together openly, where heterosexual couples live together and where one child in three is born to unmarried parents. The hostility of the far Right, including elements of the UDF and RPR, was immediate and vehement and the initial reading of the bill was delayed by a host of hostile amendments and by a filibuster in the National Assembly led by Christine Boutin (UDF), angrily opposing what they described as 'homosexual marriages'. The bill was reintroduced in April 1999 when the contractual nature of the proposal was emphasized: it is a 'contract entered into by two people to organize their life together'. It excludes brother-sister couples, people already married or in another Civil Solidarity Pact contract. None of this will placate in any way the defenders of the traditional family model who see this proposal as another step in the deliberate weakening of the traditional family model.

The Women of the Extreme Right

Christine Boutin was first elected to the National Assembly from the Yvelines constituency in 1986. She is also deputy mayor of Rambouillet and vice-president of the Yvelines General Council. Although she is linked to the UDF, she led her own electoral list in 1986 when she was suspended from the PR (a component of the UDF) and enjoys considerable support in her constituency for her pro-life, pro-family position. She is the founder of the Alliance for the Right to Life; the President of the parliamentary group of ninety traditionalist Catholic deputies who work together in defence of the family (*Oser la famille*); John Paul II made her a 'consultor' to the Sacred Congregation for the Defence of the Family. She is linked to the Association for the Promotion of the Family and close to *Opus Dei*. She is a founder member of Philippe de Villiers' traditionalist *Combat pour les Valeurs*. On 3 November 1998 she spoke for five and a half hours in the National Assembly to oppose the Government bill on the PACS, effectively delaying its passage for five months. Mme Boutin's opposition, supported by long biblical quotations, was motivated by what she sees as the recognition of a form of 'marriage' by the State for homosexuals. Her speech produced uproar in the National Assembly where the majority of Socialist members barracked her and the mainstream Right was embarrassed that the person who was to present the views of the Opposition should appear so narrowly partisan and out of touch with the realities of contemporary France. Yet the letters received afterwards by Dominique Gillet, a Socialist deputy and Chair of the parliamentary committee dealing with family affairs, showed that Christine Boutin had struck a chord with a number of people:

> I wish to express to you the fundamental opposition of our numerous membership to your proposal to set up any sort of contract (PACS or other) which would necessarily damage the natural family by recognizing in law what has been forbidden as abnormal and vicious since the beginning of time. Honour those men and women who are concerned primarily for our country and its future. parliamentary Government can only be respected and saved from discredit by the courage of deputies and senators who refuse to be zombies manipulated by the poof and dyke lobbies [sic].[18]

Women in France were granted the right to vote relatively late: in 1946, under the Provisional Government of Charles de Gaulle. Before then, politics was exclusively, and since then has been largely, a male preserve. In order to redress the imbalance between men and women candidates for elected office, the French Government introduced early in 1999 legislation to amend the Constitution by insisting on a measure of parity between the sexes in lists put forward by the political parties.

Bruno Mégret's Mouvement National (MN) is virtually an exclusively male organization. Le Pen's party had two European MPs, Martine Lehideux and Marie-France Stirbois, before the 1999 European elections. Not surprisingly, given its firm belief that a woman's place is in the home, Le Pen's FN is opposed to such a measure, which, it explains, is demeaning to women: 'it is humiliating for women to be reduced to quotas'.[19]

One of his former associates remarked ironically that Le Pen was demonstrably in favour of parity: 'the proof is that he punches and insults women as well as men' (Stirbois, p. 50). This was an allusion to the incident during the 1997 Legislative Election when he assaulted Annette Peulvast-Bergeal, the Socialist mayor of Mantes-la-Ville, which resulted in his being declared ineligible for public office for a year in November 1998.

The originality of Le Pen's FN was that women became candidates (and were elected) after their husbands had been disqualified from running for office, with the tacit understanding that they were there only to keep the seat warm for their husbands. Once the disqualification had been purged, the women would once again take a back seat. Catherine Mégret became mayor of Vitrolles in this way and it is an open secret that her husband (given the title of 'adviser') really runs the town. He is referred to ironically as 'the mayor-consort'. Cendrine Chevallier (wife of Jean-Marie, currently mayor of Toulon and briefly deputy for the city) replaced her disqualified husband as FN parliamentary candidate. Already a city councillor, she is depicted by *Présent* in the 1997 Legislative election campaign as the model candidate's wife: 'a stylish, high-powered woman [...] who combines in a pleasant way, femininity, elegance and action' and who remains a devoted mother, returning home each evening to say the rosary with her children.[20] In answer to the question 'As the wife of the mayor, what is your role?' She replies: 'First and foremost, I lend him a sympathetic ear. I am active but I remain in the background.'

She went on to fight two by-election campaigns against the Socialist Odette Casanova: she lost the first by a mere thirty-three votes (that election was annulled because a sketch on Canal+ was deemed to have interfered with the electoral process). The second was won by Mme Casanova with a majority of several hundred votes. Having been unwavering supporters of Le Pen, the Chevalliers became disabused by his increasingly outrageous behaviour. They resigned from the FN in March 1999 (but not to join Mégret's party) and remain in power in Toulon as independents. On hearing the news, Le Pen declared that he had been more moved by the death of his cat.

After his own disqualification in November 1998, Le Pen sought to follow the example of Mégret and Chevallier by having his own wife, Jany, replace him as leader of the FN list in the June 1999 European elections. She is a woman of no political experience, who has never worked and whose main interest in life (other than being Le Pen's wife) is animal welfare, like her friend, Brigitte Bardot. For Mégret, who saw himself as the second-in-command of the FN and whose supporters had been steadily gaining power in internal FN elections, this was one example too many of the arbitrary exercise of power by Le Pen. He made clear his opposition to Le Pen on 5 December 1998 and summoned an extraordinary congress of the FN at Marignane (a town with a FN majority on the municipal council) on 23 and 24 January 1999. Le Pen refused to recognize the authority of this congress which deposed him as leader and elected Mégret in his place. Le Pen took the matter to court and on 11 May 1999, the *Tribunal de Grande Instance* in Paris found in his favour, declaring that the Marignane congress had not respected the constitution of the FN and making Le Pen sole owner of the title, logo, symbols and property of the FN. Mégret was reduced to founding a new party, the MN. The catalyst which brought about the split was the proposal by Le Pen that his wife should head the FN list in these European elections when he was still ineligible to stand, a decision which proved to be one manipulation too many of FN women within the political process.

In spite of the split within the FN which many commentators have seen somewhat prematurely as the beginning of the end of the far Right in France, this is a constituency in French society which is tenacious, bringing together as it does strongly held political and religious convictions. In the 1995 Presidential elections and in the 1997 Legislative elections, support for the FN remained constant at about 15%. In the 1999 European elections, Le Pen's list scored 5.71%, Mégret's list 3.28%, a decline of 6% compared with the Presidential election but of only 1% compared with the previous European elections when the two lists are taken together. However, in terms of the issues which this chapter has examined, there was a third list, the RPF, that of Charles Pasqua and Philippe de Villiers, which represents very similar convictions (and includes Christine Boutin among its supporters) which scored 13.09% so that, in total, some 22% of the French electorate may be said to lend some measure of support to a nationalist and traditionalist agenda and one which, ultimately, can be seen as adopting a patriarchal attitude to women.

References

1   Integrist Catholics reject the reforms of the Second Vatican Council and support the retention of an unchanging Tridentine tradition. The most visible proponent is Mgr Marcel Lefebvre who founded his own seminary to preserve Tridentine traditions. Following his consecration of four bishops without permission, he was excommunicated, leading to the Lefebvrist schism. See William Smith, 'The Church', in *Aspects of Contemporary France*, ed. by Sheila Perry (London and New York: Routledge, 1997), pp. 153-74.

2   *Fideliter* (Publication of the Fraternité Sacerdotale de Saint Pie X), July-August 1987. Quoted in Claudie Lesselier and Fiammetta Venner, *L'Extrême Droite et les femmes* (Villeurbanne: Editions Golias, 1997), p. 64.

3   See *Lumen Gentium*, reproduced by Donal Flanagan, *In Praise of Mary* (Dublin: Veritas, 1975).

4   See Bernard P. Robinson,'Musings on the Magnificat', *Priests and People*, 1: 8 (December-January 1987-88), pp. 332-35.

5   In the view of many biblical scholars, this episode is most unlikely to have taken place. Luke uses the narrative device of summing up the major themes of his subsequent account of the life of Jesus in the first chapter of his Gospel. The whole thrust of his narrative is the notion of Jesus' journey to Jerusalem, to Crucifixion and Resurrection. This invented childhood journey to Jerusalem prefigures the journey he would make in his public ministry.

6   Characteristics formulated by Jean Vanier, 'Know them by their fruits', *The Tablet*, 15 March 1997, pp. 346-47.

7   Quoted in *Golias,* 27 and 28 (Autumn 1991), pp. 145-49.

8   See Lesselier and Venner, *L'Extrême Droite et les femmes*, p. 44.

9   Jean-Marie Le Pen, 'Le Banquet des 10.000', *La Documentation française*, 10 May 1987.

10   Bruno Mégret, *L'Alternative nationale: Les priorités du Front National* (St Cloud: Ed. Nationales, 1996).

11   *L'Heure de vérité*, Antenne 2, 13 February 1984.

12   Jean-Marie Le Pen, *Les Français d'abord* (Paris: Editions Carrère, 1984), quoted in *L'Extrême Droite et les femmes*, p. 56.

13   Reported in *Présent*, 18 October 1986.

14   T. Grimaux, 'Le Flop des avorteurs', *La Nef*, March 1992, p. 11.

15   Speech by Jean-Marie Le Pen, Balard, *La Documentation française*, 13 May 1984.

16   Speech by Jean-Marie Le Pen, St Franc, quoted in *Présent*, 3, 5, 6 June 1991.

17   Reported in *L'Express*, 11 June 1998, p. 29.

18   François-Marie Algoud, *L'Œuvre chrétienne de la cité vivante*, reported in *Le Nouvel Observateur*, 12-18 November 1998, p. 28.

19   Marie-France Stirbois, quoted in 'FN: Parité, connais pas', *Le Point*, 27 February 1999, p. 50.

20   'Trois jours de campagne avec la femme d'un candidat', *Présent*, 24 May 1997, p. 12.

Bibliography

Action Française, http://www.citeweb.net/affe/af/webaf.html.

Flanagan, Donal, *In Praise of Mary* (Dublin: Veritas, 1975).

Front national, http://www.front-nat.fr.

Le Pen, Jean-Marie, *Les Français d'abord* (Paris: Editions Carrère, 1984).

Lesselier, Claudie and Fiammetta Venner, 1997, *L'Extrême Droite et les femmes* (Villeurbanne: Editions Golias, 1997).

Mégret, Bruno, *L'Alternative nationale: Les priorités du Front National* (St Cloud: Ed. nationales, 1996).

Robinson, Bernard P., 'Musings on the Magnificat', *Priests and People*, 1: 8 (December-January 1987-88), pp. 332-35.

Smith, William, 'The Church', in *Aspects of Contemporary France*, ed. by Sheila Perry (London and New York: Routledge, 1997), pp. 153-74.

4 'Licencia más amplia para matar'?
Changes to Spain's Abortion Law and the Traditionalist Catholic Response

Lesley K. Twomey

This chapter offers an overview of the way in which legislation on abortion has progressed throughout the century in Spain. It also reflects on responses from the Roman Catholic hierarchy to the issue, especially in respect of recent developments in the law. In the second part of the chapter, the way in which pro-abortionists are presented in a range of Catholic publications will be analysed.

In the 1930s, under the Republican Government, Spain led the field in promoting liberalizing policies relating to family life. During that period, an amendment to the Civil Code allowed divorce. Spain was one of the first countries to introduce abortion as a result of amending the Criminal Code and this was introduced in December 1936 in the Republican zone.[1] Family policy was, thus, one of many ideological issues which divided the two sides in the Civil War. Ever since the Second Republic introduced these two specific amendments on family policy before the Spanish Civil War in 1936, attitudes to family life became part of the fracturing of Spain into Republican or Nationalist camps. Liberal Republican policies, such as abortion, in the eyes of the General Franco and his supporters, were irretrievably allied with communist, anti-Nationalist, therefore anti-Spanish sentiments and attitudes. This meant that from 1938 onwards, in the Nationalist zone with the support of the Church, the abortion law, the divorce law and civil marriage ceremonies, were deliberately removed from the statute books.[2] This meant that Spanish women again became subject to the nineteenth-century Criminal Code and Civil Code. Abortion became illegal again in 1941.[3] In her study of the early Franco period, the desire to erase from memory all aspects of pre-Civil War Spain is highlighted by Pilar Folguera Crespo when she remarks on the fact that people who had divorced and remarried under the Second Republic were forced to return to their original partners.[4] In the case of abortions carried out during the period of legality, turning the clock back was not an option.

In the period after the Civil War, the practice of procuring abortions continued, albeit illegally. Anny Brooksbank Jones cites figures for illegal abortions from the beginning to the end of the Franco years. In 1941, for example, there were 16,605 covert abortions, whilst by 1960, the official figures had risen to 24,140 (Brooksbank Jones, p. 85). At grass-roots level, necessity drove many women to desperate measures. Women were prepared to face the statutory six months' to six years' imprisonment for obtaining an abortion. Therefore, despite the ostensible pre-eminence of Catholic morality in Spain, undercover abortion continued. In this extreme example, overt Catholicism and covert anti-Catholic morality can be seen hand in hand. In Spain official attitudes belied the reality. The words used to define current practice in the on-going Argentinian abortion campaign, 'back-street abortion: a pact of silence', could have been applied to the Franco period in Spain.[5] The very existence of clandestine abortion points to the fact that the emphasis in Audrey Brassloff's assertion that 'a triumphalist Catholicism seemed immutable' needs to be placed on appearance rather than reality.

The 'Abortion Law'

The advent of the Transition period in 1975, on the death of Franco, brought a renewed entrenchment of the two opposing views on abortion. From the 1960s onwards, various women's groups had begun to form around key issues for women, campaigning more and more openly for revision of the Criminal Code to legalize contraception and abortion.[6] At the same time, the Church was beginning to seek out an influential role for itself as defender of public morality in a State moving from dictatorship to democracy. It should not be forgotten that Spain's dictatorship had been marked for several decades by an alliance of Church and State, since both during and after the Civil War, the Church had allied itself with the right-wing regime. In the new democratic Spain, this close alliance could not continue and, with the winds of change blowing through the Church following the Second Vatican Council, the Church had already begun to distance itself from the regime.[7] Brassloff underlines the Church's desire to consolidate a new power base for itself in the new democratic Spain; she comments how, 'once the nuts and bolts of the democratisation process were more or less in place, the Church intensified its push for *social* influence, particularly on "family matters": education and marriage, with total rejection of contraception, divorce and abortion' (Brassloff, p. 85).

However, the Church soon found its ability to influence legislation was being diminished. Contraception was the first of the Church's main doctrines on the family to be contravened, but other changes to the law were to follow.[8] In 1981, the Civil Code was amended so that divorce was legalized (*Código*, ch. VI, pp. 168-74).

In the case of abortion, changes to the law took longer. It was not until 1985, under the Socialist Government, ten years after the death of General Franco, that abortion stopped being an offence in a limited number of cases. The abortion law, in reality a reform of Spain's Criminal Code (*Código*, pp. 1017-19), which was put on the statute books after a prolonged struggle, on 5 July 1985, some three years after the start of the Socialist Government's period of office, could be seen as carrying forward the work of reform; it could also be seen as breaking with the moral influence of the Catholic Church or even as a recovery of rights lost following the demise of the Republic. However, it was a profound disappointment to women's groups, who had aided the Socialist victory in 1982, that when the amendment came its scope was limited.

The 1985 amendment to Article 417 of the Law 44/1971 is incorporated into the second part of the Criminal Code, entitled 'Crimes and their punishments'. The amendment decriminalizes abortion when it is carried out by a doctor, or under a doctor's direction, in an accredited private or state-owned clinic, with the consent of the woman concerned. In Spain, abortions can still only be carried out lawfully when one of the following three circumstances pertain:

- Abortion must be necessary to avoid serious danger to the life or to the physical or mental well-being of the woman. A certificate from another doctor is required in this case.
- Abortion is also permissible where the pregnancy is the result of a reported rape and the abortion must be carried out in the first twelve weeks of gestation. In this case, one medical opinion only is required.
- Abortion is permitted, finally, when it is considered that the child will be born with serious mental or physical defects. In this case, the abortion must be carried out within the first twenty-two weeks of gestation. Two doctors must certify that the abortion is necessary (*Código*, p. 1019).

It has been argued by right-wing and Catholic groups that the 1985 law was to blame for a lowering of the birth-rate in Spain. (The birth-rate was already down to 1.33 children per female by 1990. This figure had dropped to 1.21 by 1994 and is still the lowest in Europe. According to recent figures, it is at 1.16).[9] However, legalizing abortion cannot be seen as the culprit. In conjunction with the decriminalization of abortion, from 1971, the Government had stopped promoting pro-natalist policies, such as those introduced after the Civil War by the Franco Government (Brooksbank Jones, pp. 75-76). In addition, it should not be forgotten that Spanish women had been obtaining abortions illegally in Spain as well as abroad in both UK and Holland for many years prior to the passing of the Criminal Code amendment.[10]

Attempted Amendments to the Criminal Code

The Socialist Government drew up an amendment to the Criminal Code, which came before the Lower House on 9 November 1992. Under this proposed amendment, abortions would be permitted up to twelve weeks' gestation, in the case where the woman was suffering a state of anxiety and if there were a risk to her health in continuing the pregnancy.[11]

According to the Church and right-wing parties, this proposed fourth case opened the way to 'decriminalization of abortion'.[12] However, left-wing parties were not satisfied either as they considered the proposal did not go far enough. Even pro-abortion groups were divided on the proposed amendment. A spokeman for United Left (IU) indicated that his party would only be supporting the amendment because it was better than the existing law. Feminist groups and women MPs of the then governing PSOE were against the amendment, mainly because of the way it introduced a time limit of twelve weeks, where there had previously only been time-restrictions in the case of rape. They also opposed the loss of the right to decide for the woman herself, since the amendment to the law would have left the final decision to the doctor rather than to the mother. Because of the lack of consensus on Left and Right the amendment was defeated.

In 1994, the Government made a new attempt to bring in a fourth case in which abortion could legally be permitted under the Criminal Code. This amendment would have allowed abortion up to the twelfth week of pregnancy if social, personal or family conflict would arise from continuation with the pregnancy. The PSOE Government was dependent on support from the Catalonian nationalists during its final term of office (1993-96) and the right-wing Convergence and Union (CiU) Party refused to support their allies in Government on the amendment, so that, on each occasion the amendment was presented to Parliament, it was defeated. Contemporary reports place the blame squarely on the shoulders of the PP and CiU who joined forces towards the end of the Socialists' term of office to block any proposal to extend the law and include a fourth category.[13] Criticism was directed both at the right-wing parties for their delaying tactics, as well as at the PSOE for waiting until the last moment after already being in power for twelve years.[14]

There were further attempts to amend the law in 1997 and then, in February 1998, there was a further attempt to introduce the fourth case in which abortion would be legally permissible. The voting led to three 'historic' stalemates, with the Right cancelling all affairs of State to ensure the voting power of their party. The three hung divisions of the house on this issue meant that the draft bill was thrown out on a technicality.[15]

The most recent attempted amendment led to the celebrated vote in the Spanish Parliament on 22 September 1998. The People's Party Government had used delaying tactics to avoid fixing a date for the debate, despite pressure from the Left to the extent that there was a threat to denounce the PP's tactics as anticonstitutional to the Constitutional Court in June 1998. In fact, on the date fixed for the debate, there were three proposed amendments to discuss. All three included a fourth case in which abortions could legally be carried out.[16]

The debate on the amendment saw divisions of the Spanish Parliament along ancient fault lines, with the right-wing PP ranged against the parties of the Left. Commentaries on each side of the debate became increasingly heated. The Spanish press reported on the Episcopal Conference pronouncement in the debate.[17] A statement from the Episcopal Conference was read in all churches in Spain on Sunday 13 September 1998 and was emotively entitled: 'An even more liberal licence to kill children'.[18] The Episcopal Conference declared that all three proposals to amend the Criminal Code were 'immoral' and categorized them as shameful, since they would inevitably increase the possibility of killing unborn children, who are 'nevertheless proper human beings as we all were in the early stages of our existence'.[19]

The Church stance provoked immediate reaction from the Left. Matilde Fernández, who had held office as the Minister for Social Affairs in the 1993-1996 Socialist Government, threw the Church's recent past in its face, accusing it of having supported 'a licence to kill' under the Franco dictatorship.[20] Fernández is referring to the way left-wing opponents of the victors were treated under the Nationalist Government, when executions were carried out with the knowledge and support of the Church's elite. Similarly, Cristina Almeida, one of the signatories of the New Left amendment, commented that the pressure being exerted by the Church was contrary to the exercise of democracy in the Spanish Parliament and was a 'throwback to earlier times'.[21] María

Jesús Aramburu, United Left MP and spokesperson for the parliamentary Women's Committee, also weighed in against Monsignor Elías Yanes' pronouncement in Civil War terms: 'It was all like in Begin the Begin [sic], ghosts of the past, Spain's darkest hour, the two factions. But how irresponsible the Church hierarchy have been in provoking another social rift.'[22]

The link between the Church's compromised stance in its alliance with dictatorship is a frequent charge levelled at it by those on the Left. In at least one purportedly anti-abortion statement, published on the internet, a link is made between Spanish far-right nationalism and anti-abortionism. The document ends with the old nationalist rallying cry: 'Down with the appalling crime of abortion!!! Long live Spain!!!'[23] The author designates himself *Falangista de pro*, claiming to be a died-in-the-wool Falangist.

Furthermore, in an article expressing his concern about frequent postponement of the date when the debate was to be held, Francisco Umbral bemoans the fact that the governing PP relies for support on the pillars of the old regime: the *Opus Dei*, the Episcopal Conference and some of the old 'gentlemen' who belonged to the Franco Government.[24] Once again in the context of the debate, reference is made to the long-standing division of the country and to the alliance of Church and right-wing party. It is also significant that, at the same time, the Left rallied around its historic pro-abortion stance, with separate amendment proposals being filed by the Socialists, the United Left and by the New Left / Greens.

Abortion: Crime and Punishment

In the fourteen years following the decriminalization of abortion, there have been a number of successful amendments to the Criminal Code, in the main connected with definition of requirements for abortion centres to be legally approved. However, frequently legalized centres find themselves on the wrong side of the law, as in the recent case of the Iris centre in Albacete. Following the admission to hospital of a woman due to complications from the abortion she had just undergone at the clinic, the hospital doctor denounced the clinic to the police. The judge ordered the records of all 1442 patients to be seized by the police. The woman herself was arrested and brought before the judge. The doctors working in the clinic, the only legal abortion centre in Albacete were also arrested. Politicians from across the political spectrum, including the PP, called on José Manuel Rajoy, the Minister of Health, and Margarita Mariscal, the Minister of Justice, to explain how the confidentiality of patients' records would be ensured.[25]

The trial is not an isolated case, in one celebrated case the defendants have been waiting eleven years for judgement to be pronounced. Prison sentences are not uncommon for those who fail to keep within the boundaries established by the law. In Oviedo, recently, a psychiatrist and a gynaecologist were given prison sentences for procuring an abortion.[26]

Abortion and the Pro-life Lobby

How has the Church reacted to the onslaught on its traditional stance on the sanctity of human life?[27] The response from the bishops was virulent in 1985. The bishop of Cuenca reminded all those who procured an abortion or collaborated in its procurement that they would be excommunicated. However, all those in authority who pronounced themselves in favour of the new law were also implicated: 'Those who gave legitimacy to the vote on the abortion law are not free from responsibility, whatever the reason for their vote'.[28] The bishop warned all Catholics who hold public office that 'they will not be able to escape from being labelled public sinners'. The warning and its naming and shaming inherent in the words 'public sinners' seems to have been plucked from a past day and age. A pastoral letter from the bishop of Siguenza warned the faithful that no Christian could support those who operate 'according to their individual conscience'.[29] Conscience cannot be individual but is collective, directed by the Church. Though the sense of 'support' is left undefined, it can be presumed that the type of 'support' which is envisaged and decried could be for pro-abortion groups, for pro-abortion campaigns or even for politicians in favour of the reform bill.

Subsequent attempts to amend the abortion law have met with powerful opposition. When the Socialist Government presented the draft bill, which would have allowed abortion under a fourth category that of 'anxiety' (*angustia*) to the Spanish Parliament in 1992, the Church's reaction was swift. Comparison was made between those seeking to legalize abortion and those involved in other causes such as terrorism, which also involve killing innocent victims. Such statements by the bishop of San Sebastian, José María Setién, show the depth of the bishop's feeling about legalization.[30]

In 1992 the proposed amendment to the Criminal Code led to what can now be seen as recourse to traditional weaponry, a series of declarations by the Church hierarchy, through the Sunday homily and the mobilization of the faithful in vigils and protests. The hierarchy even went so far as to call on churchgoers to stop voting for the PSOE, although in later stages of the campaign, this was toned down.

The tactics used in September 1998 in many respects paralleled those of the 1992 campaign. On the Sunday prior to the debate, priests preached on the need to defeat the abortion amendment. Parishioners were urged to write to their MPs. In churches across Spain on 13 September, the weight of prayer was placed firmly on the side of protection of human life: 'For the right to life to be respected by all, law-makers and every citizen, let us pray to the Lord.'[31] Parishioners were encouraged to join the demonstration scheduled for the day of the debate outside the Spanish Parliament building organized by the United for Life (*Unidos por la Vida*) group.

Mass demonstrations of anti-abortion activists outside the Parliament building and the exertion of enormous pressure on Catholic deputies contributed to ensuring the defeat of the amendment. These political demonstrations were, at times, violent.[32] Anti-abortion demonstrators rallied support around slogans like: 'You abortionists are terrorists', a rallying cry which recalled Bishop Setién's statement at the time of the defeated 1992 parliamentary bill. Supporters of abortion denounced the Episcopal Conference as well as the ruling, right-wing PP: 'This is what happens to us when we have a Fascist Government'; 'The Episcopal Conference should be burnt.' The denunciation of the PP for its connections to its past through the term 'fascist' (*facha*) show how the inclusion of Franco's ministers amongst the founder members of the Popular Alliance (AP), the fore-runner of the PP, has not been forgotten. It also reveals yet again that the abortion issue continues to raise the ghosts of the past in Spain.

In the event, the PSOE amendment was defeated by a single vote. The United Left and New Left proposed amendments were each defeated by ten and eleven votes respectively.[33]

Media Coverage

Reporting of the amendment took front-page status in the Spanish press, showing its continued power to arouse the deepest of feelings in the electorate. For the first time in the abortion debate in Spain, widespread internet coverage gave the public access to both sides of the debate. The Episcopal Conference published its anti-abortion statement on the web. Furthermore the full text of each of the amendments to the Criminal Code have been placed on the internet on a website advertising the services of the abortion clinic, Clínica Dator.[34] The Spanish public has been bombarded with views from both sides of the debate.

Reporting on abortion issues is carried out at a global level, not only because of the fact that the Catholic Church is an international entity but also reflecting the fact that it has chosen to take full advantage of the newest form of global communication to put its message across. Much of the abortion news round-up emanates from the United States. For example, an on-line publication entitled, *Escoge la Vida* (Choose Life) gives a monthly update on the world-wide abortion situation. This contribution to the abortion debate sets the Spanish legislation in a global Hispanic context.[35] The publication is produced by a world-wide organization, Human Life International, from its Headquarters in Virginia, USA. Human Life International also produces a prayer site. Amongst the menu of prayers are to be found a prayer for a woman who has had an abortion, a pro-life prayer, a prayer for pregnant mothers. Visitors to the site can also select a *Via Crucis de los Inocentes Abortados* (A Way of the Cross of Aborted Innocents), a version of the Stations of the Cross in which each station relates the suffering of the abortion victim to Christ's suffering on the road to Calvary, complete with a Crucifixion image incorporating a pre-term baby. A rosary for the unborn relates each of the mysteries of the rosary to the victims of abortion.

Abortion and the Church

In this second part of the chapter, some of the recent publications by the Church for the attention of Spanish Catholics will be examined. These documents can be divided into various categories. There are official statements by the Church hierarchy. There are also a number of documents which are directly related to abortion and are intended as a contribution to the on-going debate in Spain. There are also documents which ostensibly have no connection with the abortion debate but, nevertheless, include opinions on it, whilst discussing other issues. I will begin by contextualizing the way in which abortion is treated in documents intended for Catholic consumption.

The Church's Magisterium and Abortion

The Church's teaching on abortion takes as its starting point the commandment not to kill (Matthew 19:18). It also proceeds from the Church's teaching on the dignity of the human person, since 'God created humankind in his image' (Genesis 1: 27). In the document, *Declaration on Procured Abortion*, the Congregation for Doctrine of the Faith presents biblical, patristic and papal declarations condemning abortion, thus setting more recent papal declarations, such as that of Paul VI in *Humanae Vitae* and those of the Second Vatican Council (*Gaudium et spes*, art.27, 51) in the context of Catholic tradition.[36] Pope John Paul II echoes earlier documents of the Church when he reminds the faithful in *Evangelium Vitae* (EV 62C) that: 'Direct abortion will always be a serious moral disorder [...] No circumstance, proposal or law can make what is an illicit act, legal.'[37] In the 1983 revised canon law, the penalties for procuring an abortion continued to be excommunication (Canon 1398) and this law is recalled in *Evangelium Vitae* (EV 62B). The same penalty was applied to 'accomplices' in the crime, in other words, doctors or others who assisted in the abortion process (Canon 1329). The penalties laid down in canon law are reiterated in the words of the new Catechism: 'Taking part in an abortion is a serious moral sin. The Church sanctions this crime against human life with excommunication' (*Catechism of the Catholic Church*, para. 2272). As well as pointing out the penalties resulting from participating in abortion, the Catechism emphasizes each human being's right to be treated as a person from the very first instant of his or her conception: 'From this moment onwards [from the moment of conception] each person's inviolable right to life must be recognized' (*Catechism*, para. 2270). The Spanish bishops' pronouncements on public sin and excommunication at the time of the passing of the 1985 amendment must be set in the context of the Church's teaching on abortion and the Church's own penalties for involvement in it.

Family Values and Abortion

However, the way the Church regards the modern world is an important backdrop to continuing statements about the immorality of abortion. The Catholic Church and, within it, the Spanish Catholic Church appears to see itself as under threat in the modern world. Crisis, threats and warnings of doom prevail in Church discourse. This is apparent in numerous publications and in statements by the Church hierarchy. For example, this stance is apparent in the Pontifical Council for the Family publication, which is a contribution to the debate on demographic trends.[38] It could also be already be found in a statement made in 1974 by Cardinal Joseph Ratzinger, Prefect of the Congregation for the Doctrine of Faith, *The Church in the Face of the Threats to Human Life*. According to the Cardinal, there exists a new 'counter-life culture' formed from a melding of individualism, materialism, utilitarianism and hedonism. Within this culture, freedom is seen as an absolute right of the individual. The ultimate root of the hatred expressed against self and against the human race is the loss of God.[39] The Episcopal Committee for the Defence of Life in 1991 referred to the 'dangerous course' which some sections of society, even sections of society who are in power, have embarked upon. Hedonistic attitudes are also behind 'attacks on basic human rights perpetrated by large sectors in society and by the current legislation in Spain'.[40] Such attitudes are a major source of 'concern and alarm' to the Spanish bishops.

Crisis is also the subject of the collective pastoral letter, sent out by the bishops of Bilbao, San Sebastián, Tudela and Vitoria: *On being a Christian in the Present Time of Crisis*.[41] In this pastoral letter, the faithful were called upon to take a stand in an increasingly secularized world. In Spain, the Christian Family Movement (MFC) reflects this desperate need to counter the attacks of an increasingly secularized society in its publications. The opening statement in the prayer/study guide it has written, highlights this attitude which regards believers as being under attack from non-Christian influences:

> In the world of today, the crisis of Christian values as socially relevant is clear. Led astray or harassed, fooled or tempted, many Christians, instead of being the salt and light of the world allow secular and non-Catholic values to influence us.[42]

The attack on Christian values is presented in terms of an invasive external force or outside influence which overcomes the individual's resistance. This is emphasized not only by the adjectives resonant of sexual attraction, seduction or sexual acts of aggression, *seducido* (led astray), *acosado* (harassed), *atraído* (attracted), but could also be present in the highly suggestive verb *penetrar* (we allow ourselves to be penetrated/invaded/influenced).

Another handbook, produced by the Spanish Family Union (UFE), approaches the secular world in the same defensive spirit. The reader is indirectly called upon to take a stand against, or at the very least to distance him or herself from, the lack of understanding of what the true value of marriage is:

> Nowadays, laws which take their point of departure from concepts very different to Christian principles and are based on anti-life culture, can have the effect of blurring or making people forget basic concepts: marriage for life is a way of attaining happiness and is a reality of great benefit to individuals and to society.[43]

First, making these statements in a Spanish context underlines how far the State-Church divide has widened. The legislative body is perceived as completely 'other' in that 'it takes its point of departure from concepts, which are completely different from Christian principles'. 'Anti-life culture' is opposed to the Christian alternative and moral threat to the Church is linked specifically to legislation which causes misunderstanding of basic principles of the faith. Whilst the authors are referring most closely to legislation on divorce, the fact that 'laws' are mentioned means the statements can equally well be applied to abortion or to contraception. It is against this backdrop of legal threat to Christian values and of secular society embracing anti-life culture that the Spanish bishops' spokesman's response to the vote on 22 September must be read. When the bishops express their 'satisfaction, relief and hope', they are seeing the 'no' victory as a turning point in a battle to win over a Spanish society which has lost its way. There is 'moral disorientation in huge sectors of society'.[44] They see in the vote 'new ways for Spanish society and its [parliamentary] representatives to continue embracing the values inherent in the sacred dignity of all human life from the mother's womb to natural death.'[45]

The Spanish bishops' desire to influence morality and to move Spain away from a pro-abortion culture can also be seen in a publication from the Episcopal Committee for the Defence of Human Life, *El aborto: 100 cuestiones y respuestas sobre la defensa de la vida humana (*100 Questions and Answers about the Defence of Human Life*)*. This book is written in catechetical style and is intended as an 'accessible and informative book about the value of human life' (p. 12). It is explicitly directed not only at the faithful but also at 'legislators and those in power' (p. 12). The Commission calls on 'all men and women of good faith to reflect on what is happening before our eyes' because the legislation relating to abortion is condemning innocent victims to an unjust death.

Pro-abortionists

Documents given the *imprimatur* by the Church do not always concentrate solely on biblical, patristic, papal or moral teaching about abortion.[46] On occasion they are an atttempt to convince those who oppose the Church's doctrine, at others they distinguish the class of person who opposes the Church on this issue.

Whilst abortion is not covered directly as one of the ten themes which *Christian Attitudes in the Family* addresses, it does, however, feature indirectly in the section dedicated to the role of women in society (pp. 84-99). Within this chapter, ten 'types' of women are described for the lay study groups to evaluate and it is here in an indirect manner that pro-abortionists are defined.

Those women who consider themselves 'equal' to men are presented with a range of negative characteristics. Reference to reproductive rights occurs alongside the appropriation of masculine behaviour:

> There are women who consider themselves men's equals in what are thought to be typical masculine ways of behaving: they smoke, they drink, they use vulgar phrases and they boast about their many sexual partners. They think they are mistresses of their own bodies and of what nature has granted them in reproduction of the species: we have the children, we decide.[47] They do not think they are complementary to men nor do they feel called to share their life with a man.
>
> (MFC, p. 87)

The purported errors committed by this category of women are manifold. The unifying force behind the condemnation is that such women 'consider themselves equal' to men, the assumption made by the authors being that, of course, they are mistaken. Such women copy 'typical' male behaviour, which is, of course, by implication, not acceptable when transferred to females: amongst these behaviours are included drinking, smoking, using vulgar words and displaying promiscuous behaviour. This group of women uses the slogan used by the pro-abortion lobby: 'A woman's right to choose', with its literal meaning in Spanish, 'We bear the children, we decide'. Once again the authors suggest that the women are misguided: 'they think'. The final charge of unnatural behaviour is that they do not feel in the least 'called' to settle down and plan a life together with any man. It may be that this 'unnatural behaviour' is intended to show that such women are themselves untrue to their gender. These women are clearly not celibate for they make great play of their promiscuity. It is noteworthy that this category of sexually active women, passing from partner (male or female) to partner, is characterized as the pro-abortionist *par excellence*. In theological terms, there is a further condemnation. This woman, who dares to consider herself equal to men, commits the sin of overweening pride in stating that she is in control of her own body and in daring to control procreation, which she fails to recognize as a gift from God. In other words, she fails to recognize her own dependence on God, and her own natural vocation, and tries to take on a God-like role, deciding when human life shall be brought into being.

Pro-abortion activism is regarded as sinful in that it makes the will of the mother 'paramount'. The same stance is to be found in the pastoral letter read in the majority of Spanish churches on 13 September 1998:

> What they are after now is for mothers to take the final decision and for their children to be got rid of at will. After a short period of reflection, the mother can decide the future child is not going to live. The State does not just look on passively but the State connives in the death and even takes an active role.[48]

The pastoral letter takes condemnation of abortionists in theological terms one step further by implicating the State in this act. The pro-abortion State is guilty of each abortion carried out, since by passing the legislation, it is an accomplice in sin.

The picture of the woman who thinks herself equal to men and who imitates male behaviour, thus, reunites several deeply negative images for the authors of the book. This non-feminine woman is pro-abortion and this leads to its inverse: pro-abortionists are non-feminine. Such women are categorized as promiscuous or lesbian, since they do not wish to dedicate themselves to one man, and it is clear that such a portrayal is intended to distance this female type from the likely adherents of a Catholic family workgroup. In this way, women who usurp masculine roles are intended as an example of the dangers which ensue when women take on non-traditional roles in society. True Catholic women are called to share their lives with their husband.

MFC presents one other main category of women treated negatively in relation to abortion. This time it is childless women, the women who choose career over family, who are to be condemned. This type of woman chooses the 'masculine model', valuing competitiveness and aggressive behaviour over unspoken feminine virtues:

> There are women who call themselves feminists and who defend the idea of the competitive woman, of the aggressive woman, because they think this is a necessary step forward. They go for the masculine model and put into practice the man's model rather than the woman's. In their scale of values, career comes first and they often choose not to have children.

(MFC, p. 86)

Once again, rather than complementing male behaviours, this type of woman apes male behaviours which are considered inappropriate for her. This time she is categorized as a 'feminist' and, for this reason, she is held up for opprobrium. It has been noted that Spanish women are notoriously reluctant to name themselves as feminists and for this reason it can be assumed that the women who pin the label on themselves must be hardened cases. MFC suggests that the feminists take the same anti-life stance as the previous category of women.

In the introduction to the study of the role of women, moreover, MFC has taken the opportunity to distance Spanish women from the struggle for women's rights. The suffragette movement is set in an Anglo-Saxon context only, which has the effect of preventing present-day Spanish Catholic women from associating themselves with Spanish suffragettes, such as Clara Campoamor, who fought for the vote in the Republican Parliament of 1931.[49] Furthermore, this aspect of liberation is seen as *passé*: 'the achievements of the suffragettes are a thing of the past' (p. 83). The other way in which the women's struggle is distanced from the present-day is that the suffragette movement is set in a time-frame which is non-Spanish. It becomes 'the determined action of a few women to become part of the paid workforce, made possible by the need to stand in for the male workforce, depleted by the Second World War' (p. 83). The authors seek to characterize the suffragette movement as alien to Spain. By describing events in which Spain did not participate, Spain is seen as outside the feminist movement. For a second time, the struggle is distanced from Spanish women and fails to take into account the struggles of working women in the Trades' Union movement in Spain as well as political movements of the Republican era. Even the Catholic women's groups of the 1950s, who took up the struggle for women's rights from within the regime, do not merit a mention.

The negative approach of this Catholic group to feminism can be seen in contrast to that of the more liberal Catholic group, the Workers Brotherhood for Catholic Action (*Hermandad Obrera de Acción Católica*).[50] The organization was originally founded in 1951 to assist in the work of bringing Spain back to Christianity after the Civil War, but soon became imbued with ideas drawn from liberation theology. In a recent volume of the on-line journal, *Cristianisme i justicia* (Christianity and Justice), members of the organization declare themselves both Catholic and feminist.[51] They accept the fact that feminism is a world-wide movement but take the view that its effects include rather than exclude Spain.

To come back to the MFC study guide, the perceived error of this 'feminist' female type is, as with the sexually liberated woman, to equate herself with masculine norms of behaviour. Aggressive behaviour and competitiveness, whilst acceptable in the male, are deemed unnatural in the female. By implication, the MFC suggests women should behave in a more passive and co-operative manner, and this suggests, by implication, that these characteristics are more appropriate to women. Indeed, these characteristics are affirmed in the eighth type of woman listed, where we see a positive affirmation of the authentic femininity for today:

There are women who try to cultivate the specific qualities of their 'feminine being'. Women have always valued life at a very deep level. Tenderness, patience, understanding and delicacy have been the qualities most characteristic of women.

(MFC, p. 88)

It is significant that giving value to human life is one of the characteristics of this 'authentic femininity'. There is suggested positive value given to these characteristics which are opposed to the refusal to conceive and the anti-life stance of the sexually liberated woman and the feminist.

What then is 'authentic femininity' thought to be like? The next section of the workbook sheds light on this. Participants are asked to identify with one of the ten types of womanhood. But in fact so few of the types are presented positively that choice is limited to four and one of these is the religious life; 'they make their life a prayer, setting God and their brothers and sisters in first place in their scale of values' (p. 88). Amongst the rest, the types which are given positive value, are the full-time mother, the mother who combines work and motherhood and the woman who cultivates true feminine qualities. The first sees her role as fulfilling an important social need. The second still chooses family over selfish personal ambitions, even though it is recognized that undertaking two social roles often means that such women pay the highest price. Thus, apart from the nun, it is still the family-centred type of woman, which is valued by this Church family group. Looking deeper, it is the self-abnegation of both the family-orientated women and the nuns which is valued, just as it is the self-seeking approach of their more ambitious sisters, including being in favour of abortion, which is condemned.

Family Values Right the Wrongs of Society

In another series of materials, intended for marriage guidance or pre-marriage groups, the Catholic umbrella group, UFE, takes a catechetical approach to a study of the nature of marriage. Like *Christian Attitudes in the Family*, it refers only in passing to abortion but those references serve to give a picture of the group's attitude to it. Divorce and abortion appear amidst a series of family-life problems. For example, they are included alongside the refusal to care for children and old people, which are negative aspects of modern society:

> The worst aspect of our age is that sometimes we do not manage to make a family in spite of trying to do so (as is shown by the divorce rate, number of abortions and of abandoned children, the old people left to their fate, the rejection of life as if it were no good). The key thing is that these failures are treated as though they were the ideal to be followed and that the foundations of the notion of the family with its positive human influence is rejected and discriminated against. Going back to this idea and putting it forward again as something accessible and desirable is the aim of this book. For this reason this book in setting out its theory takes no account of present-day non-functional families and does not present such families as alternatives when really they are broken families.

(UFE, p. 19)

Within this failure to create families, non-standard family groupings (presumably one-parent families, broken families and alternative family groupings) are described in terms of being 'diseases' or 'breakdowns' (*patologías*) of the family unit. UFE decries the fact that such non-standard family groupings are being presented as alternatives to the family when, in reality, they are symptomatic of its breakdown.

UFE does admit that it is proposing an ideal family unit, although it asserts that a family unit of two parents and children is an achievable ideal, noting that many families are managing to live out that ideal across the world. There is, therefore, no recognition that the family unit may be anything other than effective (in an undefined manner) and positive in allowing family members to reach true humanity. There is, moreover, a refusal to recognize any possible negative impact that the family may have. Nor is there any recognition that the family unit may have different effects on each member of the unit. Such opinions are categorized as 'pernicious'. Indeed a rediscovery of the family is seen as able to right many of the wrongs in Spanish society:

> Rediscovering the family [...] is exactly what our society needs to defeat a number of the evils which afflict it. These include lack of solidarity between generations, an increase in the number of abandoned children and young people drifting into drugs and alcohol. There are people broken-hearted because of marriage breakdown. There are old people left alone and friendless. There are relationships bought and sold. Human sexuality has been brought low.
>
> (UFE, p. 18)

An examination of the wrongs which rediscovery of family will right is salutary. The first category of problems mentioned is functional. Emphasis is put upon care for the weaker members of society: children and old people who are, currently, abandoned or left to fend for themselves. It is significant to note that the role of carer has been traditionally that of the woman. The remaining ills which true understanding of family can cure are wide-ranging: for example, at the door of family breakdown is laid the increase in drug culture among young people as well as increased pressure on the education and social services. In the traditional family unit, supervision of young people's education and care for the elderly has been, and is, carried out by women. If she abrogates the role, refusing to co-operate with it, then State services have to step in, stretching them to breaking point. What UFE is advocating is a return to traditional family values which will reinsert the woman in her role of carer within the family unit.

The second category of social problems, to be righted by rediscovery of the family, is demographic. UFE assumes that increased focus on family life will, automatically, lead to an increase in the birth-rate, palliating the 'demographic depression' from which Spain is suffering: in other words, correct understanding of family life equates to willingness to invest in the family by having more children. As we have seen, the birth-rate in Spain is the lowest in Europe although the number of births is beginning to rise.

However, although this point seems to be addressed evenly to male and female group members, it is of course, the female members who would make the heavier investment in the family, especially in respect of increasing the birth-rate.

The third category focuses on crimes, in the main sexual. Some of these appear to take little account of social reality. For example, UFE advocates that a correct understanding of family will obviate violence, ignoring the fact that most violence against women occurs within the family, not outside its boundaries.

Conclusion

The current abortion law in Spain allows women to have recourse to legal abortion in a limited number of cases. During the 1990s the Socialists and other left-wing parties have attempted to amend the law and remove the penalty from abortions carried out for the further reason of maternal anxiety. However, since the defeat of the proposed amendment in 1998, the Socialists have not made any further attempt to amend the Criminal Code.

Legislation dealing with issues relating to human sexuality is specifically seen as anti-Catholic, set in place with a view to destroying family values and this is particularly the case for the abortion legislation. It is for this reason that the Church makes every effort to resist any attempt to broaden such legislation and this explains its reaction to the most recent attempt made by left-wing parties in September 1998, as well as its response to the defeat of the amendments.

Furthermore, the Church's opposition to anti-life legislation leads it to construct a negative picture of those women who support women's right to choose. The behaviour, lifestyle and personal beliefs of women, who do not conform to the Church's perceived norm of womanhood and motherhood, are demonized in the pro-family Catholic literature reviewed. Women who are very different in lifestyle and in manner from the Catholic ideal are presumed to be abortionist. The caricaturized vision of what pro-abortion campaigners are thought to be like can only contribute to a deepening of divisions on the issue of abortion. 'Authentic femininity' incorporates valuing of human life. All other women are condemned to being non-feminine.

Despite the fact that the bishops pronounced that the defeat of the amendments in September 1998 represented a turning point for Spanish society and that they regarded it as a sign of hope for the future defence of human life in Spain, the question must be asked as to how long abortion legislation can be held from the statute books. The proposed amendment was defeated by one vote only, meaning that almost half the MPs were in favour of the extension of women's rights to abortion or rather of their right not to be judged by the law if they did have recourse to abortion.

The issue of abortion strikes to the heart of those tensions inherent in modern Spain's political baggage. Given twentieth-century Spain's history of opposing forces: Right versus Left, Catholic versus atheist, Republican versus Nationalist, supporter versus opponent of Franco and, given the association of abortion with the Republican cause, it is hardly surprising that this issue has inordinate power to mobilize opinion on both sides of the political spectrum. It is unlikely that Spain will be able to resolve the issues surrounding abortion until some of that historical baggage can be left behind.

References

1   Mary Nash, *Rojas: Las mujeres republicanas en la Guerra Civil* (Madrid: Taurus, 1999), pp. 233-47.

2   Mercedes Roig, *La mujer en la historia a través de la prensa: Francia, Italia, España, s.XVIII-XX* (Madrid: Ministerio de la Cultura, 1989), p. 316.

3   Anny Brooksbank Jones, *Women in Contemporary Spain* (Manchester: Manchester University Press, 1997), p. 85.

4   Pilar Folguera Crespo, 'El franquismo: El retorno a la esfera privada (1939-75)' in *Historia de las mujeres en España*, ed. by Elena Garrido González, Pilar Folguera Crespo, Margarita Ortega López and Cristina Segura Graiño (Madrid: Síntesis, 1997), pp. 527-48, p. 527.

5   Mujeres en Red, http://nodo50.org /mujeresred/aborto-repem.html#2, consulted 2 November 1999.

6   Pilar Escario, Inés Alberdi and Ana-Inés López-Accotto, *Lo personal es político: El movimiento feminista en transición*, pp. 180-85. This celebration of Spanish feminist movements also contains a series of slogans used up until 1978 in Spain, included among which are those protesting for the legalization of abortion, such as 'Decriminalization and legalization of contraception and abortion', 'free abortion on demand', pp. 131-32.

7   Georgina Blakely, 'The Holy Trinity in Spain: State, Civil Society and Political Parties', *International Journal of Iberian Studies*, 10:1 (1997), 15-32, p. 29. The Joint Assembly of Bishops and Priests in 1971 approved a resolution which, Blakely indicates, amounted to an apology for the Church's partisan role in the Civil War. See also Audrey Brassloff, *Religion and Politics in Spain: The Spanish Church in Transition 1962–96* (Houndsmill, Basingstoke: Macmillan, 1998)

8   Carmen Pujol Algans, *Código de la mujer* (Madrid: Instituto de la Mujer/Ministerio de Asuntos Sociales, 1992), Law 45/1978 modifying Articles 416 and 7 of the Criminal Code, pp. 994-95. Further references to this text will be cited as *Código*.

9   *Las mujeres en cifras: 1997* (Madrid: Ministerio de Asuntos Sociales/Instituto de la Mujer, 1997), p. 16; Irene Hernández Velasco, 'Sube la natalidad por primera vez en 20 años', www.el-mundo.es, 25 July 1998.

10 Once Family Planning Centres had been set up to administer contraception from 1978 onwards, they assisted in channelling the abortion traffic overseas. See Pilar Escario, Inés Alberdi and Ana Inés López-Accotto, *Lo personal es político: El movimiento feminista en transición* (Madrid: Instituto de la Mujer/Ministerio de Asuntos Sociales, 1996), pp. 142-43.

11 Cited by Julia Pérez, 'La angustia del aborto: La decisión del Gobierno de legalizar implícitamente el aborto hasta los tres meses desata las críticas', *Cambio 16*, 21 September 1992, p. 28).

12 Luisa Fernanda Rudi, cited by Julia Pérez, 'La angustia', p. 30.

13 Their delaying tactics included requiring at least thirty people to appear before the Justice and Home Affairs committee, as well as adding a further week's delay to the time-limit for putting forward amendments, which ensured that in the few months remaining in the life of the Parliament, further attempts to reform the Criminal Code would be blocked. See Rosa Paz, 'Una treta del PP y CiU impide que la ampliación del aborto se apruebe en esta legislatura', *La Vanguardia*, 18 October 1995, p. 12.

14 Both the CiU and United Left spokespersons criticized the Government. The tardy approach is indicative of the sensitivity of the subject but it also indicates a consciousness of the power of the issue to sway socialist voters. This may be one explanation for its appearance late in the PSOE term of office. Criticism

also came from the Trade Union movement with criticism of PSOE from the Workers' Commissions Union (*Comisiones Obreras*), see 'Sólo por un voto. El Parlamento dijo no a la modificación de la ley del aborto', *Trabajadora,* October 1998, p. 5.

15 'El congreso debatirá de nuevo la introducción del aborto libre el 22 de septiembre', http://www.aliento.net/ Actualidad/ 09/98/09.A.1.0.htm, consulted 9 February 2000.

16 The proposed fourth case was worded as follows: 'When carrying on with the pregnancy would in the woman's view mean a conflict for herself, for those around her or for her family and this prevents going ahead with the pregnancy.'

17 'La postura del Comité ejecutivo de la Conferencia', http://www.el-mundo.es/diario/1998/09/14/ sociedad/14N0024.html, consulted 21 September 1998.

18 'Licencia más amplia para matar a los hijos', http://www.conferenciaepiscopal.es/aborto.htm, consulted 13 September 1998.

19 http:// www.conferenciaepiscopal.es/aborto.htm, consulted 13 September 1998.

20 Borja Echevarría, 'Yanes contra la libertad de voto sobre el aborto', http://www.el-mundo es/diario/09/15/sociedad/15N0055.html, 15 September 1998.

21 'Todos los sectores sociales participan en el debate', http://www.el-mundo.es/diario/1998/09/22 /sociedad/22N0054.html, consulted 15 December 1998. Almeida is said to have used the words 'un atraso'.

22 María Jesús Aramburu, 'La OPA eclesiástica: Por la ampliación, contra la "intromisión" eclesiástica', http://www.el.mundo.es/diario/1998/02/21/sociedad/21NOO69.html, consulted 21 September 1998.

23 'La ley del aborto: una licencia para matar', http://euskadi. hispavista.com/foros/política, 16 September 1998.

24 Francisco Umbral, 'El aborto', http://www.el-mundo.es/diario, 29 May 1998.

25 Amaya Iríbar, 'El colegio de médicos se desentiende de la clínica abortista intervenida en Albacete', http://www.elpais.es/p/d/19980315/sociedad/albacete.htm, consulted 15 March 1998.

26 'La Audiencia de Oviedo contra el aborto', *Trabajadora,* 22 May 1997, p. 5.

27 For a summary of recent pronouncements on abortion see http://www.vidahumana.org/ vidafam/aborto/resumen.html, consulted 15 February 2000.

28 http://www.vidahumana.org/vidafam/aborto/magisterio.html, consulted 15 February 2000.

29 http://www.vidahumana.org/vidafam/aborto/magisterio.html, consulted 15 February 2000.

30 Julia Pérez, 'La angustia del aborto: La decisión del Gobierno de legalizar implícitamente el aborto hasta los tres meses desata las críticas', *Cambio 16,* 21 September 1992, pp. 44-50.

31 José Manuel Vidal, 'La Iglesia convoca para hoy una manifestación ante el Congreso', http://www.el-mundo.es, 21 September 1998.

32 Borja Echevarría, 'La "guerra" del aborto se traslada a las puertas del Congreso', http://www.el-mundo es/diario/1998/09/23/23N00.html, 23 September 1998.

33 'La izquierda y la derecha llevan la bronca al pasillo', http://www.el-mundo.es/diario/1998/09/23/ sociedad/23N0056.html, consulted 23 September 1998.

34 http://www.tutormedica.com/FAQ.htm, consulted 15 February 2000.

35 http://www.vidahumana.org/que_es_vhi.html, consulted 15 February 2000.

36 http://www.vidahumana.org/vidafam/iglesia/ensen_aborto.html. The summary article was written by José María López Riocerezo; first published in *Ya,* 27 April 1982.

37 http://www.vidahumana.org/vidafam/iglesia/ensen_aborto.html, consulted 15 February 2000.

38 Pontificio Consejo para la familia, 'Evoluciones demográficas: Dimensiones éticas y pastorales', http://www.serviciato.com/doctrina//evoluciones_demograficas.htm, consulted 9 December 1999.

39 http://www.vidahumana.org/vidafam/iglesia/ensen_aborto_amenaza.htm, consulted 18 February 2000.

40 Comité Episcopal para la Defensa de la Vida (CEDV), *El aborto: 100 cuestiones y respuestas sobre la defensa de la vida humana y la actitud de los católicos* (Madrid: Palabra DL, 1991).

41 Luís María Larrea, *Ser cristiano en la actual situación de crisis: Carta pastoral de los obispos de las diócesis de Bilbao, San Sebastián, Tudela y Vitoria*, Colección documentos y estudios, 79 (Madrid: PPC, 1982).

42 Movimiento Familiar Cristiano, *Actitudes cristianas de la familia* (Santander: Sal Terrae, 1997), p. 9. Further references to this text will appear in the form MFC.

43 Unión Familiar Española, *El matrimonio y la familia* (Madrid: EDICE, 1998), p. 7. Further references to the text will appear as UFE.

44 In his article on the 'Struggle against Legalization of Abortion in Latin America', Adolfo Castañeda refers to the battle against abortion as a spiritual battle. He cites Ephesians 10: 6.

45 http://www.elmundo.es/diario1998/09/23/sociedad/23N0055.html, consulted 15 December 1998.

46 Examples of such 'catechetical' books for the faithful often take a question and answer format. See, for example, Comisión de Estudios de S.O.S. Familia, *Aborto: 50 preguntas, 50 respuestas: en defensa de la vida inocente* (Madrid: TFP Covadonga, 1998); CEDV, *El aborto: 100 cuestiones y respuestas sobre la defensa de la vida humana y la actitud de los católicos.*

47 'We give birth, we decide' is a pro-abortion slogan dating from the early post-Franco pro-abortion campaigns. It is used here to link the 'masculine' women to the abortion campaign. Conversely, it also presents a negative image of abortionists by linking them with unnatural and masculinized modes of behaviour.

48 http://www.el-mundo.es/diario, 14 September 1998; 'Licencia más amplia para matar a los hijos', http:// www.conferenciaepiscopal.es/aborto.htm, consulted 130 September 1998.

49 See the chapter on Spanish feminism by Mercedes Carbayo-Abengózar in this volume.

50 For further information about the HOAC and its relationship with the state, see Georgina Blakely, p. 29.

51 María José Arana, *Rescatar lo femenino para re-animar la tierra*, http://www.fespinal.com/espinal/es78.htm, consulted 1 December 1999.

Bibliography

Alberdi, Inés, *La nueva familia española* (Madrid: Taurus, 1999).

Arana, María José, *Rescatar lo femenino para re-animar la tierra*, http://www. fespinal.com/espinal/es78.htm, consulted 1 December 1999.

Barreiro, Belén, 'Judicial Review and Political Empowerment: Abortion in Spain', in *Politics and Policy in Democratic Spain: No Longer Different*, ed. by Paul Heywood (London and Portland, Oregon: Frank Cass, 1999), pp. 147-62.

Blakeley, Georgina, 'The Holy Trinity in Spain: State, Civil Society and Political Parties', *International Journal of Iberian Studies*, 10:1 (1997), 15-32.

Blanco Corrujo, Olivia and Isabel Morant Deusa, *El largo camino hacia la igualdad: Feminismo en España 1975-1995* (Madrid: Ministerio de Asuntos Sociales/ Instituto de la Mujer, 1995).

Brassloff, Audrey, *Religion and Politics in Spain: The Spanish Church in Transition 1962-96* (Houndmill, Basingstoke: MacMillan, 1998).

Brooksbank Jones, Anny, *Women in Contemporary Spain* (Manchester: Manchester University Press, 1997).

Camps, Victoria, *El siglo de las mujeres*, Feminismos (Madrid: Cátedra, 1998).

Comisión de Estudios de S.O.S. Familia, *Aborto: 50 preguntas, 50 respuestas: en defensa de la vida inocente* (Madrid: TFP Covadonga, 1998).

Conde, Rosa and Teresa Carballal, 'La familia española: Continuidad y cambio', in *La mujer española: De la tradición a la modernidad (1960-1980)*, ed. by Concha Borreguero, Elena Catena, Consuelo de la Gándara and María Salas, Semilla y Surco, Serie Sociología (Madrid: Tecnos, 1985), pp. 95-107.

Conferencia Episcopal Española, *El aborto: 100 cuestiones y respuestas sobre la defensa de la vida humana* (Madrid: Palabra, 1991).

————, *Abortar con píldora también es un crimen: Declaración de la Conferencia Episcopal Española*, Documentos de las asambleas plenarias del Episcopado Español, 27 (Madrid: Edice, 1998).

del Campo, Salustiano, *Tendencias sociales en España (1960-1990)* (Madrid: Fundación BBV, 1994).

Echevarría, Borja, 'La "guerra" del aborto se traslada a las puertas del Congreso', http://el-mundo es/diario/1998/09/23/sociedad/23N0057.html, 23 September 1998.

————, 'Yanes contra la libertad de voto sobre el aborto', http://www.el-mundo.es/diario/09/15/sociedad/15N0055.html, 15 September 1998.

García de León, María Antonia, Marisa García de Cortázar and Félix Ortega (eds), *Sociología de la mujer española* (Madrid: Editorial Complutense, 1996).

Garrido González, Elisa (ed.), Pilar Folguera Crespo, Margarita Ortega López and Cristina Segura Graiño, *Historia de las mujeres en España* (Madrid: Síntesis, 1997).

Iríbar, Amaya, 'El colegio de médicos se desentiende de la clínica abortista intervenida en Albacete', http://www.elpais.es/p/d/19980315/sociedad/albacete.htm, 15 March 1998.

Instituto de la Mujer, *La mujer en cifras: Una década, 1982-1992* (Madrid: Instituto de la Mujer/Ministerio de Asuntos Sociales, 1994).

————, *Las mujeres en cifras: 1997* (Madrid: Instituto de la Mujer/Ministerio de Asuntos Sociales, 1997).

Larrea, Luís María, *Ser cristiano en la actual situación de crisis: Carta pastoral de los obispos de las diócesis de Bilbao, San Sebastián, Tudela y Vitoria*, Colección documentos y estudios, 79 (Madrid: PPC, 1982).

María Adelaida, *Mi madre quiso abortarme* (Madrid: Palabra, 1990).

Miranda, María Jesús, *Crónicas del desconcierto: Actitudes básicas y demandas políticas de las españolas*, Serie Estudios, 8 (Madrid: Ministerio de Cultura/Instituto de la Mujer, 1987).

Movimiento Familiar Cristiano, *Actitudes cristianas de la familia: Temario para grupos*, Colección pastoral, 55 (Santander: Sal Terrae, 1997).

Nash, Mary, *Rojas: Las mujeres republicanas en la Guerra Civil* (Madrid: Taurus, 1999).

Pérez, Julia, 'España queda sin niños y las parejas entran en crisis', *Cambio 16*, 14 December 1992, pp. 44-50.

————, 'La angustia del aborto: la decisión del Gobierno de legalizar implícitamente el aborto hasta los tres meses desata las críticas', *Cambio 16*, 21 September 1992, pp. 86-96.

Pontificio Consejo para la Familia, *Evoluciones demográficas: Dimensiones éticas y pastorales*, http://www.serviciato.com/doctrina//evoluciones_demograficas.htm, consulted 9 December 1999.

Pujol Algans, Carmen, *Código de la mujer* (Madrid: Ministerio de Asuntos Sociales/Instituto de la Mujer, 1992).

Roig, Mercedes, *La mujer en la historia a través de la prensa: Francia, Italia, España s.XVIII-XX* (Madrid: Ministerio de la Cultura, 1989).

Sánchez-Rivera Peiró, Juan M., 'Interrogantes interculturales sobre la mujer en el mundo de hoy' in *Mujer, trabajo y maternidad*, ed. by María José Carrasco, Ana García Mina, Jesús Labrador and Carlos Alemany Briz (Madrid: UPCO, 1995), pp. 1-12.

Telo, María, 'La evolución de los derechos de la mujer', in *La mujer española: De la tradición a la modernidad (1960-1980)*, ed. by Concha Borreguero, Elena Catena, Consuelo de la Gándara and María Salas, Semilla y Surco, Serie Sociología (Madrid: Tecnos, 1985), pp. 81-93.

Unión Familiar Cristiano, *El matrimonio y la familia: 100 cuestiones y respuestas sobre el concepto cristiano de familia y matrimonio*, second edition (Madrid: Edice, 1998).

5 'Still Working on it'
Recent Steps towards Employment Equality in France

Jean Burrell

In December 1998, the French Prime Minister, Lionel Jospin, whose Socialist Party had somewhat surprisingly won the 1997 general election given his previously modest, schoolmasterly image, invited the MP for the Pas-de-Calais, Catherine Génisson, to carry out a study and make recommendations on the unequal situation of working women *vis-à-vis* their male colleagues.[1] In his letter, he acknowledged that serious inequalities still existed 'at all stages of womens' working lives':
- Inequality in career choices
- Inequality in pay
- Inequality in rights to promotion and ongoing vocational training
- Inequality in unemployment and job security.

This situation pertains despite the legal equality of men and women enshrined in the preamble to the post-war Constitution of 1946 and despite the law introduced by the new Minister for Women's Rights, Yvette Roudy, in 1983, following the triumphant election in 1981 of the first Socialist President and Assembly for nearly half a century and, more pointedly, despite the obligation placed on member states of the European Community to transpose into national law Directives on equal treatment and equal pay issued by the Commission in the 1970s.

This chapter attempts first to account for the failure of the 1983 law to live up to its billing; then moves on to consider why, despite a raft of legislation, workplace equality continues to be a live issue for France, as for other supposedly sophisticated economies; it examines some wider social and educational factors that complicate the picture, drawing on fieldwork undertaken in the hospitality industry in France; and finally it assesses the prospects for progress in the first decade of the new century.

Employment Equality: Issues
It had appeared, as Génisson remarks in the introduction to her report, published in early September 1999, that the issue of employment equality had gone underground since the end of the 1980s. It had no doubt been assumed in official circles that the Roudy law had done its work. In any case, as the second Mitterrand presidency wound to a scandal-riven close and Governments of both Right and Left wrestled with the problems thrown up by the deep recession of the early 1990s, the Socialist Party seemed to have

moved on to other preoccupations, among them the more rarefied question of political rather than economic equality. This new battleground, and one which Jospin was quick to invest after June 1997, was parity, the attempt to ensure equal access of women and men to public office.[2] However, the 1983 law, in spite of its enabling intentions, was deeply flawed in both substance and implementation, as Génisson points out and as Yvette Roudy today recognizes: 'I was a bit naïve […] I thought financial incentives would be enough. I didn't realize how little this mattered to Government, Trade Unions and business leaders.'[3] Amy Mazur has traced the battle between Roudy and her colleagues in the cabinet or *Conseil des Ministres* that ended with a considerably watered down bill.[4] Nevertheless, certain of the law's provisions could have provided a framework for progress at workplace level, if the social partners had shown the will and effective enforcement structures (through the *Inspection du Travail*) had been in place.

As well as including clauses outlawing discrimination in all areas of employment (hiring and firing, training and promotion), as the Directive required, the Roudy law contained a distinguishing and innovative feature, compared with similar legislation in other European member states (a comparison is drawn with Italy, Spain and the UK.[5] This was an obligation laid on companies with over fifty employees to produce a detailed annual audit of the comparative situation of male and female workers, together with an analysis of measures taken in the previous year to promote workplace equality, that would be discussed in works councils and used to plan future measures. Government money was made available for companies to carry through approved 'equality plans' based on these discussions.

But Génisson notes that fewer than half the companies covered by the provision actually produce a report and fewer still make any constructive use of it. She suggests that the resulting absence of hard facts on the comparative situation of men and women at work may go some way towards explaining women employees' silence on the issue of unequal opportunities at work. Where the few 'equality plans' and the more numerous individualized training plans designed to prepare women to take on functions normally occupied by men and first introduced in 1987, *contrats pour la mixité des emplois* were implemented, it was usually in situations where employers urgently needed in any case to make changes to their workplace organization (e.g. introduction of new technology), as is noted in Jacqueline Laufer's 1992 report on the effect of the measures adopted during the preceding decade.

The question of women's employment has acquired increasing prominence over the last twenty years as their numerical presence (women form over 45% of the French labour force today against 35% in 1968, and this proportion is predicted to reach 48% by 2040), and more importantly their pattern of work over their life-span, have evolved.[6] The contrast with Spanish women's relationship with the labour market has been more directly and fully explored by Jean Burrell and Hilary Rollin.[7] But in summary the most notable development in France, almost unique in Europe, is the determination of French women to remain in the workforce through their children's early years and into middle age, so that their employment profiles have come to resemble men's. Marie-Thérèse Letablier noted that the percentage of women in the labour force in the 25-49 age-group had risen from 42% in 1962 to 76% in 1990 and that half of women aged 55 were still in the labour market (this was true for the whole 55-59 age-group by 1997).[8] In France, as in other European countries, women's employment has been rising while men's has been falling (between 1986 and 1996 the number of women in work rose by 850,000 as that of employed men fell by 92,000). A partial explanation for these developments may be found in a survey for the daily *Le Monde* in April 1999 which found that, at a time of radical change in the structures of both society and the economy, French women put financial independence above relationships and children in their list of priorities for their lives. And this includes making provision for their later years in order to avoid the dependence or impoverishment of previous generations of ageing women.

There are other less obvious reasons for the greater importance issues surrounding female employment have taken on. As is the case elsewhere, the mounting burden on the social security system of an ageing population, added to the massive withdrawal of the under-20s from the labour market because of extra years spent in education, must be counter-balanced by ensuring that the maximum proportion (including women) of the intermediate age-group is paying taxes and social contributions.[9] This means that women are offered various incentives (including an extensive network of childcare arrangements and allowances) to work rather than add to the welfare bill. In addition, it has been shown that those economies that most fully exploit their available resources of work and skills are the most likely to remain prosperous.

Yet in the 1990s and into the new millennium the same stubborn problems that have for decades faced French women, like their sisters elsewhere, and have been the subject of frequent analysis, still defy legislative remedies. First there is the persistent pay gap when compared with men (an average of 27%, rising to 30% at management level, that cannot be explained entirely by differences in seniority or sector).[10] Then women workers tend to be concentrated in relatively few branches of the economy; six sectors – teaching, health, social services, office work, retailing, and domestic service – employ 60% of women workers, while offering only 30% of the jobs present in the economy. They also progress more slowly (if at all) than their male colleagues who started at the same level, and often have more difficulty securing a post that matches their level of qualification. Furthermore, women are far less likely than men to be offered training. This can be explained partly by their massive presence in sectors that traditionally train relatively little (e.g. retailing) and in small businesses. But even in those sectors where men and women are more evenly represented and training is offered, they often lose out: a report published by the Department for Women's Rights and Vocational Training cited the example of the insurance sector where 53% of male employees had received training as against 39% of women.

Then women have borne the brunt of the drive for labour-market 'flexibility' and job creation. They occupy most of the rising number of part-time posts (over 3 million in 1997 as against under 700,000 occupied by men),[11] which until the mid 1980s were relatively rare in France, but have mushroomed since employers have been offered a reduction in social security contributions in return for creation of part-time posts.[12] They are slightly more likely than men to be on short-term contracts (CDD or *contrat à durée déterminée*). Furthermore, they account for 51% of job-seekers (affecting 13.5% of the female workforce, whereas this situation affects under 10% of economically active men). This last phenomenon, the high number of women registering as unemployed rather than simply withdrawing from the job market, demonstrates both their determination and their need to work; more and more women today find themselves heading a lone-parent family or living with an unemployed partner. In addition, part-time work, which is most often seen as women's choice, given their family responsibilities, may in reality be enforced and irregular; it is estimated that this is the case for well over a third of women working part-time.[13]

Finally, it is now explicitly recognized, since women have begun to play such a prominent role in the world of work, that there can be no division between that world and the wider society, and that behaviours and attitudes conditioned by the prevailing ideology have numerous consequences for the preparation for work and for its structure and organization. These attitudes are largely responsible for determining girls' educational choices and their roles in the family unit and the workplace. It is true that there is a generational effect that will take some time to work through. However, although young French women are achieving success at school in scientific and technical disciplines, they are still the overwhelming majority (82%) in arts streams preparing for the *baccalauréat,* and even those who opt for a science stream often do not follow through into tertiary-level science or technology courses.

As far as the issue of reconciling home and work responsibilities is concerned, there has been little movement either in the division of labour at home or in the organization of working time. The determination with which succeeding French Governments since the early 1980s have pursued a policy of worksharing (that is, an attempt to reduce unemployment by sharing out the work available among a larger number of people in the name of Republican 'solidarity', an insistent topos of French political rhetoric) has reached a climax in the Aubry laws (sponsored by Jacques Delors' daughter, Employment and Solidarity Minister, Martine Aubry). The aim of this legislation is to reduce the statutory working week from 39 hours, which has been the norm since 1981, to 35 hours by 2002. Employers, who are largely hostile because of the estimated increase in labour costs, are being offered subsidies as an incentive to comply speedily. This major force for change in French working life, which is looked upon with approval by the European Commission, could be seen as an opportunity to introduce a new flexibility into the work-home relationship and one for men and women to rethink their roles and responsibilities in the context of a society that has traditionally given high value to family activities and to shopping for and preparation of food.[14]

However, this seems initially not to have been the case. In her report, Génisson quotes a survey carried out by the left-leaning Trade Union Confederation CFDT (*Confédération Française Démocratique du Travail*) in late 1997 among 1600 employees in companies that had been operating the 35-hour week for more than six months. This survey showed that over half the men interviewed were spending their extra free time on leisure activities, whereas less than a third were devoting it to their families. On the other hand, nearly half the women surveyed were spending additional time with their families.

In addition, various provisions designed as 'family-friendly', and allowing either parent to take leave – unpaid in the case of the French version of the European

Directive on parental leave, paid in the case of the child-raising allowance *(Allocation Parentale d'Éducation* or APE) – to care for young children, have in the vast majority of cases been taken up by mothers rather than fathers.[15] When the APE was extended in 1994 to families with two children (it was previously restricted to three), at least one of whom was under the age of three, the activity rate of women in this situation is estimated to have fallen from 70% to 55%. This large-scale withdrawal from the labour market, which is thought to have affected around 250,000 women, is bound to have serious consequences in terms of their ability to return to work without suffering downgrading in level and salary.[16]

The unequal burden of family responsibilities also goes some way towards explaining women's less frequent involvement in Trade Union activity than men's, despite the efforts of the CFDT and more recently the Communist Confederation CGT *(Confédération Générale du Travail).* Both of these trade unions have suffered a drop in membership, never very large in France, accompanying the decline of heavy industry since the late 1970s. Deprived of the voices of women members at meetings and in negotiation, union branches have been slow to press on issues that might be seen as mostly benefiting women (such as application of the Roudy law or work organization).

Employment Issues in Practice

Many of the interlinked features of French women's employment outlined were identified in practice in the context of a small-scale study carried out in four European member states (France, Italy, Spain and the UK) over the period 1995-97. The purpose of the project was to examine how the European Directives relating to equal opportunities at work had been transposed into national law and then to investigate the implementation and impact of the resulting legislation within a sample industry. The industry selected was hospitality, in part because this is a sector in all four countries that employs large numbers of women and men (in France at the 1990 census the 'hotel and restaurant' category comprised about 700,000 workers, half of them men and half women, according to the INSEE) and in addition is an expanding and fast-changing one. A report produced by one of the French industry bodies (the *Fédération Nationale de l'Industrie Hôtelière*) in the mid 1990s showed that the level of qualification of women working in the sector was in general lower than that of men, but another source claimed that they formed an increasing proportion of students on post-18 professional courses and were starting to make their mark at management level.[17]

A postal questionnaire on composition of staff and on employment practices in relation to equal opportunities was sent to a total of 800 hotels, concentrating on one region of each country (Brittany in the case of France), chosen because of the presence of both an important city (Rennes for France) and a resort area (the south Brittany coast). France produced the highest response rate (29%) of the four countries studied.[18]

Analysis of the completed questionnaires showed that considerable functional segregation persisted, though varying in nature from country to country, apparently according to the status of the different functions. For example, it was in France that women were least well represented among kitchen staff (11% of kitchen posts), perhaps reflecting the strong male domination of the prestigious craft-based function of chef, whereas in Spain, where very often hotel personnel mirrors family structure and roles, 50% of kitchen staff were women. The dominance of men in restaurant waiting jobs, though to a lesser extent (at 62%), was also marked in France, where this function carries considerable prestige, compared with the UK and Spain (39% and 36%). On the other hand, women were in the overwhelming majority in reception in France and the UK, while men still just held on to the role in Spain. Needless to say, the one area where women occupied nearly all the positions in all four countries was housekeeping.

There was evidence for all countries except the UK of quite strong preferences for either women or men in certain functions (for example, 58% of the French employers expressed a preference for men in the kitchen and in general French employers also stressed appearance as an important recruitment criterion for receptionists). While not constituting direct proof of discriminatory practice, this does tend to suggest prejudice and stereotyping. Taken together with a reliance on personal recommendation and contacts when recruiting, which was less common among the UK respondents, such preferences seemed likely to lead to the perpetuation of functional segregation.

In the area of pay, the survey showed unsurprisingly that the more feminized the job, the lower the rate. It was interesting that in Italy and Spain, where reception staff were more likely to be men, there was a greater pay differential between them and waiting or room staff than in France, where receptionists tended to be female. This appears to confirm the suspicion that salaries are depressed for the functions that women normally carry out.

Even though childcare provision in France is good by comparison with the other three countries studied, the degree to which it failed women working in an industry where non-standard hours are the norm was revealed by the number of women who relied on family and friends (mentioned eighteen times, as compared with state childcare and school, mentioned twenty-two times each).[19]

The questionnaire was followed up by visits to the hotels that had indicated they would be willing to take part in in-depth interviews and also to allow a female member of staff to be interviewed. For France this fieldwork concerned twelve hotels; the clientele for those in Rennes (four hotels) was mostly business people passing through or people who worked in Rennes during the week but returned home, some distance from the city, at weekends, whereas the hotels on the coast attracted holidaymakers in the main, plus local people to the restaurant where there was one (especially for weddings and other group occasions). This pattern of custom indicated a situation where atypical work was likely to be the norm: seasonal short-term contracts, part-time hours and split shifts.

Although the sample was small, nevertheless some constant themes ran through the structured interviews, linking with the general points made above about women's employment. Among employers there was some ambivalence as to whether they preferred men on reception (for security reasons and because they were calmer) or women (because they were welcoming and were preferred by male clients). However they were clear about preferring women as housekeepers (because they were 'thorough' (*rigoureuses*) and even 'obsessive' (*maniaques*), and because of the 'intimate' nature of room work) and on the whole about men in the kitchen (though two had no preference). Reasons given for this latter preference were the heat and heavy physical work, the jealousies and resentment that could arise if women encroached on a 'macho environment'. It was interesting that in the three hotels where the general manager was a woman (in one case jointly with her husband), she expressed similar preferences and views to the male interviewees.

The interviews with employees were also revealing; about half of them were student trainees on work placement and they confirmed that relatively few young women followed the 'cuisine' stream of the course when it split into options after the common first year. This confirms Rutter and Teare's assessment of the situation of women students in their survey of education and training for hospitality.[20] The trainees interviewed gave similar reasons as their employers, adding one negative one (swearing and rude behaviour) but also stressing a positive motive for their choice of, for example, restaurant or reception work; they greatly enjoyed the contact with clients that these functions offered.

These interviews confirmed that the hospitality industry is one where stereotypes are changing only slowly, and where it is hard for women to get permanent full-time work (although part-time work may suit some well enough). When they do, they will probably have to accept long hours and split shifts, which are difficult to reconcile with family life. In addition the industry is not widely unionized and pay is in general low, particularly for those functions seen as 'women's jobs'. The first industry-wide negotiated agreement on pay and conditions (*convention collective*) was signed in 1997, a sign that some regulation is being introduced into a sector unused to negotiation.[21]

On the other hand most of the employees interviewed had made or intended to make a career in hospitality, claiming that the work was less demanding than it used to be (in the kitchen and in housekeeping notably) because of technological advances, and that the customer service aspect and the opportunities for travel were attractive.

At first sight, then, the 1990s appears in France to have been a decade of stagnation and apathy in the area of equal opportunities in the workplace since the heady days of the 1970s women's movement, the European Directives and then the triumphant accession of the Socialist Party to power in the 1980s, voted in, it should be said, largely by women and younger people on the strength of social and economic policies attractive to these groups. However, Jospin's Government shows signs of reviving these concerns and of demonstrating a firmer political will to make concrete progress, always recognizing that the easy bit (legislation) has been done and the hard part (changing hearts and minds) remains to be tackled and will only show its effects in the medium to long term.

In June 1999, Nicole Péry, appointed six months earlier to the post of Secretary of State for Women's Rights and Training, announced a comprehensive programme of work designed to improve women's access to the world of work as well as to influential positions and promised to carry out an initial evaluation of its progress in March 2000.[22] She recognized the complex nature of women's unequal position, which she called 'an issue that affects all areas of society and requires an overarching policy', reflecting the turn to 'mainstreaming' (the inclusion of reflection on the differential gender effects of all policies) that has now become the emphasis of European equal opportunity initiatives. Among other measures, Péry's programme includes increasing gender disaggregation in official statistics, so that the realities of women's situation can no longer be ignored, targets for proportions of women undergoing training by the end of 2000, and planning and monitoring an increase in the numbers of women in the upper ranks of the Civil Service.

Then Catherine Génisson's report, which draws on evidence from Trade Unions and employer bodies, companies, groups representing women's concerns, civil servants, MPs, researchers and regional officials, makes a series of detailed recommendations. She sees the overall aim as, first, helping women to reconcile work and home life (as opposed to requiring them to make a choice, which she claims is the position of German women) and secondly working towards genuine equality of employment throughout the economy (rather than creating special conditions favourable to women in the public sector, as is the case in Scandinavian countries). She judges that a fresh approach, and not a legislative one, is required to the interlinked complex of issues facing working women.

Of course this revival of interest on the part of the French Government is partly a result of the renewed emphasis in the Amsterdam Treaty, signed in October 1997, on equality between men and women. According to a European Parliament publication, it now has 'the status of a fundamental right' by virtue of new articles that extend and make more explicit member states' commitment to, for example, equal pay for equal work (adding 'or work of equal value' – Article 141).[23] In November of the same year, at the Luxembourg European Council on Employment, member states reached agreement on guidelines to underpin national employment policies, and notably the inclusion of equal opportunities among the four pillars of such policies (with employability, adaptability and entrepreneurship). And more recently at the Paris Conference held in May 1999, the third European Conference on Women in Power in the Union, Lionel Jospin announced for the year 2000 a national action plan on equal opportunities in all fields, political, economic, professional and social.

Jill Rubery and her co-authors have argued, in response to those who ask why it is still necessary to attend to patterns of women's employment separate from men's (given this is no longer a minority phenomenon), that large differences persist both between women's situation in the various member states and, as we have discovered, between the employment experiences of men and women.[24] They note that the rapid development of women's labour market participation has taken place against a background of change in education and family patterns and economic restructuring that is likely to continue well into the next decade, and express the view in their conclusion that progress on the equality front will involve negotiation between men and women on the whole range of shared issues and priorities (work, family and home, leisure, personal development).

Whatever the outcome over the next few years of that negotiation and of the flurry of Government initiatives recently announced or embarked on, one thing is certain: having demonstrated their determination to retain and extend their foothold in the labour market, French women will not be easily deterred.

References

1   Catherine Génisson, *Femmes-Hommes: Quelle égalité professionnnelle?* (Paris: Documentation Française, 1999), p. 3.

2   As addressed by Sheila Perry and Sue Hart in this book.

3   Pascale Kremer, 'Les inegalités hommes-femmes persistent dans le monde du travail', *Le Monde*, 3 September 1999, p. 10.

4   See Amy Mazur, 'Symbolic Reform in France: *Egalité professionnelle* in the Mitterrand Years', *West European Politics*, 15: 4 (1992), 39-56, and *Gender Bias and the State: Symbolic Reform at Work in the Fifth Republic of France* (Pittsburgh; London: University of Pittsburgh Press: 1995), pp. 206-28.

5   Jean Burrell, Simonetta Manfredi, Liz Price, Hilary Rollin and Lindsay Stead, 'Equal Opportunities for Women Employees in the Hospitality Industry: A Comparison between France, Italy, Spain and the UK', *Conference Proceedings of the Sixth Annual Conference of the Council for Hospitality Management Education* (1998).

6   Daniel Brondel, Danièle Guillemot and Pierre Marioni, 'Population active: Facteurs d'évolution et perspectives', *Données sociales 1996* (Paris: INSEE, 1996).

7   Jean Burrell and Hilary Rollin, 'Equal opportunities at Work in France and Spain: Theory and Reality', in *Women and Work: The Age of Post-feminism?*, ed. by Liz Sperling (Aldershot; Brookfield, Vermont: Ashgate, 2000).

8   Marie-Thérèse Letablier, 'Women's Labour Force Participation in France: The Paradox of the 1990s', *Journal of Area Studies*, 6 (1995), 108-16.

9   Gino Raymond (ed.), *France during the Socialist Years* (Aldershot: Dartmouth, 1994), pp. 184-86.

10 Rachel Silvera, 'Les salaires: toutes choses étant égales par ailleurs', in *Les nouvelles frontières de l'inégalité* ed. by Margaret Maruani (Paris: La Découverte, 1998).

11 INSEE (Institut National de Statistique et d'Etudes Economiques), *Annuaire statistique de la France* (Paris: INSEE, 1998), p. 135.

12 'Worksharing in Europe', *European Industrial Relations Review*, 300 (1999), 14-16; *European Industrial Relations Review*, 301 (1999), 14-15.

13 Margaret Maruani (ed.), *Les nouvelles frontières de l'inégalité: Hommes et femmes sur le mer* (Paris: La Découverte, 1998).

14 'Working Time Continues to Dominate Social Policy', *European Industrial Relations Review,* 306 (July 1999), p. 1.

15 'Parental and Family Leave in Europe', *Equal Opportunities Review*, 6 (1996), pp. 22-29.

16 Michèle Aulagnon, 'L'allocation parentale a incité plus de 200.000 femmes à quitter leur emploi', *Le Monde*, 8 June 1998, p. 9.

17 Evelyne Jauffret, 'Au bonheur des dames', *L'Industrie Hôtelière*, July/August 1994.

18 For further details see Jean Burrell, Simonetta Manfredi, Liz Price and Hilary Rollin, 'Women's Employment in Hotels in France, Italy, Spain and the UK', *Conference Proceedings of the Sixth Annual Research Conference of the Council for Hospitality Management Education* (1998).

19 For further details see Shirley Dex, Patricia Walters and David M. Alden, *French and British Mothers at Work* (Basingstoke: Macmillan, 1993).

20 Duncan Rutter and Melvyn Teare, *Catering Education and Training in France*, occasional paper no. 8, Institute of Education (University of London, 1992), pp. 41-42.

21 'Hôtellerie: 43 heures, c'est pas du luxe', *Libération*, 29 July 1997, p. 16.

22 Pascale Kremer, 'Le gouvernement s'engage à réduire les inégalités entre femmes et hommes', *Le Monde*, 24 June 1999, p. 12.

23 European Parliament, *Women's Rights and the Treaty of Amsterdam* (1998), pp. 36-41.

24 Jill Rubery, Mark Smith and Colette Fagan, *Women's Employment in Europe: Trends and Prospects* (London: Routledge: 1999), pp. 3-4 and 313-15.

Bibliography

Aulagnon, Michèle, 'L'allocation parentale a incité plus de 200.000 femmes à quitter leur emploi', *Le Monde*, 8 June 1998, p. 12.

Brondel, Daniel, Danièle Guillemot and Piere Marioni, 'Population active: Facteurs d'évolution et perspectives', *Données sociales 1996* (Paris: INSEE, 1996).

Burrell Jean, Simonetta Manfredi, Liz Price, Hilary Rollin and Lindsay Stead, 'Equal Opportunities for Women Employees in the Hospitality Industry: A Comparison between France, Italy, Spain and the UK', *International Journal of Hospitality Management*, 16: 2 (1997), 161-79.

——————, Simonetta Manfredi, Liz Price and Hilary Rollin, 'Women's Employment in Hotels in France, Italy, Spain and the UK', *Conference Proceedings of the Sixth Annual Research Conference of the Council for Hospitality Management Education* (1998).

——————, and Hilary Rollin, 'Equal Opportunities at Work in France and Spain: Theory and Reality', in *Women and Work: The Age of Post-feminism?*, ed. by Liz Sperling (Aldershot; Brookfield, Vermont: Ashgate, 2000).

Dex, Shirley, Patricia Walters and David M. Alden, *French and British Mothers at Work* (Basingstoke: Macmillan, 1993).

Equal Opportunities Review, 'Parental and Family Leave in Europe', *EOR*, 6 (1996), 22-29.

European Industrial Relations Review, 'Worksharing in Europe', *EIRR*, 300 (1999), 14-16; 301 (1999), 14-15.

European Parliament, *Women's Rights and the Treaty of Amsterdam* (Strasbourg: EP, 1998).

Génisson, Catherine, *Femmes-Hommes: Quelle égalité professionnnelle?* (Paris: Documentation Française, 1999)

INSEE (Institut National de Statistique et d'Etudes Economiques), *Annuaire statistique de la France* (Paris: INSEE, 1998).

Jauffret, Evelyne, 'Au bonheur des dames', *L'Industrie Hôtelière* (July / August 1994).

Kremer, Pascale, 'Le gouvernement s'engage à réduire les inégalités entre femmes et hommes', *Le Monde*, 24 June 1999, p. 12.

——————, 'Les inégalités hommes-femmes persistent dans le monde du travail', *Le Monde*, 3 September 1999, p. 10.

Laufer, Jacqueline, *L'Entreprise et l'égalité des chances* (Paris: Documentation Française, 1992).

Letablier, Marie-Thérèse, 'Women's Labour Force Participation in France: the Paradox of the 1990s', *Journal of Area Studies*, 6 (1995), 108-16.

Libération, 'Hôtellerie: 43 heures, c'est pas du luxe', 29 July 1997, p. 16.

Maruani, Margaret (ed.), *Les Nouvelles Frontières de l'inégalité: Hommes et femmes sur le mer* (Paris: La Découverte, 1998).

Mazur, Amy, 'Symbolic Reform in France: Égalité professionnelle in the Mitterrand years', *West European Politics*, 15: 4 (1992), 39-56.

——————, *Gender Bias and the State: Symbolic Reform at Work in the Fifth Republic of France*, (Pittsburgh; London: University of Pittsburgh Press, 1995).

Raymond, Gino (ed.), *France during the Socialist Years* (Aldershot: Dartmouth, 1994).

Rubery, Jill, Mark Smith and Colette Fagan, *Women's Employment in Europe: Trends and Prospects* (London: Routledge, 1999).

Rutter, Duncan and Melvyn Teare, *Catering Education and Training in France*, occasional paper no. 8, Institute of Education (London: University of London, 1992).

Secrétariat d'Etat aux droits des femmes et à la formation professionnelle, *La Formation professionnelle* (Paris: Secrétariat d'Etat aux droits des femmes et à la formation professionnelle, 1999).

6   Gendered Structures in the City

Management in Spain and Professional Identity in Etxebarría's *Amor, curiosidad, prozac y dudas*

Lesley K. Twomey

This chapter sets out to examine gendered structures in two contexts: management in Spain and the construction of professional identity in Lucía Etxebarría's *Amor, curiosidad, prozac y dudas* (*Love, Curiosity, Prozac and Doubts*), published in the late 1990s.[1] Before moving to either of these contexts, I propose to briefly assess the importance of work in the late twentieth century. According to the Spanish Constitution, one of the characteristics of the citizens of Spain, both male and female, is their right to work. The principle of the right of all citizens to work in equal conditions and for equal pay is, therefore, enshrined in the Constitution:

> All Spaniards have the obligation to work and the right to work, to choose their profession or job freely, to obtain promotion at work and to be paid a sufficient salary to satisfy their needs and the needs of their family, without there being any discrimination at all on the grounds of sex.
>
> (Spanish Constitution, Article 35, para. 1)

The value of work to the individual is bound up in the fact that the right to work, and to the subsidiary rights allied to it, has a close correlation to the concept of citizenship. Because modern societies have moved away from a situation of full employment, work has become a desirable attribute and has been converted into one of the main ways in which identity is constructed for both men and women.[2] This concept is taken up by Victoria Camps in the chapter in her book dedicated to 'Women's work', where she contends that full citizenship implies possession of an income.[3] According to Camps, work, together with its resultant income and status, affords full autonomy as a person since independence as a person is based on purchasing power. For this reason, a distinction must be made between work within the domestic sphere, unremitting and unpaid, and work in the public sphere, valued by society, limited to a finite number of hours and normally remunerated. The nature of remunerated work can be further subdivided into jobs, with their connotations of mundane necessity and professions, the domain of the elite of the labour market.

Professional Women in Spain: The Current Situation

Female professionals in Spain must be contextualized within the workforce as a whole.

However, it must be kept in mind that factors pertaining to female workers as a whole will, to an extent, have an impact on professional women.[4] Some of these factors are positive whilst others can be viewed as negative. The first positive feature to be noted in relation to the workforce is an increasing female presence. From representing a mere 29% of the available workforce in 1976, the number of women working or actively seeking employment has continued to grow, so that, by 1996, twenty years later, they represented over 37% of the working population. The figure has continued its slow upward trend with 37.8% of women available for work by 1998; however, the number of women actually employed by 1999 was only 29.6%.[5] Women's success in becoming employed seems likely to increase opportunities for progress of women in management, even though the advances still leave Spain lagging behind. Spanish women have 'erupted into the workplace', with all the social changes and need for change in attitudes that this has meant,[6] but, nevertheless, Spain's female workforce '[remains] one of the lowest in Europe'.[7] Women in other EU countries fare considerably better in the workforce with an average of 42% of women in employment (on average 15% more than in Spain).[8]

Inherent within this undoubted progress in female employment are a number of aspects which fail to square with what has been achieved. The first of these is a parallel increase in the numbers of women out of work. Spain's rate of female unemployment in 1995 was more than double that of other EU countries (García Sanz, p. 31). The figures for women actually in employment is currently lower by more than ten percentage points than those available for work, reflecting the continuing over-representation of women among the ranks of the unemployed as well as among those on temporary contracts. By 1998, the number of women actually employed had reached 27.7% as opposed to 54.5% of men yet the rate of unemployment for women was 26.6% in 1998, approximately double the rate for male unemployment (13.3%) (*Employment Survey [EPA]* 43). Statistics show that in 1998, 1,696,000 women were unemployed in total, whereas only 1,364,300 men were (*EPA* 33).

A second important feature of the labour market which will have detrimental effects on availability for promotion is the feminization of casualized, part-time working. In 1996 women were in the majority amongst workers with a part-time, temporary contract (73.64%) and they also were over 85% of those contracted to permanent posts on a part-time basis (*Las mujeres en cifras 1997*, p. 71). With high levels of female unemployment and with more of those who do work on temporary contracts, it means that fewer women will be in a position to take up professional advancement.

Furthermore, the most recent set of figures available, showing employment per sector of activity, continues to point to clear horizontal segregation of the labour market (*EPA* 04), another limiting factor on promotion opportunities. For example, the total number of employees in the construction sector in 1996 stood at 1,123,700 men in employment and only 51,700 women, with women representing a mere 4.39% of all construction employees. By 1998, the number of employees had risen in the construction sector to 1,481,000 for male employees and 64,900 for female employees. However, in overall terms, this represented a lower percentage of female employees (3.99%, own calculations based on *EPA* 04). In the service sector, in 1996, 44.9% of the total workforce was female (*Las mujeres en cifras 1997*, p.72) and this had risen to 48.1% by 1998 (own calculations based on *EPA* 04). However, by 1998 this rise meant that over 68% of the female workforce was concentrated in the service sector. This horizontal segmentation of the workforce, which can be reinforced by examination of other sectors of employment, will have consequences for management opportunities in that it will mean that women are all competing for promotion within a few sectors of the labour market, and reducing their ability to apply for and succeed in obtaining a wider range of promoted posts.

If the numbers of women in employment are generally low, and if women are employed in certain limited sectors of the labour market, what is the situation with regard to their entry into managerial levels? The figures published in *EPA* 11 give some indication as to how many of the women in employment in Spain are in posts of responsibility, although from the figures it is not easy to distinguish layers of management, since public sector and other managerial positions are incorporated into the same category. The number of women at managerial level in the Civil Service or companies with ten or more employees stood at 31,000 in 1996, an increase of almost 2,000 on the previous year. By 1997 it had risen to 35,900 and by the following year to 38,600. The number of women managers in the public sector and in large companies represents 14.2% of the total number of managers (own calculation based on *EPA* 11).

It is, however, significant that the number of women managing companies with less than ten employees is more than double the number managing over ten employees or at managerial level in Public Administration (87,800), whilst the number of male managers with less than ten employees (272,800) is only slightly above the number of men working at top level in the Civil Service or working as managers in companies with more than ten employees (233,000). Women make up 24.3% of the total number of managers in this category (own calculation based on *EPA* 11).

Finally, in the category of persons managing companies with no employees, the percentage of women 'self-employed' is very close to that of men. Whilst 256,000 men manage this type of company, 239,200 women also do so. The percentage of women managers in this category is a healthy 48.8%. The numbers look good, almost half the total are women. However, from this data we see that the larger the company or number of people to be managed, the smaller is the percentage of women managing them. Whilst, conversely, the fewer the number of employees and the smaller the company, the higher the number of female managers.

From the data available we can deduce that women managers are still a small minority in Spain and their largest numbers tend to be concentrated within the ranks of the self-employed as the last figures cited indicate. For this reason, we can continue to agree with Francisco Alvira Martín's assessment of the situation for women managers. He commented in 1994, 'Women managers are ... "a rare breed". The higher up the ranks you go, the rarer they become'.[9] Alvira Martín's words can still be applied to the management situation at the end of the 1990s.

Despite the declaration of equality for all citizens in 1978, and despite the passing of a number of laws such as the Worker's Statute and the Basic Employment Law to ensure equality in law, it can be argued that legal recognition of equality in terms of work remains a formality since, in practice, womens' pay, working conditions and basic job opportunities have never been on an equal footing with mens'.[10] Studies of women professionals regularly site disadvantage for women in certain factors: double shift (*doble jornada*), lack of opportunities both at the level of initial contract and in terms of promotion, the division of the labour market into sectors of majority female employment and sectors of majority male employment, and negative attitudes to female employment, including perception of women's level of commitment to the job.

Management studies also explored whether women did not come forward for promotion because of perceived commitments they were not prepared to make. According to Manuel Elías Olarte's study, one of the key factors dissuading women executives from seeking promotion in Spain in the late 1980s was the number of hours required in the office. Judy Wajcman, in her study of male and female managers in the UK, cites research which shows that the number of hours worked is on the increase for managers.[11] Research has shown that the scenario is no different in Spain. Elías Olarte, for example, cites a number of female managers who comment negatively on the number of hours they are required to work: 'I think that nobody should work fifteen hours: neither man nor woman, and that's because of their quality of life.'[12] Paola Vinay concludes, in a study with close parallels to the Spanish case, that 'it is possible to reach the higher functional levels only if one is ready to be available full-time for work'.[13] Both the words 'available' and 'full-time' have the connotation of complete sacrifice of self to the work machine. 'The length of the working day and availability for work' form an important section in a study, commissioned by the Institute for Women, in the late 1980s, which incorporates quotations from various managers in the Civil Service denouncing the length of the working day: 'The working day is so long drawn out in this country that it's out of all proportion.' 'It's a working day which is out of hand.'[14] Full-time availability for work has, as a subset, the concept of self-sacrifice. According to Wajcman, 'the idea is that being a manager requires total commitment and sacrifice to the organization and that the job comes first' (p. 266). High and increasing number of hours spent at work continues to be a fact of life for executives, both male and female and may be a factor dissuading women from seeking promotion.

Hours worked in the management sector continue to be high, as figures from 1998 show. The *Employment Survey* distinguishes between the number of hours worked in a given week and the number of hours per week normally worked. Male company directors indicated that they had worked 46.3 hours in the survey week (a slight rise on figures for 1997). However, they indicated that they normally worked 48.1 hours per week (an increase of 0.3 hours on the previous year). Women worked fewer hours weekly, on average five hours less than men, although their hourage shows a percentage point rise of 0.9 hours.

Self-sacrifice is expressed also in the need to limit choices in personal life. The need to choose between family commitments and work is explored in various management studies, such as that of Alvira Martín, which identifies a high correlation between childlessness and professional success, although only in the case of female executives. For example, according to the survey, women at management level were less likely than their male counterparts to have children. Carmen Martínez Ten's research found that often American professional women had taken a conscious decision not to have children.[15]

Other limiting factors on women's advancement within management have traditionally lain within the working environment itself. Management studies carried out in the late 1980s identified business culture as a limiting factor on women's advancement: 'The main obstacle to women being promoted is in the nature of the present business environment not women's qualifications nor their readiness to take on the job' (*Informe*, p. 11).[16] Professional image is another. The way successful businesswomen present themselves has been identified by various studies of Spanish businesswomen as crucial to promotion.[17] Women managers themselves identify the need to present a particular image of self to a male hierarchy as being necessary to success. External gaze focused on women because they are different continues even once promotion has been secured. One businesswoman commented: 'It is just like being on constant view in a shop window' (*Resultados*, p. 37).

In studies into women and management, new technology was specifically mentioned as a possible equalizing or liberating factor, in that it would allow managers to be connected from home and would facilitate a reduction in the number of hours spent in the office to the benefit of female managers. Research collaborators felt, somewhat paternalistically, that the technological revolution might bring a breakthrough in the lives of professional women, facilitating their entry into the workforce in greater numbers (*Informe*, p. 128). They were convinced that women would benefit from a new flexible style of working, which would in turn allow them new opportunities for advancement in the workplace.

Concentration of women in certain sectors of the labour market, high female unemployment, the double shift at home and in the office, the length of the working day together with the concept of sacrifice of personal life, the nature of business culture and the requirement to project a particular image of self have been and continue to be features of working life for women in Spain. It is against this awareness of reality for the reader that the novel constructs a professional identity for the 1990s. In the second part of the chapter, I intend to examine aspects of that identity and the techniques used in its structuring.

Construction of Identity

To construct the feminine within the novel, *Love, Curiosity, Prozac and Doubts*, Etxebarría draws on what Camps has identified as the difficult balance between the various roles women must adopt both at home and at work: 'Women are victims of a type of schizophrenia' (p. 106). Camps envisages schizophrenia as being the result of the need for women to live in different spheres and of the necessity to construct different identities to suit the domains within which they move. In the novel, Etxebarría chooses to fragment the female 'I', dividing it into a tripartite self and this fragmentation of the narrative voice into multiple identities symbolizes women's fragmented life experiences. The first female 'I' is centred on professional life (Rosa), the second on home life (Ana) and the third on alternative ways of being, on challenge to the accepted norms of behaviour for women (Cristina). The three narrative voices represent three identities in process, since the novel charts discovery of self as well as discovery of the links which bind each to the other. If David Carroll's words, relating to his discussion of *The Grass,* are appropriated, then they provide an indication of the way in which fragmentation of self is envisaged in the novel: The 'voices (the irreducible multiplicity within each voice) of the novel […] do seem to converge and culminate at one "moment" near the end of the novel'.[18] His commentary seems to point to the way in which the multiple perspectives offered by the tripartite narrative voice in *Love, Curiosity, Prozac and Doubts* ultimately converge close to the end of the novel. The three main narrative voices, the three Gaena sisters, each narrate their perception of current events intercalating their individual version of childhood events to weave 'her-stories' which the reader must take part in reconstructing.[19] This story turns out to be so interwoven that it is all but one and the same: 'and if the blood of the same father and the same mother runs through our veins, who says we are so different? Who is telling us that at bottom we are not the same person' (p. 267).

It is my intention in this chapter to focus particularly on aspects of one of the narrative voices, on Rosa, the narrator whose domain is the professional sphere. The novel's presentation of the professional 'I' in chapter P: *Poder (Power)* is, at first sight, powerful and positive: 'My career path was meteoric. I finished university with excellent grades and began working at twenty-two. At twenty-eight, I was appointed Director of Finance […]' (p. 163). However, in chapter E: *Enclaustrada, enamorada, empleada, y encadenada (Cloistered, in Love, Employed and in Chains),* the first encounter between two of the sisters takes place. Exchange of opinions about work issues is the vehicle for exploration of inherent discrimination in the workplace. In this conversation, the limiting factors placed on women's professional lives spill out against the background of Cristina at work in the bar (pp. 46-48). Initially, the readers' attention centres on a general resumé of women's difficulty in making sense of responsibilities at home and at work. The double shift because of husbands who do not share the burden of housework is highlighted: 'He [the husband] doesn't help them [the women at work] in the home, he doesn't get up if the child cries, he doesn't bother going to parents' evenings.' As we have seen in the first part of this chapter, the 'double shift' is an aspect of working life with which women workers, Etxebarría's female readers, are likely to identify.

Next, women's concentration in feminized sectors of the labour market is highlighted in a throw-away remark which allows the author to jolt the reader into realization that success is not all it seems. The readers' expectations that the women being discussed are work colleagues on the same level as Rosa are defrauded when these women are labelled 'secretaries' in Cristina's reply. The surprise effect of this differentiation of the majority of women workers from the lone professional allows Etxebarría to focus attention on the uniqueness of the female executive. At this point, attention shifts to concerns important to the executive. The focus of the conversation turns to the blocking of promotion opportunities for the lone professional: 'I am a woman so they won't promote me' (p. 46) and to complaints about the mediocre ability of those (male) colleagues occupying promoted posts: 'I should be Deputy Managing

Director. I am the best qualified by far, more so than the duffer who is in the post' (p. 46). As attention moves from issues affecting women in general to the way in which alleged discrimination affects the professional individual, there is a repetition of the 'I' pronoun, underlining personal involvement: 'I should', 'I am'. The contrast is marked between the solidarity of the previous group 'they', who face problems with an individual 'he', and the case of the lone professional for whom 'I' stands alone against a faceless 'they'.

Passivity and lack of control over her destiny, with regard to what goes on in the office and in the boardroom, make up another aspect of the work identity created for Rosa. However, such negative aspects of life a the top contrast starkly with descriptions of her arrival and departure from the bar. In external appearance, Rosa is observed through the eyes of the main narrator and described, on entry, as possessing 'an air of authority' (p. 42) and, on departure, as 'an Amazon' (p. 51), both indicating strength of character. These two descriptions provide a framework to the personal revelations about frustrated ambitions exchanged in the bar. The framework and the revelations form, at the same time, the two sides of Rosa's character, the outward, decisive, hard-nosed executive and the inner doubts of the soft core.

David Carroll refers to an 'irreducible multiplicity' within each narrative voice and this multilayered 'I' is best exemplified in *Love, Curiosity, Prozac and Doubts* by the clothing Rosa possesses. Her wardrobe is used to typify two faces of identity, allowing present professional identity to be contrasted with former self. The constructed self is exemplified in the novel by adoption of a particular dress code. The accepted norms of executive dress, according to the novel, includes dark suits: 'grey, navy blue and black'; designer labels, 'Loewe, Armani and Angel Schelesser'; demure blouses: 'silk blouses buttoned up to the neck' and matching accessories: 'three pairs of matching shoes [...] all exactly the same style by Robert Clergerie: court shoes with low one-and-a-half inch heels' (p. 55). The description of the work outfits, three tailored suits with matching accessories, is contrasted with the tumbled heap of clothing which represents another self from the past: 'Hats, raincoats, [...] hippie shirts and psychedelic T-shirts' (p. 56). The constructed self, defined by work, can be seen as submerging the past self, depicted in terms of the outdated hippie clothing, in order to mould her self to society's norms. Additionally, the differentiated piles of clothing point to the fact that Extebarría conceives of Rosa's professional life as well ordered, but her private life as jumbled. Moreover, the swing between power and inner core or between professional success and limitation on success, which have already been discerned as part of professional identity, are revisited through observation of the pile of clothing. The possession of the trappings of professional identity as well as the outward indicators of a more anarchic, youthful being are a sign of the fact that the present constructed self has not eradicated the former self: the jumbled clothes have not been disposed of.

Professional identity in *Amor, curiosidad, prozac y dudas* is constructed by Etxebarría around recognizable norms of working life for women in Spain in the 1990s in terms of the problems with double shift, limited access to promotion opportunities and professional image. I will now examine the strategies used in the novel to construct a professional identity for women.

Textual Strategies

We have already seen how professional identity is characterized by struggle between professional self and former self. One of the key ways in which this is achieved is through presenting the different options available to women as mutually exclusive 'life choices'. To do this, Etxebarría constantly counterpoints the experiences of the three sisters. Polarization of female experience is exemplified through the very different aspects of women's lives: between maternal/non-maternal; professional/non-professional. Ana with her child and home, centred in the private sphere provides the opposite pole of female experience to Rosa, the workaholic, epitome *par excellence* of the public sphere. Etxebarría's counterpointing of identities has a dual purpose: at one and the same time, it differentiates and unites female experiences. It differentiates because the two selves are clearly set in separate spheres: one in the private and one in the public. Yet, at the same time, the counterpointing technique has the effect of unifying the two identities. There are several strategies used to unite the two women, Ana and Rosa, whose experiences are set in very different arenas. The first is the fact, in the novel, women's existence, whether in the public or private sphere, is reduced to mechanistic compliance. For example, Rosa is metaphorically converted into a worker ant because of the excessive length of her working day: 'There's only my sister, the worker ant, who is capable of leaving work at 10 o'clock at night' (p. 43). The metaphor serves to dehumanize both Rosa and the world of work in commentary by the first narrative voice, Cristina, on the executive role carried out by her sister in the multinational company. By being equated to a worker ant, executive identity takes on connotations of mindless activity and minuscule importance in the vast scale of the universe, thus defrauding the readers' expectations about work at executive level. However, in the next chapter, another image of the nature of work is offered, this time through the medium of the professional 'I' reflecting on the sacrifices required by professional life. Now the length of time to be spent at work shifts to equivalence to the number of hours worked by the drones of the Industrial Revolution: 'In spite of advances in society and important changes, I am having to work twelve to fourteen hours a day, just like the worst exploited of the workers in the nineteenth century' (p. 54).

Both Ana and Rosa are depicted as carrying out tasks 'in a mechanical way' (p. 172), highlighting the fact that in the novelistic world created by Etxebarría, dehumanization operates within the private sphere as well as within the public. The way in which drugs are shown bolstering existence and providing coping strategies in a dehumanized world is another means of linking public and private spheres. Tranquillizers serve as a symbol of the unifying force binding the selves together: The mother figure, Ana, is shown resorting to tranquillizers to manage her depression as her life falls apart; the professional figure, Rosa, is shown turning to tranquillizers to manage the disparity between outward success and inner turmoil. Drugs are not, however, the only elements which unify the sisters, other unifiers include the state of their mental health as well as their suicidal tendencies. There is another factor unifying the three narrators. Commenting on both *El cuarto de atrás* (*The Back Room*) and *El mismo mar de todos los veranos* (*The Same Sea As Every Summer*), Catherine Davies points to recovery of memories, as a recurrent feature of Spanish women's writing, and, in fact, in *Amor, curiosidad, prozac y dudas*, the three narrators are also united in a more positive vein by their collective memories.[20] The memories of each narrator are partial: sharing such partial understanding has the function of enabling the reader to reconstruct past events and influences on the three sisters but it also points to the way in which constructing identity is a collective not an individual task.

Counterpointing of Cristina and Rosa also allows deeper insight into the work environment. Through this technique, Etxebarría exploits the theme of working with technology, both at non-executive and executive level. The first aspect of this theme occurs in chapter C: *Curro* (*Grind*) where Cristina's work experience in a multinational company is described. Etxebarría's treatment of the work theme has many features in common with the way in which she presents Rosa's working life: the computer, the long hours in front of a screen and the need for escape into personal life. The reader has been given Cristina's memories against which to set the experiences of Rosa. We already know how working with technology was resolved in the case of Cristina, since the novel's timeline begins after the period of working in the multinational has been brought to a close: 'I suddenly realized that my youth was passing me by in an office with opaque glass windows' (p. 33). The reader is presented with the concept that working life means loss of liberty, from which the worker only has the option to escape by walking out. An end is brought to the work experience through deletion of the hard disk, which brings relief from the computer-centred existence which work has meant: 'I went to my desk and typed a command into the computer: "Delete All"' (p. 34).

The experiences of working with technology serve as a parallel to the alienation and isolation which affect the professional narrative voice. Once again control through technology is a feature, although in the description of Rosa this is taken a stage further in that identity itself is expressed in technological terms. The professional self is identified with technology and has become subsumed into it meaning that the professional self is expressed in terms of the attributes of the modern world of communications: 'I am exactly the same as my computer' (p. 220). According to this image of mechanized existence, even if the electricity fails, the emergency battery will allow the computer to continue to function. The effect is to show that professional identity functions in a technically correct manner; the professional is described as 'programmed' (p. 220). In the novel, therefore, self-discovery of a worker in the new technological age leads to questioning of a machine-like existence: 'How can you live with a hard disk for a brain and a modem for a heart?' (p. 254) and to recognition that human beings have been colonized by technology. Technological advances cause progressive elimination of human feelings. The same or greater alienation at work is shown to be affecting both narrators but the resolution of self-discovery is left open-ended in respect of Rosa. How the reader is to construe the realization that that work is dehumanizing and what resolution can be proposed for it remain open questions. Etxebarría provides the reader with one possible response through Cristina's comment in the final chapter: 'If she could be the best in what's practically an all-male profession, could she not change her life whenever she chose?' (p. 254). The wider question also left unanswered is what constitutes a successful career path for women.

The novel points to the fact that the successful woman of the 1980s is as unfulfilled as the traditional *materfamilias*. The implication is that a new, unknown route must be carved out by women for themselves.

Amidst the shifting sands of information given, reworked and reinterpreted as a textual image of fragmentation of self, I next want to consider the techniques for presenting tensions between motherhood and professional identity within the domain of the female professional narrative voice. Roberto Manteiga, writing about Rosa Montero's protagonists has commented how women are 'caught between two diametrically opposed systems of values' and the dilemma he discerns could equally well be applied to the professional identity in *Amor, curiosidad, prozac y dudas*.[21] Chapter F: *frustrada* (*Frustrated*) is the first chapter of the novel in which the narrative voice shifts to Rosa. The chapter descriptor immediately centres the attention of the reader on 'frustrated'. It is not until the narrative voice is returned to Rosa in chapter T: *Triunfadores* (*Victors*) that possible insight into that chapter heading 'frustrated' is discernible. The move from twenties to thirties, a key turning point in life, is selected by Etxebarría as a vehicle for exploration of Rosa's achievements. But, at the heart of professional success, emptiness is the central theme of Rosa's birthday celebration: 'Thirty years old. Ten million pesetas a year. An Alfa Romeo. My own apartment. No possibility of getting married or having children' (p. 216). The discourse, with its elliptical juxtaposition of age, possessions and prospects underpins the psychological distress of the narrator, as she reflects on the imbalance between her professional life and her private life. The personal-public dichotomy is now internalized as a source of anguish for the protagonist, providing an interpretation of 'frustrated'. Public success is typified by its own trappings: the car, the money, the flat. Success is seen in terms of purchasing power. Another, shorter shopping list marks personal success: husband, child. From the identification of acquisitions and needs the novel indicates that personal success is also consumer driven.

Simone de Beauvoir has argued that for women 'fundamental assumptions dominate all aspects of social, political and cultural life'[22], and this provides a useful way of examining the device by which the novel is self-consciously divided into sections. Reader expectations are subverted in that each chapter is indicated by letter and each letter is amplified by the addition of a term beginning with that letter. Thus, the chapter heading 'frustrated' does not belong to the female professional's discourse but could be seen as having the function of providing or imposing a framework of 'fundamental assumptions' on the narrator's perceptions. This framework serves to constrain the narrative voice. This technique has the effect of converting the female narrative voice into both subject and object since she is objectified by the 'assumptions' of the external commentary. Beauvoir goes on to comments on internalization of 'fundamental assumptions' by women showing how this leads women to live in a 'constant state of "inauthenticity"' (Moi, p. 92), and this view casts light on the process at work through the chapter headings. The chapter heading sets up a question which will be responded to by the female narrators in a number of different ways. For example, after chapter T, Rosa's reflections in chapter F may now be reinterpreted as an internalization of comments made about single professional women by the apparently unspoken assumptions behind the chapter heading '*Frustrada*' (*Frustrated*). A further mediation of external comments is provided in the final chapter of the novel, where analysis of the professional woman's imprisonment in her daily routine is provided through the indirect speech reported by another narrative voice (Cristina):

> I suppose there are a lot of people who pity her, who in their own minds picture her as a neurotic old maid, who think my sister's life is like a race against the clock, trying to give sense to her existence before her biological clock runs out.
>
> (*ACPD*, p. 254)

The words 'a lot of people', followed by reported comments from that source, provide further evidence of an imposed view which the narrative voices must challenge.

We have already begun to explore how identity is externally imposed on women in the professional world. To emphasize the external pressures on executives, the novel juxtaposes metatextual intercallations from a self-help manual, which serve as commentary to the argument being put forward by the narrative voice. The purpose of the extratextual narrative voice, mediated by Rosa, is to provide an independent reference point for the expected norms to which the narrator must conform in order to have any hope of success. The '*Dress for Success Report*' by Robert T. Molloy is of Anglo-Saxon origin, presumably North American. The metatext in itself highlights the importance of following the lead of other western nations, giving an ironic twist to the fashion of preferring foreign brands and ideals to native Spanish.[23] The metatext is conceived as a series of pieces of advice, directed at women professionals, on dress and behaviour in the office environment: 'Women who wear discreet clothing are 150% more likely to feel they are treated as executives (p. 55). The metatext highlights women's anxieties about not being taken seriously in the office environment. It also imposes a fixed dress code, conforming to asexual norms. The textual and external narrative voice, mediated via Rosa, is explicitly identified as masculine. Rosa, as the sister who represses and does not express her sexuality, follows the tenets of the manual to the letter. Once again, the narrative voice, Rosa, reveals familiarity with expected norms of behaviour and, in line with her recitation of the tenets included in the manual, conforms. The advice given has been internalized and becomes an unquestioned part of work identity. The process of internalization is expressed for the reader by means of the progression through pronouns from the impersonal to the personal. Thus, 'Women' from the first quotation becomes 'I': 'I have to keep a close eye on how I behave' (p. 56). The pressure to conform is translated even into the realm of personal relationships. Relationships are carried out by the book: 'If an office romance has started, put a stop to it ... So we finished our relationship' (pp. 166-67).

Before we reach the conclusion that using such metatextual advice manuals is a ludicrous device, let us not lose sight of the advice given on image by *Estrategias de carrera para mujeres directivas* (*Career Strategies for Women in Management*), published in 1989. Following studies and surveys, the manual offers the following advice on image:

> Personal image has been shown to be a very important aspect which influences women's (as well as men's) access to the workplace. But it is also important at promotion time and in high levels of the company.
>
> (*Estrategias*, p. 15)

The image designated for the female executive, therefore, is an image defined by the masculine norm, whether Robert T. Molloy or male executives. It is significant that the link between men's access and image is only an afterthought, as indicated by the parenthetical inclusion of reference to male image.

Commentary on the professional 'I' is achieved also through the use of newspaper reporting:

> My career path was meteoric. I finished university with excellent grades and began working at twenty-two. At twenty-eight I was appointed Director of Finance and my photo appeared in the Business section of *El País*.
>
> (*ACPD*, p. 163)

The reference to newspaper reporting on one level has the effect of underlining the singularity of the appointment in that it is newsworthy, recalling Alvira Martín's commentary on the scarcity of women managers. On another level, this reference to newspaper reporting taps into the whole aspect of female image as presented in news-reporting and into the way in which news reporting provides an external commentary on women's achievements.[24] Indeed, given women's limited access to promotion, actual newspaper headlines have been dramatic with regard to female advancement in the workplace. Depiction of such success in terms of imagery taken from revolution or battle is not uncommon, with headlines like 'Assault on Power' and 'Women Conquer Key Government Posts' in *Cambio 16* or 'The Silent Revolution: Why Women are Getting Ahead of Men' from *Tiempo*.[25] These magazine headlines categorize the advances made by women in terms of conquering territory, or in terms of subversive activity. The newspaper headlines, as well as the novelistic reference to newspaper reporting of the female executive's success, serve to underline the fact that female power is not the norm.

The use of intertextuality provides Etxebarría with another strategy enabling her to point to the way that masculine definitions of the female have been imposed on women. For this reason, creation of an identity for professional women is set in the novel in both a biblical and mythological context. The sisters are universalized in a number of ways. First, through their surname, Gaena, the three are imbued with universalizing pre-Christian symbolism, since the name has resonances of Gaea, the earth. The use of mythology provides links through the maternal line with a matriarchal past. However, the three sisters are also linked to universalizing Christian typology. The three can be seen as a female Trinitarian grouping, since they are, by the end of the novel, seen as three faces of the same universal being, woman. They are the one in three and three in one, whose unity affords them god-like powers. The fragmentation of identity exlored earlier must then be set in a Christian context

The three could also be seen as echoing traditional paintings of St Anne, the Virgin Mary and Christ.[26] St Anne is represented by Ana, the eternal mother. The Virgin Mary is encapsulated in Rosa, with her celibate lifestyle and a name resonant of the flowers of the Virgin and of the rosary. Cristina's name, and her many self-inflicted wounds, recall the suffering Christ. The universal female experience of the three, as well as the link to Christian myth, is underlined by the name of their mother, Eva, as the reader is informed in the final lines of the novel: 'I haven't told you yet but my mother's name is Eve' (p. 267). Each of the three is, thus, a daughter of Eve and this means that their story is swathed in the biblical creation myth of subjection, suffering and sin.

It should be recalled that 'work' was one of the curses inflicted on humankind in Genesis 3: 'So Yahweh God expelled him from the garden of Eden, to till the soil from which he had been taken' (Genesis 3: 24). The sphere of work is construed as masculine and this element of the curse is directed at Adam. Women workers, participating in the male sphere, thus, share in the curse. However, as women and daughters of Eve, they still take responsibility for the other part of the curse since childbearing is the other major consequence of the Fall, this time specifically directed at women (Genesis 3: 16). Women now bear the burden of a double curse to face. It is to this interpretation of work as part of the impact of sin on human life that Etxebarría refers in Chapter C: *Curro (Grind)*: 'God created the world in seven days. A bit later he threw Adam out of paradise and condemned him to earning his bread by the sweat of his brow. Apple makes several million computers a year' (p. 29). Juxtaposition of the second creation story and modern consumerism, typified in the name of the computer multinational, Apple has the effect of replacing the biblical deity by the God of technology. The sheer scale of the production figures of Apple (millions) as opposed to God (seven days) is intended to show how technology has surpassed the deity in scale of operation.

Etxebarría's narrators provide a technologically aware viewpoint and their sense of restriction is typified by the comparison between the natural world, created by God, in which they can have no part, and the alien world of the office created by technological giants like Apple. The automatic doors, digitalized instructions in the lift and the closed blinds of the office contrast with the 'golden caress of the sun' (p. 33). The technological world of the modern office is rejected in favour of rediscovery of nature, which is at the same time a pseudo-science-fiction return to Earth: 'I felt like the freest woman on Earth.' (p. 34).[27] At the end of the novel, the same contrast is repeated. The natural world is described as an Eden and the city, the working environment is described as man-made and menacing:

> The road snaked across ochre-coloured fields and the evening fell on the golden pollen. The cornfields waved in the wind soft and yellow. In the distance, Madrid stood proudly, a monstruous construct of concrete and cement, huge, threatening and grey on the horizon [...]
>
> (*ACPD*, p. 267)

For this reason, instead of being seen as a means of liberation for the three 'daughters of Eve', work is seen as a constituent part of 'existential alienation' and a contributing factor the 'isolation of the individual' in an uncomprehending society.[28] For the protagonists, to rediscover themselves implies a rejection of the limitations and external requirements imposed by the workplace, which shuts out the natural world and imposes an alien culture of technology on those subject to it.

Conclusion

In this chapter, gendered structures have been explored in two complementary ways. Study of the available data relating to women's employment opportunities in Spain, show that women's management opportunities will be limited by features of the job market as a whole: high unemployment, concentration of women's employment opportunities in one sector of the labour market, and high representation of women amongst those workers on temporary contracts. Women are also found to be concentrated in management sectors of smaller firms or to be self-employed. For this reason, from the data, we know that the business organization continues to see masculine as the norm, particularly at executive level. Female executives are still not common and their otherness is typified by female managers' comments about being 'on show'. Furthermore, business has failed to capitalize on making working practices more flexible with the arrival of new technology and, indeed, has constructed them more rigidly by the late 1990s since longer hours of work are now required from businessmen and women.

Many of the issues Etxebarría chooses to explore are those highlighted by management reports and surveys of the late 1980s and early 1990s: Etxebarría explores the dichotomy of work and home, decisions on childbearing, length of the working day, working with technology as well as the way in which external commentaries on women, such as advice manuals or newspapers, create images of women which individual women have to contest. However, the final position of the novel with regard to women's professional identity at the end of the 1990s is full of hope. Following the description of Ana's self-discovery and transformation through nervous breakdown, the other two sisters, united, are depicted returning to the city. In the creation of a mythology more fitting for the modern age, biblical creation myths and the biblical curse, are finally confronted and displaced. The sisters' return is depicted through the image of 'warriors' returning to the Star of Death, Madrid. In their cry to Darth Vader, they are now identified with the Jedi warriors returning to defeat the darker side of the force.[29]

References

1   Lucía Etxebarría, *Amor, curiosidad, prozac y dudas* (Barcelona: Plaza y Janés, 1997). References to the text will take the form *ACPD*. A version of this chapter under the title 'Gendered Structures in the City: Women Managers and Lucía Etxebarría's *Amor, curiosidad, prozac y dudas*' was presented at the conference held by the Association for Contemporary Iberian Studies, Edinburgh, 6-8 September, 1998.

2   On the relationship between work and identity, see for example, Ulf Himmelstrand, '"Soluciones sin problemas " y "problemas con o sin solución" en el trabajo, en el mercado laboral y en el Estado', *Sistema*, 140–41 (1997), 25-37.

3   Victoria Camps, *El siglo de las mujeres* (Madrid: Cátedra, 1998), p. 44.

4   María Antonia García de León, *Las elites discriminadas: Sobre el poder de las mujeres* (Barcelona: Anthropos, 1994), analyses the way in which 'business women' (women who own a company or who are on the Board) are a special case in that they may be in that position through inheritance or through family connections.

5   *Las mujeres en cifras: 1997* (Madrid: Ministerio de Trabajo y Asuntos Sociales/Instituto de la Mujer, 1997), p. 55. Figures for 1998 are from the *Encuesta de la Población Activa* (*EPA*) 41, http://www.mtas.es/Estadisticas/ANUARIO/EPA/epa41_1.html, consulted 18 February 2000. All references to *EPA* figures are from this source; 1999 figures from http://www.elpais.es/p/d/20000308/espana/cuadre34.htm, consulted 8 March 2000.

6   Benjamín García Sanz, *Mujeres y empleo (1976-1996)* (Madrid: Instituto de la Mujer/Ministerio de Asuntos Sociales, 1997), p. 7.

7   Anny Brooksbank Jones, *Women in Contemporary Spain* (Manchester: Manchester University Press, 1997), pp. 78-83.

8   European Commission, *Employment in Europe*, Table reproduced by García Sanz, p. 31. Percentages of female employment in EU countries range between 72% in Sweden and 32% for Spain.

9   Francisco Alvira Martín, Marta Torres Ruis, Francisca Blanco Moreno and Ana M. Cruz Chust, *La empresa del futuro y el acceso de la mujer a puestos directivos: Informe realizado para el Instituto de la Mujer* (Madrid: Instituto de la Mujer, 1994), p. 128. Further reference to this work will be given in the text as *Informe*.

10 Juan M. Sánchez Peiró, 'Interrogantes interculturales sobre la mujer en el mundo de hoy', in *Mujer, trabajo y maternidad*, ed. by María José Carrasco, Ana García Mina, Jesús Labrador and Carlos Alemany Briz (Madrid: Universidad Pontificia Comillas, 1995), pp. 9, 11.

11 Judy Wajcman, 'Women and Men Managers' in *Changing Forms of Employment: Organizations, Skills and Gender,* edited by Rosemary Crompton, Duncan Gallie & Kate Purcell (London: Routledge, 1996), pp. 259-77.

12 Manuel Elías Olarte, *Resultados de la encuesta sobre mujeres en puestos de dirección: Análisis de la carrera profesional de las mujeres directivas* (Madrid: Instituto de la Mujer/ Ministerio de Cultura, 1988), p. 90. Subsequent references to this study will appear in the text in parenthesis as *Resultados*.

13 Paola Vinay, 'From Informal Flexibility to the New Organization of Time', in *Women of the European Union: The Politics of Work and Daily Life*, ed. by María Dolores García Ramón and Janice Monk (London and New York: Routledge, 1996), pp. 202-16.

14 *Oportunidades y obstáculos en el desarrollo profesional de las mujeres directivas: Informe elaborado a partir del estudio realizado por Studia S.A.*, Serie Estudios fuera de colección (Madrid: Studia / Instituto de la Mujer, 1990), p. 52.

15 Carmen Martínez Ten, 'Las mujeres en la empresa, desarrollo de su carrera profesional y la mujer directiva', *Mujeres e igualdad de oportunidades en el empleo*, Serie Debates, 7 (Madrid: Ministerio de Asuntos Sociales/Instituto de la Mujer, 1989), pp. 57-61, p. 59.

16 See also, Carmen Macías Sistiaga, *Las actitudes del empresario ante la contratación de mujeres* (Getafe: Servicio de Comunicación/Ayuntamiento de Getafe, 1996).

17 Instituto de la Mujer, *Estrategias de carrera para mujeres directivas* (Madrid: Instituto de la Mujer, 1989), p. 15. Subsequent references to this text will appear as *Estrategias*; Julián Carrasco Belinchón, 'Condición femenina y management', *Boletín Citema*, 89 (n.d.), July-August, 14-47, p. 46; consulted as a photocopy, undated, at Instituto de la Mujer, Madrid.

18 David Carroll, *The Subject in Question: The Languages of Theory and the Strategies of Fiction* (Chicago & London: University of Chicago Press, 1982).

19 María Socorro Suárez Lafuente, 'La mujer como tema intertextual en la literatura inglesa', in *La imagen de la mujer en la literatura*, María Ángeles Calero Fernández, Scriptura, 12 (Lerida: Edicions de la Universitat de Lleida, 1996), pp. 153-71.

20 Catherine Davies, *Spanish Women's Writing 1849-1996*, Women in Context series (London: Atlantic Highlands, N.J.: Athlone Press, 1998), pp. 240-41, 264-65.

21 Roberto Manteiga, 'The Dilemma of the Modern Woman: A Study of the Female Characters in Rosa Montero's Novels', in *Feminine Concerns in Contemporary Spanish Fiction by Women*, ed. by Roberto C. Manteiga, Carolyn Galerstein and Kathleen McNerney (Potomac: Scripta Humanistica, 1988), pp. 113-23, p. 116.

22 Toril Moi, *Sexual/Textual Politics: Feminist Literary Theory* (London: Methuen, 1985), p. 92.

23 A similar questioning of the fashion of slavish adoption of North American ideas takes place in *Amado Amo* by Rosa Montero (Madrid: Debate, 1995).

24 For further discussion of newspaper reporting of women, see Petra Secanella and Montse Quesada, 'Prensa de elite y mujer', in *Literatura y vida cotidiana: Actas de las cuartas jornadas de investigación interdisciplinaria del Seminario de Estudios de la Mujer de la Universidad Autónoma de Madrid*, ed. by María Ángeles Durán and José Antonio Rey (Zaragoza: Prensas Universitarias de la Universidad Autónoma de Madrid y la Universidad de Zaragoza, 1987), pp. 359-72; see also Concha Fagoaga 'La imagen de la mujer en los medios de comunicación. Notas sobre la percepción selectiva de los medios', *Sistema*, 64 (1986), 103-13; see also, Mercedes Carbayo-Abengózar in this volume.

25 Encarnación Valenzuela, 'Mujeres al poder', *Cambio 16*, 19 December 1994, pp. 21-3; Ricardo Herrén, 'La revolución silenciosa: Por qué las mujeres superan a los hombres', *Tiempo*, 4 November 1996, pp. 72-80.

26 *Rosa sine spina* is a traditional title of the Virgin Mary; cf. Marina Warner, *Alone of All her Sex: The Myth and Cult of the Virgin Mary* (London: Weidenfeld and Nicolson, 1976).

27 Pilar Escabias Lloret, 'The Millennial Woman: The Quest for a Female Voice in Lucía Etxebarría's *Amor curiosidad, prozac y dudas*', Paper presented at the Association of Hispanists of Great Britain and Ireland Conference, University of Hull, April 1999.

28 Davies, p. 263. Davies is commenting on the protagonist's relationship to Catalan bourgeois society in Esther Tusquet's *El mismo mar de todos los veranos*.

29 http://www.starwars.com/.

Bibliography

Alvira Martín, Francisco, Marta Torres Ruis, Francisca Blanco Moreno and Ana M. Cruz Chust, *La empresa del futuro y el acceso de la mujer a puestos directivos: Informe realizado para el Instituto de la Mujer* (Madrid: Instituto de la Mujer, 1994).

Brooksbank Jones, Anny, *Women in Contemporary Spain* (Manchester: Manchester University Press, 1997).

Camps, Victoria, *El siglo de las mujeres* (Madrid: Cátedra, 1998).

Carrasco Belinchón, Julián, 'Condición femenina y management', *Boletín Citema*, 89 (n.d.), July-August, 14-47.

Carroll, David, *The Subject in Question: The Languages of Theory and the Strategies of Fiction* (Chicago & London: University of Chicago Press, 1982).

Davies, Catherine, *Spanish Women's Writing 1849-1996*, Women in Context series (London; Atlantic Highlands, N.J.: Athlone Press, 1998).

Elías Olarte, Manuel, *Resultados de la encuesta sobre mujeres en puestos de dirección: Análisis de la carrera profesional de las mujeres directivas* (Madrid: Instituto de la Mujer/Ministerio de Cultura, 1988).

Escabias Lloret, Pilar, 'The Millennial Woman: The Quest for a Female Voice in Lucía Etxebarría's *Amor, curiosidad, prozac y dudas*', Paper presented at the Conference of the Association of Hispanists of Great Britain and Ireland, University of Hull, April 1999.

García de León, María Antonia, *Las elites discriminadas: Sobre el poder de las mujeres* (Barcelona: Anthropos, 1994).

García Sanz, Benjamín, *Mujeres y empleo (1976-1996)* (Madrid: Instituto de la Mujer/Ministerio de Asuntos Sociales, 1997).

Herrén, Ricardo, 'La revolución silenciosa: Por qué las mujeres superan a los hombres', *Tiempo*, 4 November 1996, pp. 72-80.

Himmelstrand, Ulf, '"Soluciones sin problemas " y "problemas con o sin solución" en el trabajo, en el mercado laboral y en el Estado', *Sistema*, 140-41 (1997), 25-37.

Instituto de la Mujer, *Las mujeres en cifras: 1997* (Madrid: Ministerio de Trabajo y Asuntos Sociales/Instituto de la Mujer, 1997).

————, *Estrategias de carrera para mujeres directivas* (Madrid: Instituto de la Mujer, 1989).

Macías Sistiaga, Carmen, *Las actitudes del empresario ante la contratación de mujeres* (Getafe: Servicio de Comunicación/ Ayuntamiento de Getafe, 1996).

'Las mujeres conquistan puestos clave del Estado', *Cambio 16*, 2 January 1989, pp. 34-36.

Manteiga, Roberto, 'The Dilemma of the Modern Woman: A Study of the Female Characters in Rosa Montero's Novels', in *Feminine Concerns in Contemporary Spanish Fiction by Women*, ed. by Roberto C. Manteiga, Carolyn Galerstein and Kathleen McNerney (Potomac: Scripta Humanistica, 1988), pp. 113-23.

Ministerio de Trabajo y Asuntos Sociales, http://www.mtas.es/Estadisticas/ANUARIO/EPA/.

Sánchez Peiró, Juan M., 'Interrogantes interculturales sobre la mujer en el mundo de hoy', in *Mujer, trabajo y maternidad*, ed. by María José Carrasco, Ana García Mina, Jesús Labrador and Carlos Alemany Briz (Madrid: Universidad Pontificia Comillas, 1995).

Secanella, Petra and Montse Quesada, 'Prensa de elite y mujer', in *Literatura y vida cotidiana: Actas de las cuartas jornadas de investigación interdisciplinaria del Seminario de Estudios de la Mujer de la Universidad Autónoma de Madrid*, ed. by María Ángeles Durán and José Antonio Rey (Zaragoza: Prensas Universitarias de la Universidad Autónoma de Madrid y la Universidad de Zaragoza, 1987), pp. 359-72.

Studia, *Oportunidades y obstáculos en el desarrollo profesional de las mujeres directivas: Informe elaborado a partir del estudio realizado por Studia S.A.*, Serie Estudios fuera de colección (Madrid: Studia/Instituto de la Mujer, 1990).

Suárez Lafuente, María Socorro, 'La mujer como tema intertextual en la literatura inglesa', in *La imagen de la mujer en la literatura*, ed. by María Ángeles Calero Fernández, Scriptura, 12 (Lerida: Edicions de la Universitat de Lleida, 1996), pp. 153-71.

Valenzuela, Encarnación, 'Mujeres al poder', *Cambio 16*, 19 December 1994, pp. 21-23.

Vinay, Paola, 'From Informal Flexibility to the New Organization of Time', in *Women of the European Union: The Politics of Work and Daily Life*, ed. by María Dolores García Ramón and Janice Monk (London and New York: Routledge, 1996), pp. 202-16.

Warner, Marina, *Alone of All her Sex: The Myth and Cult of the Virgin Mary* (London: Weidenfeld and Nicolson, 1976).

7 Feminism in Spain
A History of Love and Hate

Mercedes Carbayo-Abengózar

It is difficult to predict what the new millennium is going to bring for us, particularly since the adjective 'new' seems to have become transferred to the idea of a reborn century, with all its connotations. We might agree, when we look at the end of the twentieth century, within the context of the postmodern era, that the key concept is death: death of the subject, death of reason, death of history, death of metaphysics, death of totality, and death of the project of modernity, created out of the Enlightenment project. Can we then deduce that this implies the death of feminism? The Enlightment was a project that excluded women; since the subject, the reason and the *logos* were all masculine. Feminism appeared as a reaction to this exclusion.[1] During the twentieth century many women fought to be included in this masculine project. During the twentieth century these women's lives have undergone an extraordinary transformation. During the waning of the twentieth century, it has been particularly true that women have reacted against the reasonable, unique, enlightened subject and have vindicated the multiple, plural and different subject. It has been a long and difficult battle, full of contradictions, problems and despair. But it has been a passionate struggle.

My intention in the following pages is to take a brief look at this struggle by placing it within the context of Spanish feminism and to project this view into the twenty-first century. 'The twenty-first century will be the century of women', says Victoria Camps in the first line of her book.[2] Let us take an express train journey through the twentieth century to see how the journey began and to project where it will end.

The 1920s and 1930s: The Beginning of a Long Journey

As Roser Sol points out,[3] the true origin of feminism in Spain can be centred on the work that the *krausistas* carried out in the area of education, particularly with the Free Institute of Education (1876), the *Congresos Pedagógicos* (1882 and 1892) and the reform of the School of Women Teachers.[4] Nevertheless, it should be noted that, during the first decades of the twentieth century, around 50% of women were illiterate. During the 1930s, illiteracy was a fact of life for one third of women. Between 1940 and 1970, female illiteracy was reduced from 23.2% to 12.3%, although it was still double that of male illiteracy.[5] According to Sol, targeting illiteracy conformed to a kind of bourgeois feminism, affecting those who could not pay for private education. Therefore, the immediate objective of these privileged middle-class women was to gain access to the culture which had been denied them. They were conscious that the knowledge they possessed was just enough to deal with the housework and nothing else. With this in mind, in 1915, María de Maeztu (1882-1948) founded the International Residence for Women (*Residencia Internacional de Señoritas*), a student residence for women from all over Spain who came to Madrid to study. There, they took part in conferences, talks, theatre performances, concerts, courses and exhibitions. There was also a pavilion for women intellectuals from all over the world. In 1925, the *Lyceum Club Femenino* (Women's Branch of the Lyceum Club) was founded. It was a place where, according to Carmen Martín Gaite: 'many Madrid women from the enlightened bourgeoisie (generally married and not too young) found a place to escape from family matters and to open their sights to a way to escape the domestic arena'.[6]

On the other hand, within the framework of 'social Catholicism', from the beginning of the century, groups of bourgeois women created a sort of Trade Union for working women. In 1909, María de Echarri founded the *Sindicato de la Inmaculada*.[7] In this Trade Union, women workers were treated in a very paternalistic way. To join in the Union's activities, the women had to work in administration, dress-making, shops, industries and Government companies. They had to be over sixteen and had to be regular churchgoers. In this way, these women members of the bourgeoisie, unlike María de Maeztu and others, made sure socialist or liberal ideas did not creep in.

In general, the idea of women working outside the domestic arena was somehow rejected. Working in factories or in any other professional area was regarded as being against the 'nature of women' and furiously criticized. We can distinguish this opinion in the following quotation from a priest talking about the women who were members of the *Lyceum*: 'Society should lock them up as mad or criminals instead of allowing them to speak up in this club against all human and divine rules. The moral atmosphere of both the streets and homes would benefit from the hospitalization and imprisonment of these eccentric and unbalanced women'.[8] Only women with some education and in an economically stable situation could dare to resist this sort of discourse and to confront it.

The above illustrations demonstrate that the feminist movement started quite late in Spain, compared with the Anglo-Saxon countries. This delay could be due to different reasons, such as the lack of industry combined with a strong middle class, the influence of the Catholic Church and the lack of democratic tradition. The feminist movement during the 1920s, as we have seen, was a bourgeois and liberal movement, based on getting equal rights though reforming the legal system and on the promotion of female access to the world of work and culture. It had to face strong opposition from the Church and the Conservatives. Until the impetus given by the 1930s in terms of political reforms, women's organization in Spain was élitist. Women like María de Maeztu or María Lejárraga (1881-1948) defined what feminism was for them: 'Feminism looks for women to live until their prime, for them to have the same rights and duties as men, to share the governing of the world with them in an equal manner, since women are half of the population, and in perfect collaboration with men, so that they can try to achieve their own, mutual happiness and the improvement of the human species'.[9] Despite the criticism that all these women received from the most conservative and religious sectors of society, we could agree with Pierre Malerbe that 'the condition of women is one of the most burning problems in the twenties in Spain. At that time, Spanish feminism was on the boil'.[10]

This atmosphere of struggle from above, from the middle classes, continued during the Second Republic (1931-36). Women like Clara Campoamor, Margarita Nelken, Victoria Kent or Federica Montseny fought, on different fronts for women. Clara Campoamor, a lawyer and MP, defended the right to vote for women. The feminist, Socialist and later Communist writer, Margarita Nelken, wrote against the exploitation of women, hypocritical sexual morals and ignorance about contraceptives, amongst other things. Victoria Kent, a lawyer and MP became the Director General of Prisons, in 1931, introducing important improvements in the lives of prisoners. Federica Montseny was the first European woman to become a Government minister. All of them went into exile during the Spanish Civil War and from there, they continued using strategies of resistance in order to avoid systematic marginalization of the experiences of women by the hegemonic discourse of Francoism. One of their most important strategies was to avoid forgetting, to recover collective memory, to carry on writing.

On the other hand, during the Second Republic, and particularly when the left-wing party Popular Front (*Frente Popular*) won the elections, women industrial workers who had begun to come together by the end of the nineteenth century, openly became members of Trade Unions and fought together with men to defend their rights as workers. However, they faced incomprehension from the male-dominated membership: 'While, from 1900 onwards, the presence of women in both wings of the labour movement did increase in relative terms, only in exceptional cases did women achieve leadership positions where they could influence policy or act on their own initiative'.[11] For these working women, whose primary goal was the struggle for socio-economic equality, feminism was not regarded as a political ally, since it was concerned only to extend rights within the already privileged élite of the middle classes. Besides, we should not forget that all these changes and activities belonged to urban areas and that the bulk of the Spanish population was rural, where illiteracy was even higher and the power of Church and Military, together with customs and traditions made the struggle much harder.

As in the 1920s, when Spanish women achieved the vote in the 1930s, middle-class paternalistic women were mobilized by the Church. Under male tutelage they tried to struggle against the new wave of left-wing ideals to guarantee a politically, socially and culturally conservative order.

We can sum up, by saying that although the Second Republic opened up public spaces previously denied to women in both higher and lower spheres, it never meant that women had made those spaces their own, since such spaces were mainly male-dominated. Feminism was still a middle-class concept although it counted on the increasing participation of the urban working class. Despite efforts from the Conservatives and the Church to stop it, below the surface, feminism with all its contradictions, was still on the boil.

The 1940s and 1950s: A Determined Although Unsuccessful Attempt to Stop the Train.

The Spanish Civil War mobilized women on both sides and this mobilization differed from one side to the other. Proletarian and middle-class women were involved in the actual fighting and in war-time tasks, replacing men and supporting their families, while men were absent at the front. In Republican Spain, when they were not fighting, women worked in the workshops or factories of the Republican home front, or they provided health and welfare services for both home and military fronts through the Popular Front organizations. In Nationalist Spain, there was not the same level of an industrial mobilization of women, however, through the auspices of the *Sección Femenina*, women became very involved in providing different services, such as clinics and launderettes at the front.[12] Although feminist ideas and struggles carried on during the war on the Republican side, both Nationalist and Republican women were at the same time obliged to retain their roles as mothers and wives during the crisis of the war in order to return to 'normality' after it. As the Nationalist cause began to gain ground, the *Sección Femenina* started to take over in its mission of converting Spanish women to the Falangist 'Mothers of the Nation' ideal.[13]

The victory of Franco was to abort any early achievements of feminism. When the Civil War ended, it seemed that there was to be no further advancement for women, there thus began one of the most depressing and dark periods in Spanish women's lives during the twentieth century. The 1889 Civil Code was reintroduced to replace all the laws that had been passed during the Second Republic, such as those relating to abortion, divorce and contraception. Women were confined to their homes, identified with nature in the sense that in the division of work roles, women were perceived almost exclusively as 'natural' mothers and housewives, and excluded from the civil, public and political domain. The ideology of the regime praised the traditional role of mother and wife, and homes became the only sphere of action for women. Once women were back in the homes, they were easier to control. The *Sección Femenina* was charged with this task. They started by reorganizing the Social Service (*Servicio Social*) created during the war. The *Servicio Social* became a duty for all Spanish women between the ages of seventeen and thirty-five. Completing the required period of Social Service was compulsory for every woman who wanted to work or even to get a driving licence. It consisted of six months' State service, of which at least three months constituted unpaid welfare work in hospitals, schools, orphanages, old people's homes, food kitchens, as well as the making of clothes or layettes. Other activities included summer camps for the *flechas* (Arrows: girls between eleven and thirteen years old), where they were taught womanly tasks and doctrines. They were instructed in discipline and obedience and learned how to work and participate within the Nationalist hierarchy. According to the hierarchy of the *Sección Femenina*, the objectives of the *Servicio Social* were, on the one hand, recruiting new members, improving women's cultural level and helping them to adapt to community life, and on the other, for the members to be aware of problems which should not be ignored regarding the lower echelons of society.[14]

Indeed, the women of the *Sección Femenina*, just like their predecessors in the 1920s and 1930s, had the patronizing idea that they could train Spanish women in the tasks they had been doing all their lives. They organized courses on agriculture for rural women, childcare, cooking, sewing, etc. in the attempt to raise women's 'cultural' awareness. They had what they called '*cátedras ambulantes*', a sort of travelling school which could reach every single corner of Spain where, apart from teaching them the principles of the 'new Spain', they would try to recruit new members. They also tried to change the image that Spain had abroad, by exporting the 'culture' through the different music and dance groups (*coros y danzas*). Although one can imagine that the *Servicio Social* was not very popular among the majority of women, we should not forget that, in the Spain of the 1940s, children suffered from a lot of shortages, despite the efforts of their parents to improve their situation. For some of these parents, the solution was to join the *Falange* so the children could go to summer camps where they would at least be fed and enjoy the fresh air. The problem was that, together with such benefits, came indoctrination.

Indeed, none of the earlier Spanish political regimes had codified the role of women in society so restrictively. The ideology was Falangist and 'the idea of women' had been established by José Antonio in 1935 in an speech entitled: 'The feminine and the Falange':

> We are not feminist either. We do not hold the view that the way of respecting women is to take them away from their wonderful destiny and to make them do manly tasks. It has always made me very sad to see women trying men's exercises, all sweating and straining in a rivalry in which they are always going to lose, to the satisfaction of male competitors, [...][15]

The wonderful destiny to which José Antonio is referring is that of housewife and mother. However, there was always a resistance to this official discourse on women. It was a powerful and authoritarian discourse but, as Michel Foucault points out: 'Discourse transmits and produces power; it reinforces it, but also undermines and exposes it, renders it fragile and makes it possible to thwart it'.[16] The resistance came from both inside and outside the earlier regime. Particularly interesting is the former, because in some ways this was going to define the kind of feminism that would be favoured by certain women intellectuals. It is a feminism that can be called 'well-mannered' (*modoso*). With this translation, I mean a resistance from within that does not appear aggressive, that seems to go along with power instead of confronting it, that agrees with authority, instead of disagreeing. By doing that, feminism is not seen as dangerous or suspicious and therefore it manages to penetrate into the system without being noticed. The writer Carmen Martín Gaite, a woman from the 1950s generation, explains what she understands by *modosa*:

> Perhaps what happens to me is that I could never have been described as aggressive, but none the less I have always been a rebel in my innermost heart. It is very difficult to explain [...] I try not to waste the efficacy of my protest in waffling but rather in finding

my own way [...] I try to reject what I do not like from inside me, saying I do not like this, but without carrying a flag [...] I am very well-mannered.[17]

Another woman, this time from within the *Sección Femenina* expressed this concept in almost the same way. Mercedes Formica became a lawyer in 1951. She had started university before the war, when she was one of three women in the whole institution. She worked as a journalist and writer, and at the same time as a lawyer. In 1952 she started a campaign in favour of women in the newspaper *ABC*. She examined private and public laws regarding women and this became an international issue that resulted in the changing of eighty-eight articles in the Civil Code. Three issues were particularly important: the conjugal residence became the residence of both, instead of only the husband; women stopped being 'deposited' (ditched) when separated. The previous law had established that, when the couple (in reality, the man) decided to separate, women should be deposited in another place (a friend's house, a convent or any other family house) until the process finished, often for about six or seven years, with no access to her children or possessions, even if they belonged to her. Under this system, she lost everything. The third issue concerned re-married women who lost the parental authority over the children of the first marriage. Mercedes Formica succeeded in changing these three laws in favour of women. Other issues she worked on were adoption, illegitimate children and minors. However, she was a well-known Falangist and a member of the *Sección Femenina*. When she has been asked about this 'contradiction' of being feminist and Falangist she has always answered:

> I have always defended and will defend everything that favours women or any of the marginalized minorities. What I am not is a frenzied feminist; one of those that shout the right to have an orgasm as if that sensation should be claimed at all. It goes with the person [...][18]

We are looking at only two of many women who, whilst working within the system and trying not to be too noticeable, managed to do what they wanted and to fight for women's rights 'with the help of men' as they both have said. Martín Gaite, as a very well-mannered subversive writer who managed to publish constantly from the 1950s until the present,[19] and Mercedes Formica, who despite being criticized by the women of the *Sección Femenina* to which she belonged, went as far as talking to Franco to get what she wanted. These two women attracted the attention of researchers, critics and intellectuals (particularly foreigners) because of the contradiction implied by being, in the case of Formica, Catholic, Falangist and feminist, and in the case of Martín Gaite, writing constantly about women and denying being a feminist.[20]

In my view, there is not such a contradiction but a misunderstanding of the concept of feminism. Mercedes Formica explains that José Antonio was not anti-feminist, that his words have been misinterpreted: 'as the good Spaniard he was, he felt apprehensive about women who were pedantic, aggressive, violent and full of hate against men'.[21] I would like to draw attention to the sentence 'as the good Spaniard he was' because the contradiction, if any, lies therein. Apparently José Antonio saw in

Mercedes Formica: 'not the choleric suffragette, but a young woman preoccupied by the problems of Spain, that loved her culture and tried to get through life with a career in the professional world'. Feminism in Spain seems to have been wrongly identified with women becoming men, those virile and aggressive women who José Antonio and Formica talked about, women who have lost their femininity, a concept that, although never explained, has always been in the collective consciousness, as one of those lessons that one learns and never forgets. The *Sección Femenina*, in fear of women losing their femininity, taught them how the new woman should behave for her country:

> The new woman should be a woman of her time, happy being a mother, educating her children, showing a feminine interest in her husband's affairs and giving him a quiet refuge against the problems of public life. In a few words: squeaky-clean but modern.[22]

The parameters of this sentence embrace two ideas: the new woman had to be *modosa* in order to succeed, and had to be 'Spanish', as different from the suffragettes in other European countries. To be Spanish meant to be feminine, *modosa*, non-aggressive, clean in the sense of pure, different from the images the Spaniards received from abroad. This idea would penetrate into women's hearts and minds and influence their behaviour, leading in some cases to the contradictions that, for instance, Elizabeth Ordóñez and Catherine Davies have remarked upon.

The 1960s and 1970s: We Take the High-Speed Train.

It is important to highlight the impact of the Second Vatican Council, that took place between 1962 and 1967. Since then, some sections of the Catholic Church continued the Church's mission from a left-wing, rather than from the right-wing perspective.[23] The Council in fact ended the identification of the Catholic Church with the Spanish Government. Throughout the 1960s, two pillars of tradition were to undergo a deep change: the authoritarian family and the religious culture. Feminism between 1960 and 1975 reappears in Spain from two different positions: within the anti-Francoist movements, led by the clandestine political parties and within the Catholic groups that fought for women.[24] In 1960, the Seminar for Sociological Studies about women (*Seminario de Estudios Sociológicos sobre la Mujer*) appeared; in 1964, the Democratic Movement of Women (*Movimiento Democrático de Mujeres*) was founded by the feminists Carmen Alcalde, Lidia Falcón and Merche Comavella and in 1968 the Federation of Housewives (*Federación de Amas de Casa*) was created. Lidia Falcón published *Los derechos laborales de la mujer* (*Women's Labour Rights*) in 1962, *Los derechos civiles de la mujer* (*Women's Civil Rights*) in 1964 and *Mujer y sociedad* (*Women and Society*) in 1969. The Catholic groups had an important, though not very decisive, role to play, due to lack of political freedom. With the new spirit that the Second Vatican Council brought, the different organisations such as the World Union of Feminine Catholic Organisations (*Unión Mundial de Organizaciones Femeninas Católicas*), or the Working Catholic Feminine Youth (*Juventud Obrera Católica Femenina*), among others, began to work on improving women's lives. Carmen Alcalde described them as:

Groups of women who practise the three orthodox vows of chastity, poverty and obedience to Christ. They lived in small communities on the periphery close to the working classes. They were dedicated to solving their problems and fought against the bourgeoisie that undermined them.[25]

We could say that, as opposed to nineteenth-century suffrage, which arrived in Spain very late, the resurgence that feminism enjoyed during the 1960s and 1970s in Europe, had an immediate impact on Spanish society. It is important to highlight the passing of the Law of Political and Professional Rights of Women in 1961. This law, presented in Parliament by the *Sección Femenina*, allowed women to work in almost any professional area except in military careers that implied the use of weapons, and in the Administration of Justice, particularly as magistrates, judges and public prosecutors. However, in her presentation of the law in Parliament, Pilar Primo de Rivera said: 'This law is not in any way a feminist law. It is simply a law of justice for working women [...] This law, instead of being feminist, is the support that men can give to women, the weaker beings, to make their lives easier'.[26] Once again we can see how women justify themselves in front of men, as Teresa de Cepada, better known as Santa Teresa, already did in the sixteenth century and as Spanish women have consistently had to do in order to be accepted.[27] The idea of feminism that Pilar had in mind, when she presented this law, was the concept of feminism her brother had used when he portrayed feminism as aggressive and virile and not what it was, an attempt to improve women's working conditions.

For most Spaniards, to experience 1968 was to oppose Franco. The Franco regime was coming to an end. However while opposition to Franco was in vogue, at the same time the official discourse continued, offering rewards for birth, prosecuting abortion and contraceptives and claiming that the virtue of women meant they should remain in the home and dedicate themselves to other members of the family. In the International Congress of the *Sección Femenina* in 1970, the main subjects discussed were the family, changing values, the end of marriage, the *Patria* (Fatherland) as a supranational unit, the fear of divorce, abortion, the pill and the change in women who 'dedicated only to extrafamilial tasks are in danger of becoming physically and psychologically a dry human product with no plenitude'.[28] Equally in 1975, International Women's Year, while the first Conference on Women's Liberation was celebrated in Madrid, the *Sección Femenina* attended an International Conference on Women in Paris, celebrated under the auspices of UNESCO. The report that these women wrote about this conference displayed shock and anxiety at developments, as they perceived them. They thought that the conference intended to brainwash the younger generation that attended, in order to push women's emancipation and break with tradition, and to use the conference as a platform to impose Socialism as the only emancipating philosophy.

All the above show that a range of different discourses was taking over in the Spain of the 1960s. Together with the official discourse of the *Sección Femenina* that promoted a 'feminine feminism', based on defending women in the public area but maintaining traditions in private, there appeared widely different views of women's problems. There were the Catholic associations, which have been already mentioned, that worked more in the sphere of class differences. There was also a more radical discourse of women, like that of Lidia Falcón, who, disenchanted by Socialism, and the Left in general, for their failure to deal with women's problems, created the Feminist Party in 1977 and the magazine *Vindicación Feminista* (*Feminist Vindication*) in 1976. At the same time, there was another emerging official discourse, that of the incipient democracy that led to the celebration of conferences in Catalonia and Madrid on women's issues and to the expansion of the feminist movement. The 1978 Constitution of the new democratic Spain created a debate that: 'polarized the positions of the feminist movement and made them define its political strategy and its relation with the institutions' (Folguera, p.119). Finally, there were also those women writers who wrote in a more or less political way on women's issues such as Rosa Montero in her *Crónica del desamor* (*Chronicle of Unlove*) or Martín Gaite in her *El cuarto de atrás* (*The Back Room*) respectively. We could say that, as in the 1920s, feminism was on the boil once again, but unlike in the 1920s, it was a more pluralist kind of feminism. It was during the Feminist Conference in Granada in 1979, that the subject of feminism of difference came into the picture with the book by Victoria Sendón de León, *Sobre diosas, amazonas y vestales. Utopías para un feminismo radical* (*On Goddesses, Amazons and Vestal Virgins: Utopias for Radical Feminism*)[29] and created an ongoing philosophical debate between equality and difference.[30]

The Last Twenty-five Years: Changing Trains at the Station of Democracy

During the 1980s, the process of modernization of Spanish society was consolidated. According to Folguera, from 1982 to 1988 there was, on the one hand, a scattering of feminist groups and organizations, and on the other, the creation of the institutional or official feminism through the Institute for Women (1983). There were also the various seminars, in various universities, which dealt with women's issues.[31] Alongside this institutional feminism appears a professional or sectorial feminism and, what it is more important, the growing feminist consciousness in women who do not belong to any political, social or professional organization.

Indeed there is a clear feminist awareness in current Spain. In the field of Feminist Theory, Celia Amorós, Professor of Philosophy in the Complutense University in Madrid wrote *Hacia una crítica de la razón patriarcal* (*Towards a Criticism of Male-dominated Reason*)[32] in which she gives a new vision of philosophy from a gender perspective. Similarly, in her recent *Tiempo de feminismo* (*Time for Feminism*), she compiles research done in the seminar she set up called *Feminism and Enlightenment*. Equally, Amelia Valcárcel, Professor in the University of Oviedo, wrote *Sexo y filosofía* (*Sex and Philosophy*) in 1991, in which she talks about the need to make feminism a political theory, a theory of power. Similarly, in her latest *La política de las mujeres* (*Women's Politics*),[33] Valcárcel points out, that she has expanded and polished some of the ideas exposed in the earlier book. Victoria Camps, professor of Ethics at the University of Barcelona, writes about the need for a state welfare policy, which develops strategies to support and help the less powerful groups in society, including women. She believes that social justice should be based on values such as solidarity, responsibility, tolerance, professionalism and education. In her latest book, *El siglo de las mujeres* (*The Century of Women*), she gives a reflection on the two particular issues which in her opinion women should carry on working at in order to achieve total equality: the need for change in the private sphere and women's access to jobs with a high level of responsibility. In her view, feminism in the twenty-first century should be focused particularly on four areas. The first area is education. An educational system that encourages equal opportunities should be created. The second is employment. Since the crisis of the labour market could become a problem for future working women we should be aware of the problems and create solutions before it is too late. The third is politics. There should be equal participation of women in the political arena. And the fourth is moral discourse. She claims that women should be present in the discussions about the new ethical values that contemporary society is creating.

These three women agree on the need for achieving equality between the sexes, but Camps emphasises the positive character of feminine virtues generated during the centuries of exclusion and believes in the capacity of women to transform politics and the concepts of work and leisure in order to create a more mutually supportive and less alienated society. This view bridges the ongoing debate about equality/difference, both by understanding equality as the goal women should achieve, but at the same time enhancing differences.

Concurrently, there is important intellectual production in gender studies emanating from research groups at university level.[34] Although we are far from the 'Women's Studies' or 'Feminist Studies' of the USA, we could say that there is an intensity of activity, not hitherto experienced in this field.

In a wider sphere, or in more accessible fields such as literature or the mass media, there has been a significant increase in the production of newspaper articles,[35] monographs, television programmes, everyday news and, particularly, literature written by women or about women.

The current situation of feminism in Spain it that is has low affiliation. In a catalogue set up by by the Institute for Women, in 1987, there were more than 600 women's organizations of which only one tenth defined themselves as feminist. The feminist movement has been conditioned by the new relationship to the institutional policy on women. On the one hand, a number of feminists have been incorporated into this institutionalization and work with the Government, and on the other, this Government policy has taken protagonism away from the feminist groups. According to Riera and Valenciano, the term feminism is viewed with a certain ambiguity by young women. They are not anti-feminist, but they do not see feminism as a need.[36] They think that feminism is too aggressive. This approach, although somehow different, is not very far from that prevalent during the 1960s and 1970s. In a different field, Spanish women writers, as Davies and Ordóñez pointed out, seem to be very reluctant to be catalogued under the banner of 'feminine literature'. In an article published in *El País Semanal*, the writer, Almudena Grandes, complains about this classification:

> Because if they (the critics) wrote that among us there is a literature written by Spaniards that tends to maintain itself as Spanish literature, even the most stupid reader would call them cretinous, but of course, there have always been classes. Nobody expects a Spaniard

to write English literature, but it seems that a woman has to write masculine literature, since everything else is a subgenre.[37]

All the above shows that, on the one hand, there is still a kind of fear or reluctance towards feminism or feminine as an adjective applied to women's productivity, and on the other, there is an increase of women's writing or writing about women, along with a greater consciousness of women's issues. Instead of looking at this phenomenon as contradictory, perhaps we should look at the possible reasons for it. One of the reasons could be the way in which feminism has been portrayed over the years by the Church, the different Government or authoritarian discourses, and by most men, as we have seen. Carmen Rico-Godoy, in her article in *Cambio 16* says:

> It is sad and distressing to see how the ruling chauvinism (*machismo*) has managed to degrade feminism with the implicit or explicit acquiescence of women themselves. With admirable persistence and tenacity, Spanish society at the end of the century has managed to identify feminism with 'old fashioned', 'ridiculous', 'anachronistic', 'old' and many other words mostly just as insulting and discredited.[38]

Rico-Godoy's words encapsulate what we have been discussing so far, a society that defines feminism in derogatory terms, and the manner in which some women have helped this process to succeed in this definition. But it would be unfair and perhaps very simple to blame society for everything. We have seen that there has been a lot of resistance to these definitions. We know what women have achieved during the twentieth century. Perhaps what we need, to complete the picture is some self-criticism. We could affirm that one of the reasons why the feminist movement has been seen so negatively is because of its problematic and minor relationship with other women's organizations which, without declaring themselves feminist, have come together to defend their specific interests. Feminist discourse has been too theoretical and ideologically based. It has not always managed to approach everyday life issues very successfully, and this has created a lack of communication between it and a large number of women who, despite their commitment to fight for equality, felt somehow discriminated against by the feminists.

We can see that the reluctance to accept feminism in Spain comes from different angles, including the feminist movement itself. Is there a way in which feminism can be seen in a different light, as a liberating philosophy, which includes rather than excludes?

Feminism in the New Millennium: A New Challenge

In the introduction to this chapter we were posing the question as to whether feminism, like other ideologies of the twentieth century, was about to die. Women have achieved equality in most fields, society seems to be more conscious of women's problems and, in particular in Spain, there are Government policies to ensure equal opportunities for women.[39] However, as Victoria Camps has already pointed out, there is still discrimination against women in both professional and private spheres. Most women do not get jobs with high responsibility, and those who do, have to deal with double time at home, as the reports, debates and conferences celebrated as the *fin de siècle* approaches show.[40] In addition, there is the problem of an increase in domestic violence against women, as constantly reported in daily news reports and newspaper articles and the need to change the law in order to protect them.[41] Finally, as we have seen, there is still some reluctance to accept a misunderstood or misinterpreted concept of feminism, and in some way, there is also still in place in Spain the discourse of feminism as an old and anachronistic ideology.

All of this shows us that feminism cannot be about to die but perhaps be re-born to face new challenges, the challenges of the twenty-first century. One of the new challenges might be to come to terms with a new shift in feminism and feminist theory, sometimes called post-feminism. This concept was born in France in March 1968, and since then it has developed to take its current form as a kind of feminism that seeks to be plural and inclusive. Indeed post-feminism has developed since the late 1960s from the deconstruction of patriarchal discourses. It can be seen as a development of feminism informed by the key analytical strategies of contemporary thought: psychoanalysis, post-structuralism, postmodernism and post-colonialism. Although there are still attitudes to change and societies to transform, and, as we have said before, we cannot say that we have finished the struggle, there is also a need to understand feminism in terms of something other than a revolutionary movement. Feminism or post-feminism has to adapt to the needs of the society of the twenty-first century. Globalization, ecology, multiculturalism, post-colonialism, genetic engineering, media, consumerism, sexuality, cybernetics, are phenomena that need the input of feminist theory and feminist views. Perhaps what Victoria Camps meant when she said that the twenty-first century will be the century of women was exactly that: women and particularly for our purpose, Spanish women, have long-standing challenges to keep working on and new challenges to take up. We still have a long journey ahead.

References

1   I am referring to the 'feminist collective conscience' or the public awareness that something was wrong. Examples of feminism can be discerned from the Middle Ages onwards. The feminism which I intend to discuss is industrial feminism that appeared as a consequence of the Industrial Revolution.

2   Victoria Camps, *El siglo de las mujeres* (Madrid: Cátedra, 1998), p. 9.

3   Roser Sol, 'Arraigo y desarrollo de la conciencia feminista', *Historia 16*, 145 (1988), 80-85, p. 81.

4   These were intellectuals, who converted to the doctrines of the German philosopher Karl Friedrich Krause, after having studied law at university in the 1850s. In general terms, Krausist ideals looked for social and cultural change. Krausists looked for modernization of the country through industry, democracy and education. They created the *Institución Libre de Enseñanza* (Free Institution of Teaching), a revolutionary institution whose methods of learning were based on a new concept of pedagogy, in which authoritarian, memory-based and book-orientated techniques were laid aside, and more active methods were employed: 'The environment in the school, therefore, encouraged the development of values and behaviour that would enable the individual to live harmoniously and productively among others in a liberal democratic society: freedom of inquiry and opinion, mutual toleration and respect, personal morality and religious sincerity (as distinct from the dogmatism and external morality of Spanish

Catholicism), equality and respect between the sexes (co-education was a novel feature of the Institution, vigorously condemned by Catholic critics), artistic sensibility (including appreciation of Spanish popular arts), healthy habits and exercise, and indifference to luxury and ostentation'. Carolyn Boyd, *Historia Patria. Politics, History and National Identity in Spain, 1875-1975* (Princeton: Princeton University Press, 1997), p. 34.

5   Amparo Moreno Sardá, 'La réplica de las mujeres al franquismo', in *El feminismo en España: Dos siglos de historia*, ed. by Pilar Folguera Crespo (Madrid: Pablo Iglesias, 1988).

6   Elena Fortún, *Celia, lo que dice* (Madrid: Alianza Editorial, 1992), p. 16.

7   A Catholic Trade Union with the Immaculate Conception as its patron saint.

8   Antonina Rodrigo, *Mujeres en España, las silenciadas* (Barcelona: Plaza y Janés, 1979), p. 136.

9   Guilio de Martino and Marina Bruzzese, *Las filósofas: Las mujeres protagonistas en la historia del pensamiento* (Madrid: Cátedra, 1994), p. 563.

10 Pierre Malerbe, 'La agonía de la Restauración', *Historia 16*, Extra XXIII (1982), 7-35, p. 14.

11 Helen Graham and Jo Labanyi (eds), *Spanish Cultural Studies: An Introduction* (Oxford: Oxford University Press, 1995), p. 120.

12 *Sección Femenina*, the women's section of the *Falange* was set up in 1934 and Pilar Primo de Rivera, sister of José Antonio, was asked to take the leadership. The aims of this organization were: the co-operation of women in the formation of an even greater imperial Spain; the encouragement of a national-syndicalist spirit (otherwise known as vertical syndicalism) in all aspects of life; and promoting the love of the *Patria* (Fatherland) for the fight against everything that was perceived as being anti-Spanish. The *Sección Femenina* was a hierarchical and authoritarian organization. It had a national head, a provincial head, a national secretary and a provincial secretary. As women were the surest means of enlargement of the future Spanish empire, they were expected to carry out several tasks. During the war, their mission did not lie in the actual fighting, but rather in the distribution of propaganda; sewing and embroidering of flags and any other symbols; visiting and caring for prisoners and the wounded; carrying guns and batons to meetings and restricting their personal contact to Falangist men only. In the early stages, before Franco's regime, to become a member of the *Sección Femenina*, a woman needed a minimum cultural background. They had to have studied in a convent and to have had some knowledge of music and languages. Politically, most of them came from CEDA (Spanish Confederation of Right-wing Groups). The number of affiliated women before 1939 was around 2,000, increasing to 600,000 in 1939.

13 *La Falange* was created in 1933 by José Antonio Primo de Rivera. According to the Falangist Raimundo Fernández Cuesta, 'La Falange. Síntesis de valores', *El Alcázar*, 26 November 1974, 1-8, the *Falange* came into being as a result of the incapacity of both capitalism and communism to solve people's problems. It was based upon a concept of Christian Humanism, eternal values, the unity of Spain and national syndicalism. The representation of the people was to be achieved through the process of the following institutions: family, town and syndicalism.

14 All the information about *Sección Femenina* and Social Service comes from the archive of Alcalá de Henares.

15 Agustín Del Río Cisneros, *El pensamiento de José Antonio* (Madrid: Ed. del Movimiento, 1962), p. 204.

16 Michel Foucault, *The History of Sexuality: An Introduction* (London: Penguin, 1984), vol. I, p. 100.

17 Malén Aznárez, 'La rebeldía de una mujer modosa', *El País Semanal*, 225 (1981), 11-14, p. 14.

18 Concha Alborg, *Cinco figuras en torno a la novela de posguerra: Galvarriato, Soriano, Formica, Roixadós y Aldecoa* (Madrid: Libertaria, 1993), p. 109.

19 For an interpretation of the view of Spanish women by Carmen Martín Gaite, see Mercedes Carbayo

Abengózar, *Buscando un lugar entre mujeres: Buceo en la España de Carmen Martín Gaite* (Malaga: University Press, 1998).

20 For example, Elizabeth Ordóñez, *Voices of Her Own* (London and Toronto: Associated University Presses, 1991), p. 14 and Catherine Davies, *Contemporary Feminist Fiction in Spain* (Oxford: Berg, 1994), p. 6, find it difficult to understand why most contemporary Spanish women writers refuse to be called feminist.

21 Alborg, p. 138.

22 Geraldine M. Scanlon, *La polémica feminista en la España contemporánea 1868-1974* (Madrid: Akal, 1986), p. 234.

23 Fernando García de Cortázar, 'La cruz y las flechas. Las relaciones de la Iglesia con la dictadura de Franco: de la sumisión a la oposición', *El País*, 3 December 1992, 20-21, p. 20.

24 Aurora Morcillo, 'Por la senda del franquismo', *Historia 16*, 145 (1988), 86-90, pp. 89-90.

25 Carmen Alcalde, *Mujeres en el franquismo* (Barcelona: Flor del viento, 1996), p. 108.

26 This quotation has been extracted from the 1961 law itself. The documentation could be found in the Archive of Alcalá de Henares. Also in Mercedes Carbayo Abengózar, p. 79.

27 Teresa de Cepada wrote the *Book of her life* under rpessure from her superior, Father García de Toledo. She struggled to find a way in which to express the secrets of her soul without being criticized by the hierarchy of the Church. See Carmen Martín Gaite, *Desde la ventana* (Madrid: Espasa Calpe: 1987), pp. 49-62

28 Found in Box number 27 in the archive mentioned above.

29 *On Goddesses, Amazons and Vestals. Utopia for a Radical Feminism* (Madrid: Zero Zyx, 1981).

30 As an example of writings about difference feminism, see: María-Milagros Rivera Garretas *Nombrar el mundo en femenino* (Barcelona: Icaria 1994) or *El fraude de la igualdad* (Barcelona: Planeta, 1997).

31 Research Institutes to encourage feminist studies and to create an interdisciplinary dialogue between researchers and students have been created in different Spanish universities during the last twenty years, such as those at University of Barcelona, Complutense University of Madrid, Autonomous University of Barcelona, cf. Martino and Bruzzese, p. 581.

32 Celia Amorós, *Hacia una crítica de la razón patriarcal* (Barcelona: Anthropos, 1985).

33 Amelia Valcárcel, *La política de las mujeres* (Madrid: Cátedra, 1997).

34 As examples, the University of Malaga which has its Women's Studies Seminar and which has its own publication dedicated to Women's Studies called *Atenea*, the Complutense University of Madrid, and the University of Barcelona with its Centre of Research about women and its own biennial journal, *Duoda*, among others.

35 Particularly interesting is the article which appeared in *Cambio 16*, on 27 December 1993. It shows the development of feminism from the 1960s and the changes in women's attitudes towards it.

36 Josep María Riera and Elena Valenciano, *Las mujeres de los 90: El largo trayecto de las jóvenes hacia su emancipación*, second edition (Madrid: Morata, 1993), p. 224.

37 Almudena Grandes, 'Hay mujeres fatal', *El País semanal*, 1119, 18 March 1998, p. 82.

38 Carmen Rico-Godoy, *Cambio 16*, 1993, p. 24.

39 The First Plan for Equal Opportunities for Women was approved in 1987 and the second came into being in 1993. The third plan now in force. As Cristina Alberdi pointed out at the inauguration of the conference 'Women at the Dawn of the Twenty-first Century': 'We can say that sex discrimination has disappeared from the law and that we have one of the most egalitarian legislations in Europe', *La mujer en el umbral del siglo XXI* (Madrid: Editorial Complutense, 1997), p. 9.

40 I would like to mention two in particular: Cristina Alberdi et al., *La mujer en el umbral del siglo XXI*

(Madrid: Editorial Complutense, 1998) and Ramón Álvarez and Wendy Stokes (eds), *La mujer ante el Tercer Milenio* (Salamanca: Plaza Universitaria, 1997).

41 The article, published by Antonio Muñoz Molina, in *El País Semanal*, 4 July 1999, p. 114, with the title 'La justicia' is particularly interesting.

Bibliography

Alberdi, Cristina et al., *La mujer en el umbral del siglo XXI* (Madrid: Editorial Complutense, 1998).

Alborg, Concha, *Cinco figuras en torno a la novela de posguerra: Galvarriato, Soriano, Formica, Roixadós y Aldecoa* (Madrid: Libertaria, 1993).

Alcalde, Carmen, *Mujeres en el franquismo* (Barcelona: Flor del viento, 1996).

Álvarez, Ramón and Wendy Stokes (eds), *La mujer ante el Tercer Milenio* (Salamanca: Plaza Universitaria, 1997).

Amorós, Celia, *Hacia una crítica de la razón patriarcal* (Barcelona: Anthropos, 1985).

————, *Tiempo de feminismo: Sobre feminismo, proyecto ilustrado y postmodernidad* (Madrid: Cátedra, 1997).

Aznárez, Malén, 'La rebeldía de una mujer modosa', *El País Semanal*, 225 (1981), 11-14.

Boyd, Carolyn, *Historia Patria. Politics, History and National Identity in Spain, 1875-1975* (Princeton: Princeton University Press, 1997).

Camps, Victoria, *El siglo de las mujeres*, second edition (Madrid: Cátedra, 1998).

Carbayo Abengózar, Mercedes, *Buscando un lugar entre mujeres: Buceo en la España de Carmen Martín Gaite* (Malaga: Malaga University Press, 1998).

Davies, Catherine, *Contemporary Feminist Fiction in Spain* (Oxford: Berg, 1994).

Del Río Cisneros, Agustín, *El pensamiento de José Antonio* (Madrid: Ed. del Movimiento, 1962).

Fernández Cuesta, Raimundo, 'La Falange. Síntesis de valores', *El Alcázar*, 26 November 1974, 1-8.

Folguera Crespo, Pilar (ed.), *El feminismo en España: Dos siglos de historia* (Madrid: Pablo Iglesias, 1988).

Foucault, Michel, *The History of Sexuality: An Introduction, 3 Volumes* (London: Penguin, 1984).

Fortún, Elena, *Celia, lo que dice* (Madrid: Alianza, 1992).

García de Cortázar, Fernando, 'La cruz y las flechas. Las relaciones de la Iglesia con la dictadura de Franco: de la sumisión a la oposición', *El País*, 3 December 1992, 20-21.

Graham, Helen and Jo Labanyi (eds), *Spanish Cultural Studies: An Introduction* (Oxford: Oxford University Press, 1995).

Grandes, Almudena, 'Hay mujeres fatal', *El País Semanal*, 1119, (1998), p. 82.

Malerbe, Pierre, 'La agonía de la Restauración', *Historia 16*, Extra XXIII (1982), 7-35.

Martín Gaite, Carmen, *El cuarto de atrás* (Madrid: Destino, 1978).

————, *Desde la ventana*, second edition (Madrid: Espasa Calpe, 1987).

Martino, Giulio de and Marina Bruzzese, *Las filósofas. Las mujeres protagonistas en la historia del pensamiento* (Madrid: Cátedra, 1994).

Montero, Rosa, *Crónica del desamor* (Madrid: Debate, 1979).

Morcillo, Aurora, 'Por la senda del franquismo', *Historia 16*, 145 (1988), 86-90.

Muñoz Molina, Antonio, 'La justicia', *El País Semanal*, 4 July 1999, p. 114.

Ordóñez, Elizabeth, *Voices of Her Own* (London and Toronto: Associated University Presses, 1991).

Rico-Godoy, Carmen, 'El machismo quiere enterrar el feminismo', *Cambio 16*, 27 December 1993.

Riera, Josep María and Elena Valenciano, *Las mujeres de los 90: El largo trayecto de las jóvenes hacia su emancipación*, second edition (Madrid: Morata, 1993).

Rivera Garretas, María-Milagros, *Nombrar el mundo en femenino* (Barcelona: Icaria 1994).

————, *El fraude de la igualdad* (Barcelona: Planeta, 1997).

Rodrigo, Antonina, *Mujeres en España, las silenciadas* (Barcelona: Plaza y Janés, 1979).

Scanlon, Geraldine M., *La polémica feminista en la España contemporánea 1868-1974* (Madrid: Akal, 1986).

Sendón de León, Victoria, *Sobre diosas, amazonas y vestales. Utopías para un feminismo radical* (Madrid: Zero Zyx, 1981).

Sol, Roser, 'Arraigo y desarrollo de la conciencia feminista', *Historia 16*, 145 (1988), 80-85.

Valcárcel, Amelia, *Sexo y filosofía: Sobre 'mujer' y 'poder'* (Barcelona: Anthropos, 1991).

8 Lesbian Identity in Contemporary Spain
'One of the Greatest Taboos Ever'[1]

Jacky Collins

The position of lesbians in contemporary Spanish society has to be examined within an identification of the position of women overall. After the death of General Franco in November 1975 and the end of his right-wing dictatorship, Spain underwent significant social and political change. This has meant an increase in the visibility of women in public roles in society, including politics and various professional fields and at all levels of education. Indeed, pursuant to the Spanish Constitution introduced in 1978, considered to be one of the most advanced in Europe, women have been recognized as equal citizens with equal rights.[2] Furthermore, during the decade that followed, a range of legal reforms was introduced with a view to putting into practice the constitutional equality between women and men.

The ability of the State to guarantee in reality all the rights theoretically embodied in the Constitution is debatable. Differences still remain in the status of men and women and their equality. However – as Anny Brooksbank Jones explains – in the last twenty-five years, Spanish women have moved out of the private and into the public sphere.[3] It remains to be seen if those citizens of Spain who identify as lesbian will also enjoy this equality and positive visibility that Spanish women in general have otherwise begun to experience.

Whenever sexuality is analysed it cannot validly be done in isolation, but rather it should be examined alongside the role of gender in the formation of identity, since it is frequently argued that the sex of a person is biologically determined, whereas gender is constructed socially and culturally.

The connotations of the image produced by the cultural typification of lesbian identity have been predominately negative. Diane Richardson identifies the following four categories often used by heterosexual society to define lesbians or lesbianism: they are pseudo-males; they are men trapped in women's bodies; lesbianism is a 'sorry state to be in', and lesbianism may be defined primarily in relation to sex.[4] One of the main polemics surrounding the identification of the lesbian is pinpointing what exactly constitutes lesbian sexuality. It would be naïve to suggest that there is one single definition of what a lesbian is, since, as Liz Gibbs points out, 'prevailing concepts of sexuality vary according to the time, culture and most prominent moralities'.[5] Even within the lesbian community, there are diverse theories and positions on what constitutes lesbian identity; between the essentialist and the constructionist schools of thought, there ranges a broad spectrum of definition.[6] As Karla Jay and Joanne Glasgow have warned, there is always a danger of universalizing this fluid, multifaceted identity.[7] However, for the purposes of this chapter the definition of lesbian is broad: a female subject whose object of desire is another woman, whether or not such desire achieves physical fulfilment in a same-sex genital relationship. Or, as Wilton describes, she is the stigmatized 'other' both as female and as an identity located outside heterosexuality (p. 3).

One of the biggest obstacles to the development of a positive lesbian identity has been the invisibility of women's relationships, both heterosexual and homosexual, throughout history. This has been particularly apparent in the construction of this identity in contemporary Spain. As Brooksbank Jones points out, 'lesbians and lesbian feminists have had a low profile in Spain' (p. 118). Likewise, Chris Perriam comments that, 'as in the rest of Western Europe, lesbian voices have been particularly silenced [...]. Few bars and discos offer women-only spaces and outside the commercial scene alternative space is scarce'.[8] Their low profile means that is not possible here to offer a definitive view of lesbian cultures in Spain, as much remains hidden and inaccessible.[9] As Rosa Montero explains in an article in *El País Semanal* on the lesbian community in Spain, 'lesbianism is still a hidden homosexuality'.[10] Nevertheless, this chapter will take the first steps towards an assessment of how, in the current decade, the experience of lesbians and attitudes towards them and towards lesbianism in Spain have begun to change. Focus will be on four different ways in which lesbians are making progress: on the development of gay and lesbian organizations, on a number of legal changes, on images of the entity called 'lesbian' in the media and on the way lesbianism is presented in fiction.

As a basis for this argument, reference will be made to articles from both Spanish mainstream and gay publications. It should be noted that, in order to set the lesbian in the context of contemporary Spain, it has been necessary to revert primarily to local and national gay press since examples in local and national mainstream press are scarce. In addition, at the beginning of the 1990s, even many gay publications made little or no reference to lesbians or lesbianism.

Lesbians in Organizations

Before tracing Spanish lesbianism through the present decade, it would appear appropriate to return to the early 1970s, when the first clandestine gay group, the Spanish Gay Liberation Movement (*Movimiento Español para la Liberación del Homosexual*), was established. This organization existed illegally, since the Delinquency and Social Rehabilitation Law (*Ley de Peligrosidad y Rehabilitación Social*), passed in 1970 during Franco's regime, decreed that even the suspicion of homosexuality could be punished with imprisonment.[11] This law substituted the earlier Vagrancy and Corruption Law (*Ley de Vagos y Maleantes*), in force since 1933, and later modified in 1954 to include homosexuals.

In 1979, homosexual acts between consenting adults were decriminalized and, in 1981, the formation of gay and lesbian groups legalized. Throughout the period from the Civil War (1936-39), until the start of the Transition and the introduction of the new Constitution in 1978, to live openly as a lesbian was doubtless problematic, if not impossible. The lack of debate and identification of lesbians deprived this section of society of any form of voice or identity. Furthermore, the absence of express reference to lesbians in the laws punishing homosexuality has meant that little data is available of specific cases sustaining the official *de facto* repression of lesbians during this period.

The change in the political climate in Spain led to the formation of the first openly gay and lesbian groups. However, the lesbian presence in these mixed groups has and continues to constitute a small minority. The first Spanish lesbian-only group, the Lesbian Association (*Col.lectiu de Lesbianes*), was formed in 1977, under the umbrella of the Catalonian Gay Liberation Front (*Front d'Alliberament Gai de Catalunya* [FAGC]). A year later, the lesbian section of this group broke away to form the Lesbian Freedom Fighters (*Grup en Lliuta per l'Alliberament de la Lesbiane* [GLAL]), which was born out of the feminist movement. This development was indicative of the trend, throughout the 1970s and 1980s, of lesbians choosing to organize around a number of feminist groups, where many embraced a *doble militancia*, or activism both on feminist and on broader socio-political issues. Indeed, at one of Spain's first conferences on feminism, *Jornadas Feministas*, held in Granada in May 1979, the concept of a feminism of difference was debated alongside topics such as sexuality, abortion, violence, harassment and lesbianism.

During this period, a clear pattern was established whereby lesbians became involved in mainstream political debate alongside other progressive movements, rather than seeking to address lesbian-specific issues.[12] As the national political situation stabilized with the election of a democratic Socialist Government in 1982, many such mainstream issues were resolved and lesbians were then in a position to tackle questions that specifically affected them and the gay community.

Nevertheless, there is more recent evidence of lesbians continuing to provide solidarity and to support other social and political associations. In an article in *Ideal*, reporting on International Women's Day, the Lesbian Collective (*Colectivo de Lesbianas*) in Granada is cited as demonstrating alongside Granada Women's Assembly (*Asamblea de Mujeres de Granada*), the Women's Secretariat of the Independent Workers' Commissions (*Secretaría de la Mujer de CC.OO.*), the Faculty of Philosophy and Sociology Women's Group (*Grupo de Mujeres de la Facultad de Filosofía y Sociología*), the Young Women's Group (*Grupo de Mujeres Jóvenes*), and the Anarchist Women's Group (*Mujeres Libertarias*) (*Ideal*, 25 February 1990). An article in a later edition of the same publication concerning this event, reported on the gathering of approximately a thousand people demonstrating about issues such as the abortion law, the divorce law and the position of women in the workplace with no mention made of lesbian-specific issues (*Ideal*, 9 March 1990).

Given the current political stability and the purported equality of all Spaniards, following the introduction of the 1978 Constitution, it could be imagined that lesbian groups and communities are currently living openly throughout Spain. In fact, at present there are nationally only approximately ten exclusively lesbian groups in existence and 50 mixed gay and lesbian organizations. The majority of these are to be found in major cities or provincial capitals, for example in Madrid, Barcelona and Seville. Nearly all of these groups are allied to four umbrella organisations operating at a national and international level: Spanish Gay and Lesbian Federation (FEGAL),

National Gay and Lesbian Association (PGLEE), Joint Association of the National Homosexual Liberation Fronts (COFLHEE) and Joint Gay and Lesbian Association (CGL). In the main, the number of lesbians in mixed groups continues to be considerably smaller than the number of gay men, and the membership of lesbian-only groups is small. Indeed, on 22 February 1997, one of the main issues discussed at the first Lesbian National Conference (*Encuentro Estatal de Grupos de Lesbianas*), held in Madrid, was the amount of influence lesbians have within mixed gay and lesbian organizations and groups.

The issue of the enduring invisibility of lesbians in these mixed organizations was reinforced by a television documentary *A través del espejo* (*Through the Looking Glass*), broadcast by the state-owned TV2 channel on 26 January 1990. It examined the question of homosexuality, considered by some parts of society as a perversion, sin, crime or disease and by others simply as a way of expressing their sexuality freely. Within the documentary, an American short, *Empty Bed*, was screened, followed by a studio debate in which none of the participants were lesbians.

By contrast, four years later there were signs of progress as the private channel Canal+ broadcast the documentary *Salir del armario* (*Coming out*), on 26 June 1994, about the national and international homosexual community.[13] The programme reported that the gay and lesbian community in Spain was one of the country's most politically active groups and that, internationally, the gay and lesbian community had abandoned the fringes of society to become a movement that was participating in all aspects of contemporary culture. In addition, the value of the 'pink peseta' was discussed, including products specifically marketed for this community. In order to highlight the social and cultural reality of this minority in Spain, participants on the programme included a lawyer, a politician, Spain's first officially registered gay couple and a book shop proprietor (the only lesbian). Here it is possible to observe not only the visibility of the lesbian in the gay community, but also the emergence of lesbians into mainstream society.

Although earlier demonstrations had been held regionally, for example in Barcelona, the first national Gay and Lesbian Pride Day was celebrated on 28 June 1991. This event appeared to herald an imminent change not only in the attitude of Spanish society towards homosexuality, but also in the self-perception of the Spanish gay and lesbian community. In Madrid, various gay and lesbian organizations took to the streets calling for a society where sexual difference could be developed freely, fighting against discrimination and calling on schools and colleges to provide a sex education free from prejudice.

In 1992 in Cordoba, gays and lesbians met at the Gay and Lesbian Provincial Conference (*Encuentro Provincial de Homosexuales y Lesbianas*). The resolution of this conference was to put an end to secrecy and hiding. In *Ideal*, María José Moruno, the Town Councillor for Women (*Concejala Municipal de la Mujer*), expressed her support for this view by declaring that it was time to bring this topic out into the open and remove the stigma that had been attached to it by questioning the morality of affection (*Ideal*, 26 September 1992). At the same time, Carmen López, spokesperson for the Cordoba Women's Assembly, stated that gays and lesbians should speak openly about the subject and she made special reference to lesbians, since they suffer from being even less visible, which is a source of unhappiness and grief (*Ideal*, 28 June 1992).

Despite this support, participants at the Cordoba conference levelled criticism at a number of institutions, including the Andalusian Institute for Women, for failing to address the issue of lesbianism in any depth, at a time when gays and lesbians continued to be subjected to an ambiguous Criminal Code concerning matters of public indecency (*Ideal*, 28 June 1992). Further, complaints were made concerning the discrimination suffered by gays and lesbians in the workplace, as it was revealed at the conference that many had lost their jobs once they were open about their sexuality.

Following the establishment of openly gay and lesbian organizations in Spain, a degree of regional and state economic subsidy has gradually been made available to support their activities, for example, from the Council for Social Integration in Madrid (*Consejería de Integración Social de Madrid*). This has led to an improvement in the infrastructure and service provision that such groups are able to offer to the lesbian community. However, an article in the magazine *¿Entiendes?*,[14] published by the Madrid-based lesbian and gay group COGAM, reflects how the provision of subsidies of this kind is not unanimously supported in Spanish society. It reported that, on 5 January 1992, the right-wing national newspaper, *ABC*, had complained about gays receiving taxpayers' money. Following publication of the *¿Entiendes?* article, the right-wing People's Party (PP) minister, Jesús Pedroche, who claimed to have been misquoted in the *ABC* article, called a meeting with COGAM's spokesperson to smooth out any misunderstandings. However, he was quick to emphasize that the PP had no plans to develop a policy to work toward gay and lesbian rights. This party's stance on this issue remains unchanged to date.

Consequently, although support has been made available, it appears that certain sectors of the Spanish population would prefer that gay and lesbian organizations should use the funds available to create ghettos in which to disappear so as not to trouble mainstream society further. Moreover, the limited subsidies and grants that have been made available have mainly gone to mixed gay and lesbian groups. Lesbian-only groups have received little, if any, such support.

Lesbians and the Law

Despite opposition and discrimination, throughout the 1990s these lesbian and gay organizations have continued to present their arguments and demands before the country's judiciary and MPs. In October 1993, a particular breakthrough was achieved regarding the official recognition of same-sex partnerships. The VIII Congress of Democratic Judges submitted a proposal to the then Justice Minister, Juan Alberto Belloch, demanding a change in the law that would provide equal recognition for common-law couples, including those of the same sex, concerning entitlement to pension rights and Social Security benefits. In March of the following year, in the northern city of Vitoria, the first Register of Civil Unions (*Registro de Parejas de Hecho*) was opened to gay and lesbian couples. This development led Jordi Petit, spokesperson for PGLEE, to talk to *El Mundo* about the 'countdown' for the official recognition of gay and lesbian couples by the introduction of a Partnership Law (*Ley de Parejas*).[15]

The debate concerning the recognition of same-sex couples also attracted national media attention. On 1 March 1994, the private (national) television channel, Antena 3, broadcast a discussion programme, presented by Jesús Hermida, examining same-sex marriages and the adoption of children by gay and lesbian couples in Spain. Although the presence of gay men in mainstream Spanish society is more evident than that of lesbians, it is interesting to note that the photograph chosen by *Ideal* to advertise the programme portrayed two women kissing. It could be speculated that the choice may have been to cause less offence, to titillate the heterosexual male readers or because maternity and the rearing of children are considered to be female activities.

As a result of the recommendation by the European Parliament in February 1994 that common-law (including same-sex) couples should receive equal treatment before the law, many gay and lesbian organizations throughout Spain felt able to petition their regional Governments to establish registers similar to the one in Vitoria. In fact, within two months of the register being opened in Vitoria, a further twenty-six municipal registers were established in eight Autonomous Communities. By the end of 1997, the number of civil union registers had risen to 105.

In the light of these developments, the homosexual community demanded a change in the legal status of common-law couples at a national level. This culminated in two demonstrations by a considerable number of gay and lesbian organizations, held in Madrid in June and November 1995. A degree of progress was observed, when a number of legal changes came into force during that year. Firstly, the Urban Tenancy Agreements Law (*Ley de Arrendamientos Urbanos*), was modified to recognize common-law couples, regardless of their sexual orientation. Secondly, a new Criminal Code was approved that penalized any discrimination on the basis of gender, ethnicity or religion, with sexual orientation listed as one of the categories. Finally, gay and lesbian couples were also included in the new Assistance Law (*Ley de Ayuda*) legislation that covered the victims of violent crimes. Such changes encouraged Spanish gay and lesbian organizations to continue to press for the full legal recognition of same-sex partnerships.

What appeared to be a favourable start to the 'countdown', was to prove a slower process than anticipated with regard to the introduction of a Partnership Law. Despite ongoing debate and frequent political lobbying, little progress has been made with regard to the legal status of same-sex partnerships and lesbian and gay marriages at a national level. However, there have been signs of change at a regional level where Civil Union laws have been passed that afford a range of civil rights to both heterosexual and homosexual partnerships.[16]

In addition, in the wider European context, Spain had taken a lead amongst other nations, with the exception of Denmark, Norway and Finland, who had already passed legislation giving certain legal recognition to same-sex couples, by at least raising the issue in political and judicial arenas. Perhaps it is only a matter of time before the national Parliament recognizes same-sex couples before the law.

Whilst the issue of homosexual partnership rights has been apparent in contemporary Spanish political debate, the issues of lesbian and gay adoption and parenting remain relatively untouched. The renowned sexologist, Dr Elena Ochoa, participating in the gay and lesbian conference 'Homosexuality: Choice, Right or Illness?' at the Complutense University in Madrid on 30 March 1995, supported the argument that homosexuality is one of the many manifestations of sexuality, rather than an illness or a perversion. Moreover, she added that she could see no reason why gay and lesbian couples should not adopt.

Furthermore, a number of positive political comments have been made outside the sphere of central Government. The Valencian regional Parliament has approved a change in the laws governing adoption so that fostering can be granted to heterosexual and same-sex couples. Although this regional law does include permanent adoption, it holds no legal effect as this aspect is regulated by national legislation. In an interview given to the gay publication, *Zero Quincenal*, the mayor of Vitoria, José Angel Cuerda, who had been responsible for setting up the first Register of Civil Unions in Spain, declared himself in favour of gay and lesbian marriage and adoption (*Zero Quincenal*, 6, 12 March 1998). In the case of the former, he argued that to deny this right constituted grossly unfair discrimination. With regard to the latter, he held that it was essential to take into account what was in the best interests of the child, rather than to deny gays and lesbians this right on principle on the basis of their sexuality, such an approach being brutal and uncivilized. In June 1999, Inés Sabanes, the United Left (IU) candidate for Madrid in the European elections, echoed this opinion. As part of her manifesto, she argued in favour of gay and lesbian rights to civil marriage and adoption.

Lesbian Chic and the Pink Peseta

Matters of finance had already brought the gay and lesbian community into the mainstream press. On 31 October 1993, *El País*, Spain's largest selling national newspaper had carried an article on the 'Pink Peseta' under the heading 'Pink Consumerism: The Gay Market Offers Major Possibilities for Investment'. Although the author of the article, Gonzalo P. Ponfedra, includes quotations from leading Spanish gay activists, the underlying message would seem to be less supportive of the homosexual lifestyle and more interested in exploiting the section of the population's buying potential. Although the pink peseta usually refers to gay male purchasing power, the image used here to support the article was once again that of two women kissing. In this instance, the article appears to be more positive, yet the apparent change in opinion centres on the economic potential of the lesbian and gay community as contributing to, rather than taking from, the heterosexual community.

Lesbians in Literature

Given the lack of Spanish literary works that either have a lesbian as a main or central character or that deal with the subject of lesbianism, it is possible to comprehend why this identity has remained invisible until recently. In 1978 *El mismo mar de todos los veranos (The Same Sea As Every Summer)*, by Esther Tusquets was published.[17] As Paul Julian Smith points out, this was the first part of what is considered to be 'the first substantial account of lesbianism in Spanish narrative'.[18] The lesbian identity that is presented by the author in this body of work is far from affirming. She offers a collective image of a woman who is unhappy, predatory and marginalized. It is a crisis that drives her into a lesbian relationship, yet later she returns to the acceptability of a male signifier (either husband or son). Almost two decades later, Tusquets returns to the subject of lesbian relationships in *Con la miel en los labios* (*With Honey on their Lips*).[19] As in the former trilogy, the author employs the triangle dynamic where a woman has to choose between the love of a woman and that of a man. Moreover, the lesbian in this latter novel loses the object of her love as well as her dignity and self-respect in a final outburst of uncontrollable emotion and rage. She is portrayed as one who is located outside a civilized, ordered society.

In 1995, the Tusquets publishing company awarded the Sonrisa Vertical prize for erotic literature, to the author of the novel *Tu nombre escrito en el agua* (*Your Name Written on the Water*).[20] The author however refused to reveal her real name and avoided efforts made by the press to contact her, even after she was awarded the prize. This attitude may indicate either that the author was ashamed of being identified with a novel that had a lesbian as the main character, or that she was afraid of being labelled as a lesbian herself. She gave her reason for preferring to remain anonymous in a fax sent to *El País* from a public office in Rome as wanting 'to carry on living the normal life she has had up to now'. Nevertheless, in spite of the novel's success, the happiness and joy that Mariana finds in a lesbian relationship with Sofía is short-lived, since her ex-husband Santiago seeks out the lovers and mistakenly murders Sofía after assaulting and humiliating both of them. It seems there is a high price to be paid for transgressing the established order of heterosexual patriarchy, as one more lesbian character is made to disappear from mainstream literature and another is left to endure loneliness, unhappiness and marginalization.

By contrast, Lucia Etxebarría, winner of the 1998 *Premio Nadal* for *Beatriz y los cuerpos celestes* (*Beatrice and the Heavenly Bodies*) has shown no such reluctance in owning her work.[21] Indeed, she has spoken freely about the lesbian imagery portrayed in the novel and about her own life. However, it is important to bear in mind that this is not a 'lesbian' novel, nor does it focus specifically on lesbian relationships. Rather it presents lesbianism as located within a range of sexualities that women should be free to choose from. Nor is this the first time that this author includes lesbian attraction in her writing. In the earlier work, *Amor, curiosidad, prozac y dudas* (*Love, Curiosity, Prozac and Doubts*), she touches on lesbian relationships but in a less developed manner.[22]

Without doubt, lesbians have begun to appear on the pages of mainstream literature. However, it cannot be argued that Spanish lesbian literature has begun to emerge in contemporary society, since few novels have been written *by* lesbians, *for* lesbians, *about* lesbians. Gabriele Griffin states that 'lesbian cultural production [...] has proliferated in the last 20 odd years'.[23] This may be true for the UK and USA, it remains to be seen how long it will be before this will apply to Spain. It could be that these recent literary successes will encourage a Spanish lesbian literary collection, which will present the reader with a subject that is no longer deprived of happiness, fulfilment and positive recognition within mainstream society.

Lesbians and the Silver Screen

Male homosexual desire has found considerable explicit representation in Spanish cinema since the end of the 1970s, yet the same cannot be said to be the case for the female counterpart.[24] Indeed, apart from the television documentaries referred to and a handful of characters in films by the avant-garde director Pedro Almodóvar (*Pepi, Luci, Bom y otras chicas del montón* [*Pepi, Luci Bom and Other Girls on the Heap* 1980], *Entre tinieblas* [*Dark Habits* 1983], *Tacones lejanos* [*High Heels* 1991], *Kika* [1993] and *Todo sobre mi madre* [*Everything about my Mother* 1999]), there have been very few visual images of lesbians in the Spanish media. However, two recent examples merit particular mention. Firstly, on 21 June 1997, Spanish television featured its first national coming out, when one of the female characters (Bea), in the Tele 5 series *Más que amigos* (*More than Friends*), declared she was a lesbian (*Ideal*, 21 July 1997). Rather than undergoing a severe personality change to be portrayed as dangerous, unfortunate or different, she was still cast positively as 'one of the gang'. Two years on, Bea was still appearing in this programme. This is in marked contrast to many other lesbian characters in western literature, film and television who are not permitted to exist happily and who usually experience a sad demise. Secondly, the release of Marta Balletbó Coll's film, the internationally acclaimed low-budget *Costa Brava (Family Album)* could, as Smith suggests, be seen as a forerunner in Spanish cinema by its placing of a lesbian, Ana, and her bisexual lover, Montserrat, as the central characters.[25] Although the locations in the film (Barcelona/Costa Brava) suggest that sexuality is not fixed or stable, but rather a site or sites to be visited, nevertheless the relationship between Ana and Montserrat withstands the questioning of sexuality and the threat of separation. In these two examples, we are presented with lesbian subjects who are allowed to live, love and be happy.

Conclusion

Whilst gay men have traditionally enjoyed considerable visibility, as a general rule, lesbians, until quite recently, have remained a hidden element within Spanish society. Since female sexuality itself has been largely ignored for centuries, so lesbian sexuality has been almost consistently omitted from any economic, sociological, psychological and political research. It is only during the latter half of this decade that this marginalized identity has begun to be debated in the public arena. By the same token, gay men have been fighting for their rights for many years whilst lesbians have engaged in supporting them in this political activism. They have also been subsumed into the modern feminist movement, rallying to a more general cause, rather than finding a voice of their own.

Although the social status of women varies considerably, both geographically and culturally, it remains globally inferior to that of men. In general, woman suffer more poverty, ill health, powerlessness and lack of education than men, lesbians in Spain are no exception to this. In much of western society, citizenship, with its implied obligations and benefits, is a male privilege. Women, particularly lesbians, are on the whole excluded from this concept. As Carole Pateman argues, 'citizenship has gained its meaning through the exclusion of women, that is to say sexual difference'.[26] The limited citizenship that women can achieve is within the concept of a (traditional) heterosexual family as mothers. It appears that lesbians, even those who bear children, are not afforded this social recognition, for although they may be providing the next generation, they do not fulfil the other requirement of being dependent on men.

In conclusion, there is clear evidence to show that the lesbian in Spain has been able to take her first tentative steps from invisibility to begin to be recognized by and as part of Spanish society. This chapter has shown how and to what extent certain attitudes towards lesbians and lesbianism in Spain have altered during the 1990s. As the decade has progressed, so the appearance and naming of the lesbian within both the gay and heterosexual communities has gradually increased. Within a social, legal and literary framework, she has begun to establish a visible location for herself from the obscurity of being masked by heterosexual society and by gay men, although not always positively.

The media offers a reflection of society's identity and the recent appearance of lesbian characters, images and themes in Spanish mainstream culture suggests an emerging anxiety over gender and sexuality. Since the late 1970s, Spanish society has witnessed the eradication of many traditional taboos, such as sex outside marriage, adultery, pornography, which in the past provided the conflict necessary to produce dramatic tension. Perhaps the emergence of the lesbian is linked to the notion that society has explored all the possible avenues of heterosexuality. A further reason for the appearance of the lesbian in popular culture in the 1990s could be as a result of the destabilizing of the traditional gender categories and roles.

This social change has given rise to a degree of visibility for the lesbian subject. Nevertheless, it is important to remember, as renee c. hoogland points out, that:

> While a general loosening up of traditional sexual taboos is unmistakably part of larger socio-historical developments in modern Western societies, lesbianism, it appears, has not equally enjoyed growing visibility and social acceptance. [29]

It remains to be seen whether lesbian identity in Spain in the next century will experience greater representation and if so, how this is to be manifested. Since we are at this point of emergence, it is impossible to say whether recent social and cultural developments merely represent a passing phase that will end, once the lesbian's financial and economic potential have been exploited to the full.

References

1   'Uno de los más grandes tabúes de la historia', *El Mundo*, 21 June 1997.

2   A specific number of articles (Articles 14, 23, 32, 35.1, 39) deal with women's (and men's) personal, civil, political, economic, social and cultural rights.

3   Anny Brooksbank Jones, *Women in Contemporary Spain* (Manchester: Manchester University Press, 1997), pp. 1-71.

4   Diane Richardson, 'Lesbian Identities' in *The Theory and Practice of Homosexuality*, ed. by John Hart and Diane Richardson (London: Routledge and Kegan Paul, 1981), pp. 111-24.

5   Liz Gibbs (ed.), *Daring to Dissent: Lesbian Culture from Margin to Mainstream* (London: Cassell, 1994).

6   See Tamsin Wilton, *Lesbian Studies: Setting an Agenda* (London: Routledge, 1995), pp. 24-49.

7   Karla Jay and Joanne Glasgow (eds), *Lesbian Texts and Contexts: Radical Revisions* (New York: New York University Press, 1990), pp. 1-11.

8   Chris Perriam, 'Gay and Lesbian Culture', in *Spanish Cultural Studies. An Introduction*, ed. by Helen Graham and Jo Labanyi (Oxford: Oxford University Press, 1995), pp. 393-95, see especially pp. 393-94.

9   For an explanation of the multiplicity of lesbian cultures, see Annamarie Jagose, *Lesbian Utopics* (New York: Routledge, 1994).

10 Rosa Montero, 'El misterio del deseo: Así son y así viven las lesbianas en España', *El País Semanal*, 31 October 1993, 16-26, p. 16.

11 Juan Vicente Aliaga and José Miguel G. Cortes, *Identidad y diferencia* (Barcelona: Egales, 1997), p. 28; Ricardo Llamas and Fefa Vila, 'Una historia del movimiento de lesbianas y gays en el estado español', in *conCiencia de un singular deseo*, ed. by Xosé M. Buxán (Barcelona: Laertes, 1997), p. 193; Nicolás Pérez Canovas, *Homosexualidad, homosexuales y uniones homosexuales en el derecho español* (Granada: Comares, 1996), p. 18.

12 The following groups and organizations are mentioned in the article: Communist Action (*Acción Comunista*), National Labour Confederation (*Confederación Nacional del Trabajo*), Women's Liberation Front (*Frente de Liberación de la Mujer*), Revolutionary Communist Youth (*Juventudes Comunistas Revolucionarias*), Socialist Youth (*Juventudes Socialistas*), Revolutionary Communist League (*Liga Comunista Revolucionaria*), Communist Left Organization (*Organización de Izquierda Comunista*).

13 The infinitive in Spanish can be translated into English by the gerund, infinitive or imperative and this title could also be rendered 'Come out of the closet' or 'To come out of the closet'.

14 *¿Entiendes?*, May/June/July 1992, p. 13.

15 *El Mundo*, 5 March 1994.

16 Legislation has been passed by the Catalan Parliament (30 June 1998) and by the Legislative Assembly of Aragon (12 March 1999).

17 Esther Tusquets, *El mismo mar de todos los veranos* (Barcelona: Anagrama, 1978).

18 Paul Julian Smith, *Laws of Desire: Questions of Homosexuality in Hispanic Writing and Film, 1960-1990*, Oxford Hispanic Studies (Oxford: Oxford University Press, 1992), p. 91.

19 Esther Tusquets, *Con la miel en los labios* (Barcelona: Anagrama, 1997).

20 Irene González Frei, *Tu nombre escrito en el agua* (Barcelona: Tusquets, 1995).

21 Lucía Etxebarría, *Beatriz y los cuerpos celestes* (Barcelona: Destino, 1998).

22 Lucía Etxebarría, *Amor, curiosodad, prozac y dudas* (Barcelona: Plaza y Janés, 1997).

23 Gabriele Griffin (ed.), *Outwrite: Lesbianism and Popular Culture* (London: Pluto Press, 1993), p. 1.

24 Peter Evans, 'Back to the Future: Cinema and Democracy', in *Spanish Cultural Studies: An Introduction*, ed. by Helen Graham and Jo Labanyi (Oxford: Oxford University Press, 1995), p. 327.

25 Paul Julian Smith, 'Review of *Costa Brava* (*Family Album*)', *Sight and Sound*, 7: 3 (1997), 43-44.

26 Carole Pateman 'Equality Difference and Subordination: The Politics of Motherhood and Women's Citizenship', in *Beyond Equality and Difference: Citizenship, Feminist Politics and Female Subjectivity*, ed. by Gisela Bock and Susan James (London: Routledge, 1992), 17-31, p. 19.

27 renee hoogland, *Lesbian Configurations* (Cambridge: Polity, 1997), p. 8.

Bibliography

Abelove, Henry, Michele Aina Barale and David M. Halperin, *The Lesbian and Gay Studies Reader* (London: Routledge, 1993).

Aliaga, Juan Vicente and José Miguel G. Cortes, *Identidad y diferenci*a (Barcelona: Egales, 1997).

Brooksbank Jones, Anny, *Women in Contemporary Spain* (Manchester: Manchester University Press, 1997).

Etxebarría, Lucía, *Amor, curiosodad, prozac y dudas* (Barcelona: Plaza y Janés, 1997).

————, *Beatriz y los cuerpos celestes* (Barcelona: Destino, 1998).

Evans, Peter, 'Back to the Future: Cinema and Democracy', in *Spanish Cultural Studies: An Introduction,* ed. by Helen Graham and Jo Labanyi (Oxford: Oxford University Press, 1995), 326-31.

Gibbs, Liz (ed.), *Daring to Dissent: Lesbian Culture from Margin to Mainstream* (London: Cassell, 1994).

González Frei, Irene, *Tu nombre escrito en el agua* (Barcelona: Tusquets, 1995).

Griffin, Gabriele (ed.), *Outwrite: Lesbianism and Popular Culture* (London: Pluto Press, 1993).

Guasch, Oscar, *La sociedad rosa* (Barcelona: Anagrama, 1991).

hoogland, renee, *Lesbian Configurations* (Cambridge: Polity, 1997).

Jagose, Annamarie, *Lesbian Utopics* (New York: Routledge, 1994).

Jay, Karla and Joanne Glasgow (eds), *Lesbian Texts and Contexts: Radical Revisions* (New York: New York University, 1990).

Llamas, Ricardo, *Teoría torcida: Prejuicios y discursos en torno a la homosexualidad* (Madrid: Siglo XXI/De España Editores, 1998).

Llamas, Ricardo and Fefa Vila, 'Una historia del movimiento de lesbianas y gays en el estado español', in *conCiencia de un singular deseo,* ed. by Xosé M. Buxán (Barcelona: Laertes, 1997).

Lucia-Hoagland, Sarah and Julia Penelope, *For Lesbians Only. A Separatist Anthology* (London: Onlywomen Press, 1988).

Montero, Rosa, 'El misterio del deseo: Así son y así viven las lesbianas en España', *El Pais Semanal,* 31 October 1993, 16-26.

Pateman, Carole, 'Equality Difference and Subordination: The Politics of Motherhood and Women's Citizenship', in *Beyond Equality and Difference: Citizenship, Feminist Politics and Female Subjectivity,* ed. by Gisela Bock and Susan James (London: Routledge, 1992), 17-31.

Pérez Canovas, Nicolás, *Homosexualidad, homosexuales y uniones homosexuales en el derecho español* (Granada: Comares, 1996).

Perriam, Chris, 'Gay and Lesbian Culture', in *Spanish Cultural Studies: An Introduction,* ed. by Helen Graham and Jo Labanyi (Oxford: Oxford University Press, 1995), 393-95.

Plummer, Ken (ed.), *Modern Homosexualities: Fragments of Lesbian and Gay Experience* (London: Routledge, 1992).

Richardson, Diane, 'Lesbian Identities', in *The Theory and Practice of Homosexuality,* ed. by John Hart and Diane Richardson (London: Routledge and Kegan Paul, 1981), pp. 111-24.

Smith, Paul Julian, *Laws of Desire: Questions of Homosexuality in Hispanic Writing and Film, 1960-1990,* Oxford Hispanic Studies (Oxford: Oxford University Press, 1992).

————, 'Review of *Costa Brava* (Family Album)', *Sight and Sound,* 7: 3 (1997), 43-44.

Soriano Rubio, Sonia, *Como se vive la homosexualidad y el lesbianismo* (Salamanca: Amaru, 1999).

Tusquets, Esther, *Con la miel en los labios* (Barcelona: Anagrama, 1997).

————, *El mismo mar de todos los veranos* (Barcelona: Anagrama, 1978).

Wilton, Tamsin, *Lesbian Studies: Setting an Agenda* (London: Routledge, 1995).

9   An Introduction to Julia Kristeva

Sylvie Gambaudo

In 1979, Julia Kristeva advocated the advent of a third generation of feminists in Europe, whose attitude was to distance themselves from the first two generations.[1] What she called the first wave of feminist struggle was deep-rooted in the history and political reality of the nation and identified 'with the logical and ontological values of a rationality dominant in the nation-state'.[2] The second wave disputed the former generation's politics of sameness and demanded 'recognition of an irreducible identity, without equal in the opposite sex',[3] and as such sought to detach themselves from a distrusted socio-political system which fabricated identities according to its patriarchal needs. In the third wave, to which Kristeva belongs, 'the very dichotomy man/woman as an opposition between two rival entities may be understood as belonging to *metaphysics*' (Belsey and Moore, p. 214). Instead, this third wave in the feminist struggle supports 'an *interiorisation of the founding separation of the sociosymbolic contract*' (Belsey and Moore, p. 215), that is to say any process of victimization and persecution of one group by another (whether, for example, in sexism or racism) can be analysed as a socio-cultural symptom at the very root of identity whatever the sex or colour. Kristeva is interested in participating in the creation of 'a *signifying space*' (Belsey and Moore, p. 214) within which conflicts in human relationships can be uncovered in order to explicate and modify the process of marginalization inherent in society.

Over the past thirty years,[4] she has remained devoted to defining and refining a framework to analyse what she calls 'the human enigma'.[5] Her journey can roughly be divided into three stages. Starting with a linguistic approach to the human subject, and in particular the study of language acquisition, the limits of language and psychotic discourse,[6] she developed a framework enabling an apprehension of the human prior to entry into the linguistic sphere. She then shifted her methodology towards psychoanalytic theory and practice;[7] psychoanalysis was to become the cornerstone upon which she built her *oeuvre*. More recently, Kristeva's work has shifted away from her usually specialized style towards styles accessible to a more varied audience: fictional texts,[8] transcripts of her lectures,[9] her correspondence with Catherine Clément.[10] Her interests have also diversified into various cultural concerns: neurosciences, the media, politics, education and so on. However, within this diversity emanates one essential topic, central to Kristeva's concern at the end of the millennium, which is the representation of the maternal.[11]

What follows is a presentation of Julia Kristeva's work, starting with a brief summary of the Freudian legacy leading to an explanation of how Kristeva's psychoanalysis furthers the paternalistic model. It will focus in particular on three areas of her journey: semanalysis, the failure of the paternal function and the importance of re-theorizing the maternal.

From Freud to Kristeva: The Place of the Maternal in the Process of Subjectivation

In short, Freud considered the Oedipal Phase constitutive of the subject and of gender. The child and, later on, the adolescent, renounce their desire for the mother, separate themselves from her and choose to take their place in the father's society. The Oedipal Phase, or phases, marks a departure from the maternal continent and an identification with the paternal realm. In his later work, Freud expressed his awareness of the need to research into this maternal continent, in other words to investigate the importance of the maternal function in the process of subjectivation. However, Freud did not perform this research and his legacy remains mostly that of a paternalistic theory, centred around the idea of a castrating father and his law by which the subject must abide so as to attain membership of society. The importance of theorizing the maternal and its function in society is something that Kristeva has always insisted upon and which remains central throughout her work.

Jacques Lacan takes up Freud's idea of a castrating paternal function but views this function from a different angle. Well before the Oedipal Phase, he introduces the idea of the Mirror Stage (around six months old) as the point from which the baby is able to see itself and its mother in unity. Before the Mirror Stage, Lacan believes that babies only have a fragmented apprehension of themselves. It is this unit mother-child, the dyadic unity, that paternal law is going to castrate during the Oedipal Phase. Hence, for Lacan, it is not just the male child who fears castration but the mother and the child. Paternal castration irrevocably severs the link that binds them. From the moment of castration, Lacan views the pre-oedipal relationship mother-child, the Imaginary, as lost once and for all. The linguistic subject has now fully entered the realm of the Symbolic Order ruled by the Law of the Father.

With Julia Kristeva we get an investigation of the maternal that does not annihilate the maternal in favour of the paternal, but rather offers an understanding of 'maternal' which has its place in both the pre-linguistic and the linguistic experiences of the subject.

Semanalysis

In the first stages of her work, Kristeva introduces the concept of 'semanalysis'.[12] Through semanalysis, she focuses on the materiality of language rather than its communicative functions. This materiality of language she calls the 'semiotic' and proposes the mother-child dyad as the locus of its enactment:

> I have questioned the archaic secret in language, that is to say the pre-oedipal phases dealing with the child's relationship with its mother, this imprint of the maternal upon the psyche and upon language that I call the 'semiotic' (as distinct from the 'symbolic' which is characteristic of language, of its signs and its syntax).[13]

Kristeva further proposes that semiotic activity does not stop, as Freud and Lacan theorized, with the Oedipal Phase or the child's entry into the Symbolic Order. On the contrary, she finds in linguistic production 'proof' that semiotic activity remains part of the ability to symbolize and concludes that the presence of such activity in adults represents a re-enactment or reminiscence of the mother-child relationship.[14] Moreover, Kristeva theorizes that the mother already inscribes in the baby's psyche the experience of separation and rejection that will be re-enacted during the Oedipal Phase: the mother is the one who controls and regulates the satisfaction and frustration of the baby's nurturing needs, together with what goes in and out of the baby (from food to faeces). Kristeva suggests that the maternal function rather than the paternal function sets up the child's move into language and subjectivity. The pre-linguistic child moves from material/semiotic rejection (bodily matters), dependent upon the mother's body, to linguistic/symbolic representation by bringing into play a new type of rejection: rejection of the maternal. In other words, Kristeva suggests that it is the mother who initiates the capacity to reject waste matters outside the body in the child, a 'skill' the child will re-enact in its 'rejection' of inner (psychical) matters through linguistic symbols: speech. Learning to speak is then two-fold: on the one hand, the speaking subject expresses psychical matter symbolically; on the other hand, this symbolic expression means the rejection, or in Kristevan terms 'abjection', of the maternal semiotic. This two-fold process is what enables the subject to access socio-symbolic membership.[15] Contrary to Freud and Lacan, Kristeva finds that abjection of the maternal is never perfect; she notices the presence of semiotic activity within symbolic production. Her re-thinking of the pre-oedipal and later oedipal scenes leads us to interesting findings in relation to feminism.

First, Kristeva confirms the work done by researchers like Freud and Lacan in asserting the castrating effect of language acquisition. Far from rejecting the work of those thinkers, Kristeva proposes a reconsideration of the importance of the maternal in language and the role of the mother in relation to the process of subjectivation. Paternalistic approaches tended to view the separation of the child from the mother, a separation performed by the father, as constitutive of the subject. Kristeva challenges this paternalistic focus by proposing a maternal 'function', prior to that of the castrating paternal function and preparing for it. The psychoanalytic assumption that the paternal function is to suppress the maternal, and by cultural projection the conviction (found in particular amongst radical feminists) that in a patriarchal system men suppress women, is exposed as suspect. Both become two contrasted responses to the same questionable logic. Instead, Kristeva proposes an internalized dichotomy whereby both sexes face the task of 'making' sense of their selves in relation to the maternal and paternal functions that constituted them.

Second, to posit the existence of a semiotic dimension of language disputes traditional linguistic understanding. Linguists (followers of Ferdinand de Saussure in particular) endeavour to explain and categorize language within rules: language is homogenized, meaningful and functional. It can be formalized and human communicative productions can be fully apprehended.[16] Kristeva rejects the idea of language as a finite, stable, fully symbolic structure that can be studied outside the human subject. At the same time she rejects any effort to categorize the subject of enunciation (the symbolic subject) as finite, stable and fixed. Thus, categories such as 'man' and 'woman' are, for her, metaphysical concepts rather than definitions of two distinct essences born out of a biological reality. In establishing the semiotic disposition of the subject, Kristeva also is first to posit that it is impossible to fully explain gender identity solely by means of symbolic logic and rules. If semiotic activity disrupts symbolic language, a re-enactment of the mother-child experience in the adult, it is also where the authority of the 'father' can be disrupted, questioned, renewed. This aspect of Kristeva's thinking is where her feminism is found. She is suggesting that paternal law (symbolic, social, patriarchal) is constantly challenged by the resurgence of the semiotic maternal imprinted in the individual. In this way, Kristeva believes that we are experiencing a time of crisis of identity, induced by a crisis of the paternal function,[17] and that the questioning and potential renewal of our identities within the socio-symbolic sphere rests upon a return to and reassessment of the maternal function.

Fin de siècle: The Failure of the Paternal Function

From the mid 1980s, Kristeva's work displays a pessimism about the state of democracies in Western Europe.[18] She is very critical of the political arena which she defines as a 'technocratic setup' within which the guarantors of the paternal function are:

> 'answerable but not guilty', and this means that all subjective and moral dimensions have been re-absorbed, eliminated, by the inexorable march of bureaucracy that is more and more anonymous and responsible to itself alone. There are no longer any culprits [...]: since good and evil do not exist, total bureaucracy, another version of totalitarianism, has trivialized and animalized the human.
>
> (Guberman, *Julia Kristeva*, p. 174)[19]

In the absence of a clearly defined positioning of authority, the place of power is being left vacant. Instead, we are being offered a moralizing euphoric discourse, a consensual ideology which erases problems rather than addresses them and around which we rally.[20]

Following Freud's argument on the processes at play in the foundation of civilization, Kristeva recalls that any given society requires the presence of a dominant unified power (for example, an authority figure or a political party).[21] This paternal entity acts on two levels, reminiscent of the early history of the individual. On the one hand, it performs a castrating function, repressing the individual's desire to break the constraining rules of socialization, keeping semiotic activity at bay. At the same time, it offers itself to the subject as an identificatory image, an image of power that the subject desires to appropriate for him/herself. Either the individual (or collective) will subject him/herself to this paternal invitation inside the social space and away from the maternal, or s/he will revolt against that paternal power and re-place it with his/her own.

Kristeva argues that the absence of authority means that revolt is impossible. Because the subject finds him/herself incapable of revolt against the foundations of 'power', she believes that the notion of power becomes corruptible. Instead of revolting against an (absent) paternal agency, we identify with the elusive notion of power itself and target minority groups who prevent that power from functioning.[22] The paternal function, responsible for maintaining social order is being passed on, displaced onto the next person/group. Consequently, the place of power in the Freudian sense, unified and stable, unifying and stabilizing the social sphere, remains empty. The subject is then faced with an impaired paternal function, fragmenting and destabilizing the boundaries that held the social fabric together.

As a psychoanalyst, Kristeva sees a parallel between the socio-economic situation and the disquieting loss of interest in psychical life.[23] She observes a tendency in her patients' cases towards a closing of psychical activity. In most cases, she sees a disassociation between conscious representation and the expression of affects (feelings): the affective charge has been repressed from conscious memory, offering a discourse devoid of desire. In the absence of affects, some patients seem more like automatons than human beings; their subjectivity has become pure abstraction, meaningless, defined by a series of unquestioned and unquestionable automated tasks.

Kristeva suggests that the impoverishment of psychical activity means that culture and civilization are also becoming poor. She writes quite strongly against the media which replace psychical activity with soporific ready-made 'images' inducing 'sensations'. She describes the hyper-consumption of media images as 'psychical laziness, fleeting narcissistic mirages' (Guberman, p. 173) which rest on 'the careful shunting aside of the reality of suffering and the necessity to confront such suffering with a full knowledge of the facts' (Guberman, p. 173). We use those images which are provided to us, like answers to a problem. The more the media invade our lives the less we have to make our own images. We, as humans, end where a culture of illusion, running on empty images of false hopes begins. Increasingly unable to connect emotionally with real life events, we grow bored with the banality of reality and are instead excited about the spectacle of life. A new society, built on illusions, is then slowly emerging. Media productions depict a place where 'reality' is projected onto the pages of a screen. Upon that surface, 'real life' has been altered to generate an illusory spectacle of life and death and a state of everlasting excitement. Behind this fabricated surface, there is nothing to be found of the human subject. It is this vulgarization of subjectivity, of human life, mainly but not solely by the media, that Kristeva sees as dangerous, even criminal, because illusion has become the norm and because we revere those mirages like sacred images of true life. In a society where performance and spectacle prevail, images are becoming prosthetic devices replacing the subject's absent desire. The processes at play within the psyche are no longer the source of stimulation out of which we generate language. Instead, the translation of psychical activity into language is being provided by outside stimuli such as the media. The human subject no longer processes outside information but in reverse, receives ready-made information into a quasi-hallucinated reality. The unconscious 'relationship' body/mind becomes increasingly poor and, if Kristeva is right, we can imagine a future where the primary dynamics (psychical activity) generating subjective and collective meaning will have become obsolete.[24] Instead, the 'human' subject will be the locus of a technological implant of knowledge, that is to say, a new form of subjectivity and society. In the meantime, the human subject is facing the absence of a representation of his/her desire, which is translated by an invasion of his/her psychical space by the (not yet obsolete) body, in the form of modern diseases. Stress-related diseases represent symptoms of unconscious processes which have not found release in language production. We have lost the ability to separate what belongs to the real and what belongs to the domain of artifice. Psychical processes are replaced, repositioned outside the body and mistaken for the real. In this deceptive modern discourse, drives and affection are not represented, leaving us with the impossibility of verbalizing the body. In speaking a language which denies the body its expression and its potency, we are left with a diseased body:

> [...] the 'new maladies of the soul', that contemporary psychoanalysis encounters, testify to a limited ability to work on psychical conflicts: to the extent that not only are our contemporaries unable to judge good and evil and sink in its trivialization [...] but many do not manage to represent their conflicts psychically (in sensations, words, images, thoughts), and consequently expose themselves to acts of vandalism, psychosomatic disorders, drugs.
>
> (Kristeva, *Le féminin et le sacré*, p. 69)

Towards a New Millennium: Re-theorising the Maternal

Faced with these new maladies, Kristeva believes in the merits of psychoanalytic approaches in that they can make the link between the body and the psyche; the analytic process offers the possibility of finding the lost desire of modern men and women and translating it into language: a process experienced by analysands but also by writers in '*écriture*' and by 'mothers'.

The analyst's interpretative role is two-fold; on the one hand, psychoanalytic discourse is a system of representation, that is to say a theoretical, normative construct of reality within which psychical activity occurs and is known: the paternal function is thus re-instated in the person of the analyst. On the other hand, the relationship between the analyst and the patient mobilizes the emotional and psychical representations of both protagonists. Psychoanalytic discourse is also the space where the desire of the patient is respected and maintained. Through the transference of the analysand and counter-transference of the analyst, the subject's link with the semiotic maternal is also heard and interpreted. Psychoanalysis in dealing in this way with the whole of individual history becomes the place where the human subject is able to re-write his/her own story. Psychoanalysis enables the writing of another fiction, authored by the analysand now conscious of his/her relation to both maternal and paternal functions. This form of 'textual practice', which enables the subject to re-open the space of psychical activity, is not solely granted to the psychoanalytic setting. An important part of Kristeva's writing theorizes the importance of another form of self-analysis called '*écriture*'.

'*Ecriture*' can be defined as a type of literary practice which defies discursive pretensions, on the writer's part, to omniscience and neutrality. On the contrary, '*écriture*' carries within its own discourse the diversity particular to human experience.[25] Kristeva defines '*écriture*' as a process enabling the writer, analysand or *artiste*, 'to put the neutral surface of abstract words into contact with a whole dynamic of recollection that leads us at once to recall traumas, the pains or the pleasures, and the most archaic sensations' (Guberman, p. 55). She then defines style as, 'one possibility of being in contact with our unconscious [...] our sensations' (Guberman, p. 55). Style occurs when the memory of these pains and sensations are translated into language. Writing is a journey of reconciliation between the subject's body and his/her memory, which appears to the reader as changing style. For her, it implies that the novel form would appear to offer the most potential, as it sets out to tell a story and therefore a movement in time and space which theoretical texts, for instance, cannot convey so easily.[26]

Kristeva stresses the importance of reconsidering the relationship between identity and the notion of time/space.[27] She analyses for instance the move from national identity to European identity and argues that, faced with a transcending of our geographical frontiers, we are also transcending history. Identification with the Nation (paternal) rested on identification with relationships based on production typical of it; Kristeva postulates that our identities are now founded on modes of re-production (maternal). She suggests that the loss of national frontiers, Historically, equates to the loss of symbolic supremacy and leads the Historic subject to a time previous to patriarchy, that is a matriarchal order.[28] This Historical loss and return is paralleled in the history of the individual subject from symbolic time to a time prior to the entry into language (semiotic). In this, women have a privileged role to play as they are, biologically and psychically, closer to the archaic memory of reproduction. The fact that, in spite of social crises, women still desire motherhood, indicates that beyond the collapse of the socio-symbolic contract, they carry the desire to reproduce their own species.[29] Women have then an important role to play in carrying the human race over the threshold of the crisis (death drive), into a renewed contract with the social.

This aspect of Kristeva's thought is one of the most criticized. It suggests that the logic of her position remains intrinsically connected to a form of biological determinism. In my opinion, these criticisms rest on a misinterpretation of Kristevan rhetoric. She is not suggesting a return to a division of labour between the sexes, but calling contemporary thinkers to hear/represent the silent voice of 'woman' and its potential for the renewal and survival of society as a whole. Due to the collapse of the paternal function, Kristeva sees a threat in human capability to produce significance. Hence, there is a need to re-consider those processes that occur prior to language, semiotic processes, and to find a way to re-present these processes in language to 'repair' the socio-symbolic function. This means analysing what I described as the 'maternal function', the relationship between infant and mother and the desire to reproduce that function beyond the collapse of the symbolic contract. This of course means verbalizing the silent voice of women in general and biological mothers in particular. It especially means theorizing 'motherhood' and giving it a place within the symbolic realm:

> Some women, and some men!, carry out a 'symbolic maternity' in their professional and personal lives: particularly in education and therapeutic jobs, but not just in these. I call maternal vocation, not the work, extraordinary in itself, of the genitrix or of the carrying mother, but this alchemy that leads from biology to signification, via the modulation of desire into tenderness, and into representation-sense-language-thought.
>
> (Kristeva, *Le féminin et le sacré*, p. 84)

Kristeva believes the future of that which we call 'human' rests on a re-investment of the space left vacant by a crisis of the paternal function. This means a return to the maternal time that inaugurated the onset of the symbolic. As mentioned earlier, women would have a privileged role to play because they are, biologically and also psychically, closer to the archaic memory of the maternal. However, Kristeva is always clear that the maternal disposition of the subject is not an experience solely accessible to women who have borne a child. The maternal disposition that she is putting forward can (though it need not always) occur in biological mothers, and in women and men who live out a symbolic motherhood on another level: *écriture*, or careers in education, for instance. Kristeva's early work tended to focus on studying the presence of the feminine in texts written by men. At the turn of the millennium, Kristeva has been increasingly turning her interest towards theorizing the maternal in women's texts.[30] In both cases, the tendency to emphasize the literary production of one sex is not to be equated with the greater importance of that sex over the other. Today, her position is that failing to represent maternal experience, 'Those who censor it open the path either to the robotization of our species which is already underway [...] or to a return of religion to fill the empty space' (Kristeva, *Le féminin et le sacré*, p. 85). I speculate that her 'choices' in authors are cleverly chosen and are an appropriation of a given cultural setting.

Since her early days, Kristeva has, overall, remained loyal to her early premise that gender identity rests on a positioning of the subject within the masculine/feminine dichotomy, and this whatever the sex. Her early work on the feminine in male authors enabled her to be promoted and recognized within a generally male-dominated academia. From this well-established position, she can now bring the subject of motherhood to the fore in a society which increasingly rejects its biological roots, preferring to imagine itself in a future where the human species will have done away with biological complications.

References

1   Julia Kristeva, 'Le temps des femmes', first published in *34/44: Cahier de recherche de sciences des textes et documents*, 5 (1979), 5-19; translated as 'Women's Time' and reproduced in *The Feminist Reader: Essays in Gender and the Politics of Literary Criticism*, ed. by Catherine Belsey and Jane Moore (Basingstoke: Macmillan, 1989), pp. 197-217.

2   Belsey and Moore, p. 197. This first wave is characterized by the suffragette movement and the struggle for women's existential equality with men.

3   Kristeva sees the second wave as a more revolutionary generation of women. They are influenced by the context of the May 1968 events in France, and they are more educated especially in aesthetics and psychoanalysis. (Belsey and Moore, p. 198)

4   Julia Kristeva arrived in Paris in December 1965 as a research student. She began writing and publishing in 1967.

5   Ross Mitchell Guberman (ed.), *Julia Kristeva: Interviews* (New York: Columbia University Press), p. x.

6   Julia Kristeva, *Séméiotiké: Recherche pour une sémanalyse* (Paris: Seuil, 1969); *La Révolution du langage poétique* (Paris: Seuil, 1974); *Des Chinoises* (Paris: des femmes, 1974).

7   Julia Kristeva, *Pouvoirs de l'horreur: Essai sur l'abjection* (Paris: Seuil, 1980); *Histoires d'amour* (Paris: Denoël, 1983); *Soleil noir: Dépression et mélancolie* (Paris: Gallimard, 1987); *Etrangers à nous-mêmes* (Paris: Arthème Fayard, 1988); *Les nouvelles maladies de l'âme* (Paris: Fayard, 1993).

8   Julia Kristeva, *Les Samouraïs* (Paris: Fayard, 1990); *Le Vieil Homme et les loups* (Paris: Fayard, 1991); *Possessions* (Paris: Arthème Fayard, 1996).

9   Julia Kristeva, *Sens et non-sens de la révolte* (Paris: Arthème Fayard, 1996); *La révolte intime* (Paris: Arthème Fayard, 1997). The transcripts of Kristeva's courses to research students are part of what she terms *discours direct*, literally direct discourse, that is a series of texts published raw. The books that resulted from her lecturing mark a departure from her usually elaborate, structured and condensed style. They convey not only her expertise but also the directness of speech delivery and interaction with an audience.

10 Julia Kristeva with Catherine Clément, *Le Féminin et le sacré* (Paris: Stock, 1998).

11 Kristeva has recently started publishing texts on women authors. The first volume published in 1999, *Le Génie féminin: La vie, la folie, les mots* (Paris: Fayard, 1999) is dedicated to an analysis of Annah Arendt's work.

12 See *La Révolution du langage poétique* (Paris: Seuil, 1974), translated as *Revolution in Poetic Language* (New York: Columbia University Press, 1984).

13 Kristeva with Catherine Clément, *Le Féminin et le sacré* (Paris: Stock, 1998), p. 26. All translations from the French are my own unless otherwise stated. As I am writing this piece, post-1996 texts by Kristeva have not, to my knowledge, been translated into English.

14 In particular, Kristeva often mentions the pitch, rhythms, melody of the voice. As re-enactment of the pre-linguistic baby's experience, for Kristeva, the voice is an important semiotic vector where semiotic activity can be found. Read, for instance, the touching account of Paul's analytic sessions in *Les Nouvelles Maladies de l'âme*; Paul was a child who violently refused to enter the symbolic realm which in the context of Kristeva's psychoanalytic work with him translated as a refusal to share the language of the analyst. Kristeva proceeded to 'sing' her sessions with the child, in order to reach the maternal in him, the place where he desired to be. With this singing (melodic, semiotic), she was also able to offer Paul access to symbolic language (the words sung).

15 Stuttering, for example, could be regarded as semiotic activity breaking the linearity of symbolic language; stuttering is usually regarded as a hindrance and in some cases an illness to be corrected in order to facilitate social interaction.

16 In the context of feminism, see for instance the work done to establish differences between the way women and men use language and how such readings of gender in language has led some theorists to proclaim the existence of a 'man-made language'. See Dale Spender, *Man-Made Language*, second edition

(London, Boston, Sydney and Wellington: Pandora, 1980) and to attempt the writing of a 'woman-made language' (see Suzette Haden Elgins, *Native Tongue* (New York: Daw Books, 1984).

17 In what follows, I shall be using the terms 'paternal function' and 'maternal function', 'masculine' and 'feminine' to indicate processes pertaining to gender identities rather than tasks performed according to a given biology. One of Kristeva's merits has been to avoid the pitfall of building a 'gynocentric' theory to rival phallocentrism. Although the above terms are traditionally equated with one sex only, Kristeva strives to articulate positionings of identity within the two ends of the masculine/feminine spectrum. She is not advocating the current blurring of gender identities but on the contrary calling for a diversification and multiplication of our definition of gender, and this includes parental functions.

18 For a more detailed analysis of Kristeva's account of contemporary crisis, I refer the reader to my essay 'Absence and Revolt: The Recent Work of Julia Kristeva', in *Theory, Culture and Society*, 17: 2 (forthcoming 2000).

19 Julia Kristeva interviewed by Bernard Sichère, trans. by Guberman, chapter 15, 'The Old Man and the Wolves'.

20 Consider how 'political correctness' erases conflicts born out of differences: for instance, the use of the term 'person' instead of 'man' reduces men and women to a single homogeneous term that erases differences and does not translate the conflictual reality of gender identities.

21 See Sigmund Freud, *Totem and Taboo: Resemblances between the Psychic Lives of Savages and Neurotics* (Harmondsworth: Penguin, 1938).

22 In the UK, this process of 'scapegoating' is often orchestrated by those in power who find culprits outside the very locus of power to explain social unrest. For instance in the context of gender politics: single mothers whose premeditated pregnancies translate into more Government spending on benefits, biological fathers whose parsimonious financial contribution to childcare leads to budgetary difficulties for the Government among other things. In both cases, the absence of the father on the family level is symptomatic of the wider picture of an increasingly 'fatherless' social organization. This phenomenon is never addressed as the translation of a socio-symbolic function in disarray. Instead, the 'father' State prefers to pass the blame onto the minority groups that threaten its image. This projectory discourse is usually reinforced by the media.

23 See *Les Nouvelles Maladies de l'âme* (Paris: Arthème Fayard, 1993).

24 The process of digitization of the human, once the domain of science fiction, is becoming reality. See for instance Philip K. Dick, *Do Androids Dream of Electric Sheep* (London: Panther, 1977).

25 See Julia Kristeva, *Sens et non-sens de la révolte* (Paris: Arthème Fayard, 1996), chapter 8.

26 Since the late 1980s, Kristeva herself has moved to writing novels along with theoretical texts (see footnote 8).

27 See Kristeva's interview with Jonathan Rée and her essay, 'Women's Time'.

28 History with a capital H to differentiate human History from individual history.

29 'Women' as a generic term representative of a biological group and potential. Kristeva is not suggesting that all women desire biological motherhood, but pointing out the significance of a social event; the fact that some women have children means that a desire to carry the species beyond the death threshold is present in them. Kristeva extends this life-giving potential beyond a mere biology by theorizing the maternal disposition of other groups too.

30 See her latest publications: *Le Féminin et le sacré* (Paris: Stock, 1998) and *Le Génie féminin: La vie, la folie, les mots* (Paris: Fayard, 1999).

Bibliography

Texts by Julia Kristeva

Sémeiotiké: recherche pour une sémanalyse (Paris: Seuil, 1969); *Desire in Language: A Semiotic Approach to Language*, ed. by Leon Roudiez, trans. by Thomas Gora, Alice Jardine and Leon Roudiez (New York: Columbia University Press, 1980).

La Révolution du langage poétique: L'avant-garde à la fin du XIXème siècle: Lautréamont et Mallarmé (Paris: Seuil, 1974); *Revolution in Poetic Language*, trans. by Margaret Waller (New York and Guildford: Columbia University Press, 1984).

Des Chinoises (Paris: des femmes, 1974); *About Chinese Women*, trans. by Anita Barrows (London: Boyars, 1977).

'Le Temps des femmes' in *34/44: Cahier de recherche de sciences des textes et documents*, 5, Université de Paris VII; translated as 'Women's Time' in *Signs*, 7: 1 (1981), and reproduced in *The Feminist Reader: Essays in Gender and the Politics of Literary Criticism*, ed. by Catherine Belsey and Jane Moore (Basingstoke: Macmillan, 1989), pp. 197-217.

Pouvoirs de l'horreur: Essai sur l'abjection (Paris: Seuil, 1980); *Powers of Horror: An Essay in Abjection*, trans. by Leon S. Roudiez (New York and Guildford: Columbia University Press, 1982).

Histoires d'amour (Paris: Denoël, 1983); *Tales of Love*, trans. by Leon S. Roudiez (New York and Guildford: Columbia University Press, 1987).

Soleil noir: Dépression et mélancolie (Paris: Gallimard, 1987); *Black Sun: Depression and Melancholia* (New York: Columbia University Press, 1989).

Etrangers à nous-mêmes (Paris: Arthème Fayard, 1988); *Strangers to Ourselves*, trans. by Leon S. Roudiez (New York: Harvester Wheatsheaf, 1991).

Interview with Jonathan Rée, 'Contemporary Philosophy: Talking Liberties', part 3, Channel 4 (1992).

Les Samouraïs (Paris: Fayard, 1990); *The Samurai: A Novel* (New York: Columbia University Press, 1992).

Le Vieil Homme et les loups (Paris: Fayard, 1991); *The Old Man and the Wolves*, trans. by Barbara Bray (New York and Chichester: Columbia University Press, 1994).

Les Nouvelles Maladies de l'âme (Paris: Arthème Fayard, 1993); *New Maladies of the Soul*, trans. by Ross Guberman (New York: Columbia University Press, 1995).

Possessions (Paris: Arthème Fayard, 1996)

Pouvoirs et limites de la psychanalyse, vol.1, *Sens et non-sens de la révolte* (Paris: Arthème Fayard, 1996).

La Révolte intime (Paris: Arthème Fayard, 1997).

Le Féminin et le sacré, with Catherine Clément (Paris: Stock, 1998).

Le Génie féminin: La vie, la folie, les mots, vol. 1 (Hannah Arendt) (Paris: Fayard, 1999).

Edited collections

Guberman, Ross Mitchell (ed), *Julia Kristeva: Interviews* (New York: Columbia University Press, 1996).

Other sources

Catherine Belsey and Jane Moore (eds), *The Feminist Reader: Essays in Gender and the Politics of Literary Criticism* (Basingstoke: Macmillan, 1989), pp. 197-217.

Dick, Philip K., *Do Androids Dream of Electric Sheep* (London: Panther, 1969).

Elgins, Suzette Haden, *Native Tongue* (New York: Daw Books, 1984).

Freud, Sigmund, *Totem and Taboo: Resemblances between the Psychic Lives of Savages and Neurotics* (Harmondsworth: Penguin, 1938).

Gambaudo, Sylvie, 'Absence and Revolt: the Recent Work of Julia Kristeva', *Theory, Culture and Society*, 17: 2 (forthcoming 2000).

Lechte, John, *Julia Kristeva* (London and New York: Routledge, 1990).

Smith, Anne-Marie, *Julia Kristeva: Speaking the Unspeakable*, Modern European Thinkers (London and Sterling, Virginia: Pluto Press, 1998).

Spender, Dale, *Man-Made Language*, second edition (London, Boston, Sydney and Wellington: Pandora, 1980).

Acknowledgement

I thank Nigel Prosser for his help in proofreading this piece.

10 The Quest for Identity in the Later Fiction of Simone de Beauvoir

Alison T. Holland

This chapter will look at the fictionalized accounts of the construction of femininity in *Les Belles Images* and *The Woman Destroyed* (*La Femme rompue*) within the theoretical framework provided by *The Second Sex* (*Le Deuxième Sexe*).[1] It will focus on the quest for selfhood of the central characters who, at a particular historical moment in a specific cultural context, the bourgeoisie in Paris in the 1960s, are struggling to recognize themselves within the terms of the definitions of femininity available to them. Attention will be paid to networks of images that evoke dissolution and loss of self. The textual strategies used to convey the women protagonists' fragile sense of subjectivity will be examined. It will be argued that Simone de Beauvoir's writing reproduces their sense of loss of self and disintegration of identity.

Simone de Beauvoir and the Quest for Identity

Simone de Beauvoir took up writing fiction again in 1966. Since the publication of *The Mandarins* (*Les Mandarins*) in 1954, her autobiography and the autobiographical account of her mother's death, *A Very Easy Death* (*Une Mort très douce*) had been the main focus of her writing.[2] Why did she turn to writing fiction again? In her autobiography Beauvoir tells us that, upon completing *A Very Easy Death* she promised herself that she would not write about herself again for a long time and began to think about themes not directly to do with her own experience and characters with lives very different from her own.[3] Besides, as Elizabeth Fallaize points out, Beauvoir had first turned to autobiography, in part, because of her unease about the novel form.[4] When she starts writing fiction again in the 1960s, she does so against the background of the development of the New Novel and her technique and style are radically different.[5] This is not to suggest that Beauvoir was a partisan of the New Novel, but it is clear from comments she made during interviews given in the 1960s that she did not dismiss the movement out of hand and shared a number of ideas typical of it.[6]

Although Simone de Beauvoir's later fiction focuses on the lives of women, and although the narrative voice in these texts belongs to women, it is important to bear in mind that neither *Les Belles Images* nor *The Woman Destroyed* was conceived as a feminist work as such. Indeed, it was not until the early 1970s that Beauvoir began campaigning on feminist issues and she first declared herself to be a feminist in an interview with Alice Schwarzer in 1972.[7]

Beauvoir's women protagonists are not feminist heroines who provide us with positive role models. As for Laurence, the central character in *Les Belles Images*, Beauvoir tells us:

> In this world that I dislike, no character could speak in my name [...]. I decided to look at it through the eyes of a young married woman sufficiently in agreement with those around her not to sit in judgment but also sufficiently honest to feel uneasy about her complicity. [...] The difficulty lay in making the ugliness of the world in which she was suffocating, show through her plight, without intervening myself.
>
> (*All Said and Done*, p. 138*; *Tout Compte fait*, p. 172)

Simone de Beauvoir actually wrote that she wished the ugliness to be seen 'du fond de sa nuit', literally 'from deep in her night'. She uses the same metaphor to speak of her project in the shorter fiction collected in *The Woman Destroyed* which is based on the lived experience of women in their forties who had written to Beauvoir about the break up of their marriages: '[...] they ended up no longer knowing who they were. In a different way to Laurence, they too were struggling in total ignorance and I had the idea of depicting their plight' (*All Said and Done*, p. 140*; *Tout Compte fait*, p. 175). Beauvoir's original words were, '*donner à voir leur nuit*', literally, 'to make their night visible'.[8] The image of night encompasses the bitter pain and suffering and incomprehension experienced by these women.

Beauvoir set out to reveal their plight; yet the portraits in the stories collected in *The Woman Destroyed* are far from sympathetic; readers are invited to track down Monique in 'The Woman Destroyed', as if they are tracking down the guilty character in a detective story, 'comme on dépiste un coupable' (*All Said and Done*, p. 140; *Tout Compte fait*, p. 176); Murielle in 'The Monologue' ('Monologue') is a bitter and tyrannical woman on the brink of madness; the unnamed central character in 'The Age of Discretion' ('L'Age de discrétion'), to whom I shall refer as the woman in my text, whilst she is shown more authorial understanding than the other protagonists, is, nevertheless, exposed as a self-deluded intellectual whose best work is behind her. Beauvoir was affected by the reaction to her book of certain feminists who regretted its lack of feminist activism and accused her of betrayal. This is how she defends herself against their accusations with regard to 'The Woman Destroyed':

> There is no reason at all why one should not draw a feminist conclusion from 'The Woman Destroyed': Monique's unhappiness arose from her having agreed to be dependent. But I really do not feel obliged to choose exemplary heroines. It does not seem to me that describing failure, error and bad faith means betraying anyone at all.
>
> (*All Said and Done*, p. 144; *Tout Compte fait*, p. 179)

This is a crucial point. The images of women constructed in Beauvoir's fiction are not images of women as they have to be. In constructing these images, Beauvoir is also challenging them and exposing the patriarchal power structures underlying women's situation.[9]

In her contribution to a 1964 debate, *Que peut la littérature?*, Simone de Beauvoir argues that to reveal the world is to act on it and so to change it.[10] Furthermore, she argues, one of the roles of literature is to overcome our separation from one another by revealing that what is most personal to us is shared by others. Thus, 'failure, outrages, death, must be spoken of, not to make readers despair, but, on the contrary, to try to save them from despair'.[11] Beauvoir's readership concurred; many wrote to tell her that Laurence's story was theirs: 'Yes, that is exactly our story; that is just the world we live in; and like Laurence we too feel imprisoned, caught in a trap' (*All Said and Done*, p. 138; *Tout Compte fait*, p. 173). When 'The Woman Destroyed' appeared in instalments in *Elle* magazine, Beauvoir was inundated with letters from women identifying with Monique.[12] Recognizing their own plight in Beauvoir's fiction, readers might act to change their situation. Even today, women readers continue to 'misread' 'The Woman Destroyed' and, significantly, read the end of the story, not as bleak and hopeless, but as a new beginning for Monique.[13]

Pointing up the social construction of gender, Simone de Beauvoir tells us in *The Second Sex*: 'One is not born a woman, one becomes one'.[14] What it means to be a woman is imposed on women and individual women are not free to shape the concept of femininity as they please (*The Second Sex*, p. 692; *Le Deuxième Sexe*, vol. II, p. 601). We read in the final chapter entitled 'The Independent Woman': 'A woman who does not wish to shock or to become devalued socially must live out her feminine condition in a feminine manner', '*vivre en femme sa condition de femme*' (*The Second Sex*, p. 692; *Le Deuxième Sexe*, vol. II, p. 602). Torn between their project as a human being and their destiny as a female, women experience a tension between their transcendent subjectivity and their identification with an alienated image of themselves. Becoming a woman is a hard lesson to learn.

Notions of gender and identity are tightly bound; to a great extent, our sense of self depends on our ability to fit into a gender category, to be a 'real woman'. Although it is beyond the scope of this chapter to develop fully the analysis, it is nevertheless interesting to bring together *The Second Sex* and Simone de Beauvoir's portraits of women struggling to be/become, with theories of gender performativity.[15] As developed by Judith Butler in her book *Gender Trouble: Feminism and the Subversion of Identity*, performativity is something we all do in order to inhabit a gendered identity and so become meaningful subjects.[16] We become ourselves through performing gender within a range of performances already scripted for us. In Judith Butler's words, 'identity is performatively constituted by the very "expressions" that are said to be its results' (p. 25). There is a sense in which Laurence, the central character in *Les Belles Images*, self-consciously performs 'woman' (being a woman), fails to integrate fully the definition of womanhood and finds herself wanting. For Laurence, performing 'woman' has ceased to seem self-evident or natural and her subjectivity, her sense of herself, is shaken.

Lacking a solid core of authenticity, Laurence observes the gender performances available to her through other mothers, daughters, wives, lovers and working women, and grasps onto messages she has learned and absorbed – messages from Mlle Houchet, her teacher, from Dominique, her mother, from her father, from Jean-Charles, her husband and from 'everyone' that break into the text – as she looks for the blueprints she needs. Alienated from others, as well as from herself, she is at once aware of the reiterative nature of the parts she plays (that is, that the roles she plays conform to pre-existing models) and distanced from them. The notion that somewhere else, somewhere 'wholly different and exactly the same', the same thing is happening to others, even to 'another Laurence' (p. 40; French edition, p. 32), is one that recurs almost obsessively throughout the narrative (pp. 10, 11, 40, 61, 72-73, 134, 166; French edition, pp. 7, 9, 32, 50, 60, 110, 137), yet, at the same time, Laurence is painfully aware of her separateness; the words, 'what have the others got that I haven't?' (p. 23; French edition, p. 19), echo in the text. For Laurence, 'the world is everywhere somewhere else, and there's no way of getting in' (p. 32*; French edition, p. 26).

Beauvoir's protagonists live in a world where women are defined in relation to men and through their roles as wives and mothers. *The Second Sex* presents readers with a bleak view of marriage. Whereas men 'look to marriage for an enlargement, a confirmation of their existence, but not the mere right to exist' (*The Second Sex*, p. 448; *Le Deuxième Sexe*, vol. II, p. 225), marriage is women's destiny and a disastrous one at that. The representation of marriage in Beauvoir's later fiction is equally bleak. Laurence's marriage with Jean-Charles is based in dishonesty, illustrating how '"conjugal love" leads [...] to all kinds of repressions and lies' (*The Second Sex*, p. 491; *Le Deuxième Sexe*, vol. II, p. 312). Her mother, Dominique, divorced and subsequently abandoned by her lover for a much younger woman, is painfully aware that a woman without a man is socially incomplete. In 'The Monologue', Murielle, twice divorced, suffers, in part, from being socially 'invisible' without a man. She is the epitome of the tyrannical housewife, obsessed with the fight against dirt and germs.[17] Monique has made marriage her 'career', living her life by proxy, only to be abandoned at forty-four after twenty-two years of marriage 'empty-handed, with no career, no other interest but [Maurice, her husband]', for a younger, ambitious career woman ('The Woman Destroyed', pp. 178-79; 'La Femme rompue', p. 205). In the later fiction, the one portrait of a marriage where there is room for optimism, in spite of the alleged bad faith (*mauvaise foi*) of the main character, is that between two bourgeois intellectuals at the end of their careers. Although 'The Age of Discretion' deals with the conflict between the woman and André, her husband, conflict over the meaning of what it is to grow old, conflict over their son and their relationship with him, the couple is reconciled and hope is held out at the end of the narrative that they will help each other live out the remainder of their lives together.

Motherhood, Beauvoir tells us in *The Second Sex*, contrary to the widely accepted preconception about it, is not enough to bring women fulfilment in their lives (*The Second Sex*, p. 536; *Le Deuxième Sexe*, vol. II, p. 383). Although maternal devotion may be completely genuine, 'maternity is usually a strange mixture of narcissism, altruism, dreams, sincerity, bad faith, devotion and cynicism' (*The Second Sex*, p. 528*; *Le Deuxième Sexe*, vol. II, p. 372). Only a woman who freely and sincerely chooses maternity and its responsibilities is capable of becoming a 'good mother' (*The Second Sex*, p. 537; *Le Deuxième Sexe*, vol. II, p. 385). In *Les Belles Images*, Laurence appears to some extent to embody the ideal mother, whose children are an enterprise to which she commits herself, who is 'capable of disinterestedly desiring the happiness of another,

[…], who without soul-searching seeks to transcend her own existence' (*The Second Sex*, p. 537*; *Le Deuxième Sexe*, vol. II, p. 385). In contrast, Beauvoir seeks to represent the woman, Murielle and Monique in *The Woman Destroyed* collection and Dominique in *Les Belles Images*, as tyrannical mothers to varying degrees. Murielle, who has driven her daughter to suicide, epitomizes the 'cruel aspect of maternity', the 'bad mother':

> Along with mothers who are frankly sadistic, there are many who are above all capricious; what they adore is dominating their child; when it is tiny they treat the baby like a toy: if it is a boy they make fun of his sex; if it is a girl they make her into a doll; later they want a little slave to give them blind obedience; if they are vain they show off their child like a performing animal; if they are jealous and possessive, they hide their child away.
>
> (The Second Sex, p. 529*; Le Deuxième Sexe, vol. II, p. 373)[18]

It is, thus, within the narrow terms of the roles defined for them that the women characters in Simone de Beauvoir's fiction live and look for meaning. They are wives and mothers, but who are they?

In Simone de Beauvoir's later fiction, her women protagonists experience loss of sense of self and face breakdown and madness. Laurence's subjectivity is fragile. She searches hopelessly for a sense of who she is, a sense of identity. 'She has always been a picture. Dominique has seen to that […]. Faultless child, accomplished adolescent, perfect young woman', we read in the early pages of the book (pp. 26-27*; French edition, pp. 21-22). Later she has become an 'exemplary young wife' (p. 162; French edition, p. 133), forming with Jean-Charles the 'perfect picture of the couple who still adore one another after ten years of marriage' (p. 171; French edition, p. 141). In *Les Belles Images*, mirrors, reflections, pictures, images, and the gaze of others form a dense network of symbolization. The text is a 'hall of mirrors' (*jeu de miroirs*). Laurence, watching her mother looking at herself in the triple dressing-table mirror, wonders: 'Behind the reflections twirling in the mirrors who is hiding? Maybe nobody at all' (p. 21*; French edition, p. 17). Images are associated with 'illusion', 'mirage', 'false', 'lies', 'disillusionment', and ultimately 'nothing' as Laurence loses her sense of identity: 'I didn't feel like I was playing the part of the young married woman coming home: it was worse than that. I wasn't a picture; but not anything else either: nothing' (pp. 206-207*; French edition, p. 170). Her watching herself in a mirror punctuates the text as, lacking an inner conviction of who she is, she seeks in her reflected performance the Laurence that others see in an attempt to find her self. Early in the novel, Laurence identifies with Midas, the king whose touch turned everything, including his daughter, into gold: 'Everything she touches turns into a picture' (p. 26*; French edition, p. 21). By the end of the novel, she finds the strength to refuse to bring up Catherine in the same way that she had been brought up (p. 160; French edition, p. 132) and tells Jean-Charles: 'Bringing up a child doesn't mean making them into a pretty picture…' (p. 220*; French edition, p. 182). At the end of the novel, Laurence appropriates the power of the gaze to which she has been subjected: 'She looks [Jean-Charles] straight in the eye, he looks away' (p. 221*; French edition, p. 182). Laurence has defeated Jean-

Charles, her gaze signifies her triumph. In the final lines of the novel, Laurence looks at herself in the mirror as she determines how she will go on. In her final gesture, it is as though Laurence truly sees her self for the first time.

The imagery of mirrors, reflections and images that forms such a dense network in *Les Belles Images* is also found in *The Woman Destroyed*. In this collection too, these images encapsulate the women protagonists' unstable sense of self and the fragile boundary between reality and delusion. When the woman in 'The Age of Discretion' wakes from heavy sleep, it is the reality around her that seems chimerical, dreamlike: it is 'the illusory, shimmering other side of the void into which [she] had sunk' (p. 48; 'L'Age de discrétion', p. 57). It is as if she finds herself through the looking glass.

In 'The Monologue', Murielle is preoccupied with her image. She fantasizes about writing her life story, telling the world 'the real genuine truth', and about how others would gripe when they saw her name and her photo in the shop windows (p. 77; 'Monologue', p. 90). Murielle's image/ photo is one more weapon in her all-consuming quest for revenge. She wants to be the woman in the pictures, to be seen to be rehabilitated. Murielle's monologue itself acts as a distorting mirror where values are inverted and where Murielle attempts to construct a positive image of herself as the best mother in the world.

In 'The Woman Destroyed', Monique loses her sense of self and with it her image:

> A man had lost his shadow. I forget what was happening to him, but it was terrible. As for me, I've lost my image. I didn't look at it often; but it was there, in the background, just as Maurice had painted it for me. [...] It is dark, I cannot see myself any more.
>
> ('The Woman Destroyed', p. 207*; 'La Femme rompue', p. 238.)

She has depended on Maurice to know who she is. Ostensibly cooperating with her psychiatrist but almost defiantly, Monique looks at herself in the mirror in an attempt to find herself: '"Help me," asks Doctor Marquet. All right. I will try to find myself again. I stood in front of the mirror [...]' (p. 209*; 'La Femme rompue', p. 240). Her action recalls Laurence's corresponding gesture. When Monique rereads old letters in an attempt to make sense of her relationship with Maurice, she becomes convinced that it is the memory of love that has replaced the real love they had; like an echo, the auditory equivalent of a reflection, memory has given things a ring not their own. And yet, Monique recalls, his smiles and looks had been no different. Her lament interrupts the text: '(Oh, if only I could get back those looks and those smiles!)' (p. 195*; 'La Femme rompue', p. 224). In her delirium, as her crisis deepens, it is as if reflections, echoes have become disembodied, free-floating:

> Those smiles, looks, words can't have vanished. They're floating around here in the flat. I often hear the words. A voice says in my ear, very distinctly, 'Poppet, sweetheart, darling...' If I caught the looks and smiles as they float by and popped them by surprise on to Maurice's face, then everything would be the same as before.
>
> ('La Femme rompue', p. 237)

In summary, in all the texts, images, reflections and echoes figure the frail line that divides the real and the illusory and the fragility of the women's sense of self.

The Metaphor of the Body in Beauvoir's Later Fiction

In *The Second Sex*, the body is defined not as a thing but as a situation. It is an essential element of women's situation, that is, part of the totality of our existence. It is through our bodies that we apprehend the world and it influences the scope of our existential projects.[19] This being said, the body does not establish a fixed and inevitable destiny for women, condemning us to remain in a subordinate role forever (*The Second Sex*, p. 65; *Le Deuxième Sexe*, vol. I, p. 71). Still, it is undeniable that the portrayal of women's bodies in *The Second Sex* is terribly negative. We must submit to menstruation, pregnancy, childbirth, lactation and menopause as to so many ordeals and crises, continually alienated in our bodies: 'Woman, like man, is her body, but her body is something other than herself' (*The Second Sex*, p. 61; *Le Deuxième Sexe*, vol. I, p. 67). Furthermore, the representation of female sexuality and desire in *The Second Sex* is, generally speaking, profoundly negative. As Toril Moi writes, 'the female sexual body [...] becomes an object of disgust'.[20]

In Beauvoir's later fiction, the body is a metaphor for the self and is intimately tied up with questions of identity. The body is manifestly a site of pain in *Les Belles Images* and in *The Woman Destroyed* too. *Les Belles Images* stands out from the other texts insofar as it incorporates a cluster of positive images related to the body. The body can express pleasure and through pleasure connect Laurence with her self and a sense of the real. Choice and consent preclude facticity and so disgust. When she first knew Jean-Charles: 'Suddenly one evening coming back from a drive, in the stopped car, his mouth on my mouth, the fire, the dizziness. Then, for days and weeks, I was not a picture any more, but flesh and blood, desire, pleasure' (p. 27*; French edition, p. 22). However, moments of wholeness, of 'self-coincidence' are rare in *Les Belles Images* and more frequently, the body is a source or an expression of pain. As Elizabeth Fallaize so aptly puts it, 'repression leads [...] to the inscription of [Laurence's] feelings in her body'.[21] Pain is associated with hardness and tightness but it is on eating, or rather the rejection of food and vomiting, that the text focuses. These take on explicit symbolic significance as the text progresses. Lack of appetite develops into an inability to eat and then a rejection of food and through this a rejection of her world and her self. Laurence's vomiting signifies a rejection of her self; she is emptying herself, ejecting her self: 'What have they turned me into? This woman who loves no one, indifferent to the beauties of the world, incapable even of crying, this woman that I'm vomiting up' (p. 219*; French edition, p. 181). She comes to see her refusal to eat as an expression of her revolt.

In 'The Age of Discretion' too, emotional pain is inscribed in the woman's body. The terms used to describe her pain are hyperbolic. The suffocation motif, present in *Les Belles Images*, reappears here as the woman writes of being choked by her resentment (p. 31; 'L'Age de discrétion', p. 37). Her emotional upset/bitterness against André is expressed metaphorically as a physical illness: 'Every second, calling his face, his voice to mind, I kindled the resentment that was consuming me. It was like one of those illnesses where you make your own suffering, every breath tears your lungs, and yet you are forced to breathe (p. 34*; 'L'Age de discrétion', p. 41). Pain is associated with stiffness, hardness and paralysis. Her pain is 'that iron bar in [her] chest' (p. 38; 'L'Age de discrétion', p. 45).

In 'The Woman Destroyed', the body is present in the symbolism of the text in a more muted way. Nevertheless, powerful emotion is still linked with painful difficulty in breathing. In a way similar to the pain experienced by the other women protagonists but far more understated, Monique's emotional pain is represented metaphorically as physical pain. Like Laurence, Monique suffers from loss of appetite. Her weight loss is emblematic of her suffering. More foregrounded in the text is Monique's constant bleeding that lasts some twenty-three days. The bleeding is noted in a restrained tone, gathering its symbolic power from reiteration. It is a metaphor for her loss of self, analogous to Laurence's vomiting: 'I am still bleeding. If only my life could run out of me without my having to make the slightest effort!' (p. 205*: '6 February, then with no date.'; 'La Femme rompue', p. 235: '*6 février, puis sans date.*'); 'I'm still bleeding. I'm afraid' (p. 205*; 'La Femme rompue', p. 237). Monique's self is seeping away. Not until the diary entry for the 23 February, do we read that the bleeding has stopped.[22]

In 'The Monologue', the body is an expression of Murielle's hurt, the site where she projects her anger and disappointment. And for Murielle, the body equates with perverted sexuality. Murielle's monologue returns obsessively to images of sex, which is consistently associated with dirt and disgust. The text is as much an instance of coprophilia (morbid pleasure in dung/filth), as a case of coprolalia (obsessive use of obscene language). 'The Monologue' is shocking for the obscenity and violence of its language. The whole text is hyperbolic, excessive. It confutes Murielle's claim to have renounced sex. One of her earliest childhood memories is filtered through the sordid lens that distorts all Murielle's perceptions; she remembers one 14 July when her father had lifted Nanard, her brother, onto his shoulders to see the fireworks while she had remained on the ground, trapped in the crowd that was like an animal on heat, with people's groins pressing into her face. Murielle is deprived of the light/joy/excitement that her brother is lifted up to see. Throughout the text, Murielle's disgust is focused on her mother. She accuses her of incest with Nanard. Murielle is also convinced that her mother seduced Murielle's first husband and manipulated her into marrying him to guarantee her own pleasure and Murielle's unhappiness. She visualizes the sex act in violent terms, preoccupied by animality and filth:

> It was she who hooked him at the gym and she had it off with him filthy as she was it can't have been very inviting to stuff her but with all the men she'd had before she must have known a thing or two she was the type who'd get astride the bloke I can just imagine her it's so disgusting the way women fuck.
>
> ('The Monologue', pp. 90-91*; 'Monologue', p. 105)

Murielle is reluctant to name the female genitalia although she might have chosen from an available repertoire of obscene terms. Instead, they figure as an empty space, a filthy gap: 'That old bag it makes you shudder to think of between her legs she drips with perfume but underneath she stinks […] she didn't wash […]' (p. 91*; 'Monologue', pp. 105-6). The term *'momie'* in French, mummy, adds overtones of putrefaction. The same emphasis on animality and filth recurs in Murielle's recollection of Albert's infidelity with Nina who had been her 'very dear friend'. In Murielle's delusion, her daughter Sylvie's suicide must also be linked in some way to what she defines as perverted sex. Murielle's need to sleep and the fact that she must take her sleeping drug in suppository form make up a constant refrain in the story. The images used to express this are sexual and obscene. She accuses the doctor of sadism and, appropriating and reversing a phallic image, complains: 'I can't stuff myself like a cannon' (p. 75*; 'Monologue', p. 88).

In *Les Belles Images* and *The Woman Destroyed* the text reproduces the sense of loss of self and disintegration of identity experienced by the women protagonists. It imitates their struggle for wholeness and coherence and their suffering. I shall now go on to examine briefly some of the ways in which this is achieved.[23]

One of the ways in which the integrity of character is undermined in the text is the use of character doubles, mirrored characters. A complex web of identifications between Laurence and her daughter, Catherine and the little Greek girl is built up through repetition and echoes. In Greece, watching the dancing girl 'out of her mind with music', Laurence identifies with her then identifies her with Catherine, as the joyful, life-affirming dance is transformed into a macabre dance of death: 'I too was possessed, possessed by the child who was possessed by the music. […] Child condemned to death, to an appalling death with no corpse. Life was going to murder her. I thought of Catherine whom they were murdering right then' (pp. 192-93*, 211; French edition, pp. 158, 174). Just as Laurence is appalled at the idea that the child will come to resemble her mother, so she will reject the idea that Catherine will suffer the same fate as herself. When Jean-Charles betrays Catherine by discussing her with others over dinner, Laurence feels he betrays her too. Laurence is appalled. In the text, the word *'trahison'* and the violent rape imagery are a direct link with Jean-Charles's earlier betrayal of Laurence, when, during an argument over Catherine, he brings up her breakdown that he refers to as 'a crisis of guilty conscience', confuting the sympathy and understanding he had feigned (*Les Belles Images*, p. 210 and pp. 161-62; French edition, p. 73 and p. 133).[24] The cumulative effect of textual links between Laurence and Catherine and the little Greek girl is to subvert solid boundaries of identity, thus duplicating Laurence's experience in the text.

The notion of a stable, unified identity is further put into question by the instability that is inherent in the I/she (*je/elle*) split in the narrative in *Les Belles Images*. The way the narrative voice shifts from 'I' to 'she' not only from paragraph to paragraph but also within paragraphs and even within sentences duplicates, on a textual level, Laurence's loss of psychic unity and feelings of alienation. Let us consider the opening scenes. The novel seems to open in the first person, at least, the only indicators of the origin of narrative voice are in the first person ('What have the others got that I haven't? why do I think that?').[25] Then, after the first, long, fragmented paragraph, the narrative shifts to the third person ('Laurence suggested they do a psychological test […]' p. 10*; French edition, p. 8),[26] before shifting back to the first person within a sentence: 'She's spent a lot of energy, that's why she feels depressed now, I'm cyclic' (p. 10*; French edition, p. 8). As the narrative continues, mainly in the third person, the first person narrative interposes a commentary on it. The narrative shifts to the first person again as Laurence recalls her breakdown of five years earlier and tries to convince herself that she is not about to be ill again. These shifts and ambiguities present in the opening section of the novel, are replicated throughout the text. However, by the final chapter, the balance has shifted.

Here, the first person narrative is much stronger, more sustained and it is the third person narrative that appears to intrude. Laurence determines: 'I'll go back over the trip picture by picture, word by word' (p. 186*; French edition, p. 153). She engages with and tells her own story in the first person. The third person breaks into the text intermittently in the present moment, perfectly conveying Laurence's alienation, for example, as Jean-Charles meets her at the airport. From this point 'she' erupts in the most painful moments of Laurence's story as if her 'I' is stifled and she withdraws and has recourse to the third person in order to protect herself. As Laurence's anguish reaches its climax, and as text-time and story-time reconverge, (story-time and narrative moment coincide), the narrative voice oscillates between 'she' and 'I':

> I'm jealous but above all, above all… She's breathing too fast, she's panting. […] The secret she blamed herself for not being able to find out, perhaps after all it didn't exist. It didn't exist. She has known since the trip to Greece. I was *disappointed*. The word stabs her. She presses her handkerchief against her teeth as thought to hold back the cry she is incapable of uttering. I am disappointed. I have cause to be.
>
> (*Les Belles Images*, pp. 217-18*; French edition, pp. 179-80)

Laurence's battle to face up to her pain is reproduced in the text as 'I' and 'she' succeed each other. When the narrative is picked up again as Laurence wakes from exhausted sleep, the first person voice fades once more and the narrative reverts to 'she' for the final three pages that relate Laurence's talk with Jean-Charles. The first person asserts itself only once: 'He doesn't want me to crack up again. If I hold out, I'll win' (p. 221*; French edition, p. 182). The intermittency of the first person voice at the end of *Les Belles Images* contributes to readers' lack of confidence in Laurence's stability and sense of self. The I/she split at the heart of the narrative encapsulates the way she is divided against herself and, struggling to hold on to her sense of identity, incapable of sustaining her 'I'.

I now want to go on to read the incoherence in Simone de Beauvoir's later fiction in the light of Peter Brooks's assertion that 'mental health is a coherent life story, neurosis is a faulty narrative'.[27] Nothing is meaningful in itself. We create meaning by organizing our experience. Now, insofar as Beauvoir's texts resist order and logic, insofar as they tend towards meaninglessness (which is the meaning of the texts), then the texts duplicate the women protagonists' struggle to make sense of who they are. In the textual universe Simone de Beauvoir creates, readers are disorientated and invited to share the helplessness of women trying to make sense of their lives. I am going to begin by looking briefly at temporal confusion and incoherence before going on to deal with textual disruption and fragmentation.

Simone de Beauvoir's later texts, *Les Belles Images* and *The Woman Destroyed*, refuse to convey a sense of chronology, a sense of linear logic. Readers have to work to impose a sequential pattern on events. I want to illustrate this by briefly analysing 'The Monologue', 'La Femme rompue', and *Les Belles Images*. In 'The Monologue', readers are drawn into Murielle's madness and obsession as they attempt to make sense of her monologue at the same time as they are repelled by the vulgarity and sordidness of her delusion. They are confused by the non-linear structure of the story. No concessions are made; readers piece together Murielle's history, learning a little of the puzzle at a time. Readers look in vain for linear logic in the text; incidents are related in disorder, prompted by seemingly inconsequential details. An associative logic carries the narrative forward. The past intrudes into the present and the present disrupts the narration of past events. Quoting a fairly lengthy passage in full will allow me to demonstrate this. It occurs towards the beginning of the narrative:

> It was bound to happen they're dancing right over my head. Now my night is fucked tomorrow I'll be in pieces I'll have to dope myself to see Tristan and it will be a balls-up. You mustn't! Bastards! It's all I have in life sleep. Bastards. They're allowed to trample on me and they're making the most of it. 'The pain in the arse downstairs can't kick up a fuss it's New Year's Eve.' Laugh away I'll find a way to get you back she'll be a pain in your arse the pain in the arse I've never let anyone trample on me. Albert was livid: 'No need to make a scene!' oh yes indeed there was! he was dancing with Nina crotch to crotch she was sticking out her big tits she stank of perfume but underneath there was a whiff of bidet and he was wiggling about he had a hard-on like a stag [...]
>
> They're going to break through the ceiling and come down on my head. I can imagine what they're doing its too disgusting they're rubbing against each other sex to sex it makes the slags cream they're proud as punch because the bloke's got his prick in the air. And all of them are getting ready to cuckold their best friend their very dear friend they'll do it tonight even in the bathroom not even lying down dress hitched up on their sweating arse when you go and piss you'll tread in the come like at Rose's the night I made a scene.
>
> ('The Monologue', p. 78*; 'Monologue', pp. 90-91)

In terms of events that make up the story, it emerges only gradually that Murielle's ex-husband, Albert, was unfaithful to her, with her best friend, Nina, at a party given by Rose and that Murielle, when she found out, made a scene. She is reliving those events in the present, imagining the same event taking place again, (only this time multiplied, as every guest, ['*chacun*'] is about to betray their partner), at her upstairs neighbour's where there is a noisy party going on. (If this sequence of events can be worked out, it is nevertheless virtually impossible to distinguish fantasy and reality.) The text presents readers with a baffling, disordered series of statements, an extremely convoluted narrative. The dancing in the present gives rise to Murielle's insistence that she will not allow herself to be trampled on ('*piétiner*') which prompts the memory of an incident in the past when Albert might have thought he could trample on her but when she refused to acquiesce. This memory in turn moves Murielle to imagine the present scene upstairs until her lurid, delusional vision of the present gives way once more to the painful recollection of the incident in the past. The past and present coalesce. A succession of textual echoes serves as a narrative thread, providing hinges on which the narrative pivots.

Textual Disruption

I now want to address the incoherence that stems from fragmentation and interruption. I am going to concentrate on the most fractured text of my corpus, *Les Belles Images*. The first page of the novel introduces readers into a disorienting textual universe. Laurence's monologue is fragmented by dialogue, which is in turn fragmented by Laurence's reflections. What is real is made insubstantial by a textual practice that deprives both descriptive monologue and interpolations of coherence and meaningfulness. This effect is felt in the shocking (from an unprepared reader's point of view) opening paragraph and subsequently, at different moments throughout the narrative. In the same way that Laurence's personality disintegrates, so too does the text. In the same way that her sense of the real becomes more fragile, readers experience the dissolution of the real on a textual level.

As the narrative recounts one Saturday evening at Feuverolles, an excerpt from a conversation about chic restaurants between Dominique and an anonymous interlocutor (there are no reporting clauses) is superseded by a snatch of conversation between Jean-Charles and Dufrène before Laurence's attention is caught once more by Dominique's voice and, mid-way, her conversation becomes the focus of the narrative (pp. 111-12; French edition, pp. 92-93). As the guests fight for a turn to speak, the conversation is represented with no typographical clues that it is in fact a dialogue. The distinction between dialogue and narrative is blurred. Two long sentences contain all the contradictory utterances of all of the participants in the conversation. There are, of course, no reporting clauses.

> You must admit there are books that can no longer be written, films that no one can watch any more, music that can't be listened to, but masterpieces are never dated, what is a masterpiece? Subjective criteria ought to be got rid of, it's impossible, excuse me all modern criticism is tending in that direction, what about the criteria for the Goncourt and the Renaudot, I'd like to know what they are, the winners are even worse than last year, […] not at all there's no other criterion, no objective criterion.
>
> (*Les Belles Images*, pp. 114-15*; French edition, pp. 94-95)

This irreverent representation of the conversation conveys the jostling of the guests for space to speak. Incoherence is exacerbated as, towards the end of the paragraph, the conversation seems to split into two parallel conversations happening simultaneously, the final comment apparently a response to an opinion expressed six inputs earlier, or perhaps it is simply the comment of someone unable to force their way into the conversation until now. Unorthodox punctuation (most commas are omitted within what I take to be individual utterances or contributions to the conversation), adds to the impression of speed. The text races on until a fervent remark from Mme Thiron stops everyone in their tracks and the text is brought to an abrupt halt. Not for long, it appears: 'Then they set off again...' (p. 115*; French edition, p. 95); this time, Laurence does not bother even to listen.[28]

Incoherence also derives from the fact that the text is multi-layered. Repeatedly, Laurence distances herself to make an observation then distances herself again to comment on her observation, then again to comment on her comment. This is disconcerting for readers. Encountering such layering in the text, this *'jeu de miroirs'*, with its concomitant contradictoriness, readers are invited to share Laurence's uncertainty and ultimately, her distress. In the following example, multi-layering translates Laurence's inner conflict. In this passage, she is recalling the moment during the family meal when she was forced to recognize her powerlessness in the face of the united opposition of everyone else:

> Her father and Dominique said it together: Well then? Hubert nodded his head knowingly. Laurence forced herself to eat, but it was then she had the first spasm. She knew she was beaten. You can't be right against everybody, she has never been arrogant enough to think that. (There was Galileo, Pasteur and the others that Mlle Houchet told us about. But I'm no Galileo.) So at Easter – she'll certainly be well again by then, its only a matter of a few days, you don't feel like eating for a few days and then of course things get back to normal – they'll take Catherine to Rome. Laurence's stomach cramps. Perhaps she won't be able to eat for a long time.
>
> (*Les Belles Images*, p. 212*; French edition, p. 175)

As Laurence is torn by painful emotions, so too the text is divided against itself. Laurence's anguish is manifest.

Multi-layering can obscure the boundary between the real and the imaginary. This effect is achieved at the point in the text where Laurence finds Dominique devastated after a violent confrontation with Gilbert:

> Gilbert rang the doorbell at ten o'clock, she thought it was the concierge, she opened the door. Patricia went straight to Gilbert to cry in his arms, and Lucile was shouting, he kicked the door shut behind him, he stroked Patricia's hair, so tenderly, soothed her, and there in the hall he'd shouted at her, slapped her, he'd grabbed her by the collar of her blue dressing-gown and dragged her into the bedroom.
>
> (*Les Belles Images*, p. 150*; French edition, p. 124)

The text acquires an hallucinatory quality as two narratives are blended in one, the receipt of the letter and Gilbert's visit. The passage is marked by abrupt shifts in tone, a convulsive rhythm. Reported in the third person, the events are, nevertheless, implicitly recounted by Dominique herself. Thus the narrative situation that prevails in the novel as a whole is paralleled here in this narrative within a narrative.

I now want examine how Simone de Beauvoir's texts are disrupted at a syntactical level. Syntax and punctuation, which establishes syntax, are important because, as Roger Fowler points out, 'syntax exercises a continuous and inexorable control over our apprehension of literary meaning and structure'.[29] I construe transgressive (disordered and fragmented) syntax as a duplication in the text of the women protagonists' fragile subjectivity. For, as Alice Jardine puts it, 'disturbances in the syntactic chain – the insurgence of rhythm and intonation into the ranks of grammatical categories for example – may be seen as an attack against the ultimate guarantor of our identity'.[30]

'The Monologue' is Simone de Beauvoir's most transgressive text and her most 'crazy'. That it is perceived as such is, to a considerable extent, owing to its eccentric syntax. It is in this text that her (mis)use of punctuation is flagrant. The text is not without punctuation but conventional rules of punctuation are flouted. A sense of disarray is generated as readers, largely deprived of boundaries normally marked by punctuation, attempt to make sense of the text. Sometimes, sentence-internal punctuation is missing. At other times, confusion arises because utterances that might normally be divided into two sentences or more are amalgamated, as when Murielle goes over Sylvie's suicide, seeking to disculpate herself: 'Yes, if I were one of those mothers who get up at seven in the morning she would have been saved I live according to another rhythm there's nothing criminal about that how could I have guessed?' (p. 96; French edition, p. 112). Whole sections of text lack punctuation. Readers encountering series of undifferentiated clauses must themselves impose order on the text. Disorientation is increased, when clauses they might differentiate appear jumbled. This is the case, for instance, early in the text where Murielle imagines her family celebrating New Year without her. Noisy, festive people in the street ('Bastards! They're shattering my eardrums […]', p. 75*; French edition, p. 87) become conflated with Murielle's family ('Bastards! They go round and round in my head I can hear them I can see them', p. 75*; French edition, p. 88) and we read:

> I don't give a shit about them only they mustn't stop me from sleeping; it makes you fit for the loony bin you admit everything the true and the false they needn't count on that though I'm strong by nature they won't get me.
>
> ('The Monologue', p. 76*; 'Monologue', p. 88)

I believe few readers are not forced to reread such utterances a number of times in order to make sense of them. In so doing, in repeating a fragment of text over and over, they replicate the obsessions that grip Murielle.

Elsewhere, disarticulated, disjointed syntax translates Murielle's distress. When she burns some incense because she imagines she smells vomit, she is reminded of Sylvie's funeral: 'This smell of incense is the same as at the funeral service; the candles the flowers the coffin: my despair. Dead; it was impossible!' (pp. 89-90*; 'Monologue', p. 104). The convulsive rhythms of this jerky syntax are unmistakable. In addition, series of short, asyntactic and disarticulated sentences suggest breathlessness, duplicating a rapid intake of breath. This can suggest Murielle's being rocked by powerful emotions. For instance, when she remembers her father: 'My father loved me. No one else. It all stems from that' (p. 78*; 'Monologue', p. 90). Or when she relives the pain of Sylvie's death: 'Sylvie died. Five years ago already. She is dead. For ever. I can't bear it' (p. 90*; 'Monologue', p. 104). This example occurs just after the example of convulsive syntax quoted above and is immediately followed by Murielle's breaking down and uttering desperate pleas: 'Help I'm suffering I'm suffering too much someone get me out of this I don't want to sink right down again no help me I can't stand it anymore don't leave me alone…' (p. 90*; 'Monologue', p. 104).

Together, the lack of sentence-internal punctuation in much of the text and series of short, asyntactic utterances have the effect of hurrying readers along.[31] Murielle's racing thoughts and rapid speech are mirrored in the text. The representation of Murielle's telephone call to Tristan is exemplary. Murielle's voice leaves no room for Tristan's. Long, unpunctuated sentences reproduce her relentless onslaught. Early in the call, Murielle puts her case to Tristan in an utterance which, without a pause, takes up thirteen lines of print in the French edition. The utterance itself appears in more than three pages of text without a paragraph break. (See p. 99; French edition, p. 115.) Tristan's brief utterances appear in the text only as blanks (ellipses), their import is gathered only from Murielle's response. (See pp. 99-101; French edition, pp. 114-17.) Readers, like Tristan, can experience Murielle's monologue, her only weapon, as an assault.[32] It seems to pin us down.

The effects identified in 'The Monologue' are not unique to that text. Many of the same techniques are found in *Les Belles Images*. It, too, is characterized by contorted, transgressive syntax. Syntax is often broken and disarticulated, conveying pain and the pangs of Laurence's anguish.[33] One of the most striking examples occurs at the point in the text where Laurence realizes the enormous responsibility she bears as a parent: 'A burning stab through the heart. Anxiety, remorse' (p. 164*; French edition, p. 135).[34] Contorted syntax recurs when Laurence remembers her depression five years earlier: 'It seemed to me that I had no future anymore: Jean-Charles, the children had one; not me; so what was the point in improving my culture?' (p. 53*; French edition, p. 43). And spasmodic syntax translates the intense emotion that destabilizes Laurence as she watches the little Greek girl dance.

Disarticulation is especially marked during the culmination of Laurence's breakdown that has been building up throughout the novel. Laurence considers and rejects the idea that jealousy is at the root of her collapse: 'Oedipus not properly dealt with, my mother still my rival. Electra, Agamemnon. Was that why Mycenae moved me so much? No. No. Nonsense' (p. 217*; French edition, p. 179). The repressed emotion that is giving rise to her inner conflict is her disappointment with her father. Laurence's pain at recognizing and naming her disappointment is conveyed by broken syntax, duplicating her breathlessness that is denoted in the text: 'I am jealous but above all, above all…' (p. 217; French edition, p. 179). Laurence dozes off, exhausted after confronting her pain and wakes to find Jean-Charles there. Her refusal to see the doctor is expressed in disarticulated syntax: '"No, never! I won't let myself be manipulated." She shouts: "No! No!"' (p. 218*; French edition, p. 180). Laurence's struggle to find a way forward is related in fractured, convulsive syntax:

She falls back on her pillow. They will force her to eat, they'll make her swallow it all; all what? Everything she's vomiting, her life, the life the others lead with their bogus love affairs, their concern with money, their lies. They'll cure her of her refusals, of her despair. No. Why no? The mole that opens its eyes and sees that it's dark, where does that get it? Close them again. And what about Catherine? Should her eyelids be nailed shut? 'No': she's shouted out loud. Not Catherine. I won't let them do the same thing to her as they did to me. What have they turned me into? This woman who loves no one, indifferent to the beauties of the world, incapable even of crying, this woman that I'm vomiting up. Catherine: not like me, open her eyes at once and perhaps a gleam of light will reach her, perhaps she'll get out. Out of what? Out of this darkness. Out of ignorance, of indifference. Catherine… She sits up suddenly.

(*Les Belles Images*, p. 219*; French edition, pp. 180-81)

This paragraph, quoted in full because it exemplifies Simone de Beauvoir's use of fragmented, disrupted syntax, begins with Laurence falling back on her pillow and ends with her sitting up, a reversal that marks a critical moment, a turning point for her. Laurence has found in herself the strength to challenge Jean-Charles and fight for her daughter. The intense emotions that are destabilizing Laurence are paralleled in the unsettled, disrupted syntax of the passage.

In conclusion, we have seen that Simone de Beauvoir's women protagonists are engaged in a struggle to recognize themselves within the terms of the definitions of femininity available to them and the roles of wife and mother, roles they must either play or be excluded from but cannot ignore. Powerful images communicate the painful sense of dissolution and loss of self that these women experience. Moreover, through the use of character doubles and unstable narration, through temporal confusion and incoherence stemming from fragmentation and interruption, and through disrupted syntax, the text itself duplicates the disintegration of their identities.

Today, *The Second Sex* remains an influential text. Moving testimony from young women at a recent international conference confirms the view that its themes are as relevant now as when it was first published.[35] Generations of readers continue to respond to *Les Belles Images* and *The Woman Destroyed*, finding in them a reflection of their concerns as they search for a sense of identity. In the third millennium, women will go on reading Simone de Beauvoir's fiction to understand who they are and to change.

References

1   Some of the material in this chapter was first conceived in a brief paper I presented at the Cinquantenaire du Deuxième Sexe in Paris in January 1999, under the title 'The Quest for Self in *Les Belles Images*'. *Les Belles Images*, coll. folio (Paris: Gallimard, 1966); translated as *Les Belles Images* by Patrick O'Brian (London: Collins, 1968). *La Femme rompue*, coll. folio (Paris: Gallimard, 1968), translated as *The Woman Destroyed* by Patrick O'Brian (London: Fontana, 1971). *Le Deuxième Sexe*, 2 vols, coll. folio (Paris: Gallimard, 1949), translated as *The Second Sex* by H. M. Parshley (Harmondsworth: Penguin, 1975). The English translations of *Les Belles Images* and *La Femme rompue* are currently out of print. My text refers to the English editions cited above and, where indicated (*), adapts inaccurate translations in quotations.

2   *Les Mandarins*, coll. folio (Paris: Gallimard, 1954); translated as *The Mandarins* by Leonard M. Friedman, (London: Fontana, 1982). *Une Mort très douce*, (Paris: Gallimard, 1964), translated as *A Very Easy Death* by Patrick O'Brian (Harmondsworth: Penguin, 1969).

3   *Tout Compte fait*, coll. folio, (Paris: Gallimard, 1972), p. 169, translated as *All Said and Done* by Patrick O'Brian (Harmondsworth: Penguin, 1987), p. 135.

4   Elizabeth Fallaize, *The Novels of Simone de Beauvoir* (London: Routledge, 1988), p. 119.

5   The French writer Alain Robbe-Grillet led debate about the New Novel (*nouveau roman*) in the 1950s and 1960s. In his avant-garde, experimental anti-novels, traditional characteristics of the novel such as plot, characterization and narrative were rejected.

6   See, for example, the interview published in Francis Jeanson, *Simone de Beauvoir ou l'entreprise de vivre* (Paris: Seuil, 1966), p. 295. (A summary of the interviews with Jeanson that lasted four hours can be found in   Claude Francis and Fernande Gontier, *Les Écrits de Simone de Beauvoir: La vie – L'écriture* (Paris: Gallimard,   1979), pp. 220-21). See also the interview with Ved Solverg Saetre, in *Vinduet*, 3 (1968), 196-201. Summary and extracts translated from Norwegian in Francis and Gontier, *Les Écrits*, pp. 233-34, p. 233.

7   Interview first published in *Le Nouvel Observateur*, 14 February 1972, pp. 47-54. Reprinted in Alice Schwarzer, *Simone de Beauvoir aujourd'hui: Six entretiens* (Paris: Mercure de France, 1984), pp. 27-51, translated by Marianne Howarth in *Simone de Beauvoir Today: Conversations 1972-1982* (London: Chatto and Windus. The Hogarth Press, 1984), pp. 29-48. See also Simone de Beauvoir's interview with Alice Jardine, *Signs*, (Winter 1979), 224-36, especially p. 235, where she explains her position on feminism.

8   O'Brian's translation reads: 'I had the idea of speaking about their darkness and making it evident' (p. 140).

9   An interesting discussion of the shortcomings of 'Images of Women' criticism can be found in Toril Moi, *Sexual Textual Politics: Feminist Literary Theory* (London: Methuen, 1985), pp. 42-49. In particular, she deals with the demand for the representation of female role-models in literature, pp. 47-48.

10 *Que peut la littérature?*, ed. by Yves Buin (Paris: Union Générale d'Éditions, 1965), pp. 73-92. Literally translated, the title means: 'What can literature do?'. Beauvoir is echoing Sartre's ideas on commitment in literature. See Jean-Paul Sartre, *What is Literature?*, trans. by Bernard Frechtman (London: Methuen, 1978).

11 'Il faut parler de l'échec, du scandale, de la mort, non pas pour désespérer les lecteurs, mais au contraire pour essayer de les sauver du désespoir.' *Que peut la littérature?*, p. 92.

12 In fact, Beauvoir believed that many of these women had misread her book. See *All said and Done*, p. 142 (*Tout Compte fait*, p. 177-78). For a discussion of the way in which Beauvoir's writing practice undermines her declared intentions in this text see Toril Moi, 'Intentions and Effects: Rhetoric and Identification in Simone de Beauvoir's "The Woman Destroyed"', in Toril Moi, *Feminist Theory and Simone de Beauvoir*, (Oxford: Blackwell, 1990), pp. 61-93.

13 Moi, 'Simone de Beauvoir's "The Woman Destroyed"', p. 61.

14 *The Second Sex*, p. 295*. Parshley's translation reads: 'One is not born, but rather becomes, a woman'. The much quoted original French is: 'On ne naît pas femme: on le devient' (*Le Deuxième Sexe*, vol. II, p. 13).

15 For a useful introduction to these theories, see Sarah E. Chinn, 'Gender Performativity', in *Lesbian and Gay Studies: A Critical Introduction*, ed. by Andy Medhurst and Sally Munt (London: Cassell, 1997).

16 Judith Butler, *Gender Trouble: Feminism and the Subversion of Identity* (London: Routledge, 1990).

17 For Beauvoir's devastating depiction of women obsessed with housework, see *The Second Sex*, pp. 470-71; *Le Deuxième Sexe*, pp. 268-69.

18 Parshley has extensively cut this passage in his English translation.

19 *The Second Sex*, p. 66; *Le Deuxième Sexe*, vol. I, p. 73. Parshley's translation reads: 'it is the instrument of our grasp upon the world, a limiting factor for our projects'. In the French, the term *'esquisse'* meaning preliminary sketch is used to convey the influence of our bodies on our existential projects. Beauvoir's text echoes what Maurice Merleau-Ponty wrote in *Phénoménologie de la perception* (Paris: Gallimard, 1945).

20 *Simone de Beauvoir: The Making of an Intellectual Woman* (Oxford: Blackwell, 1994), p. 168. As Moi suggests, there are arguments to support the view that the sexuality represented in *The Second Sex* is sexuality as it is under patriarchy, not sexuality as it necessarily must be. For a discussion of these arguments, see *The Making of an Intellectual Woman*, p. 171.

21 Fallaize, *The Novels*, p. 135.

22 This metaphor of bleeding as loss of self is taken up and developed by Marie Cardinal in *Les Mots pour le dire*, (Paris: Grasset, 1975). Her heroine's bleeding stops as she rebuilds her personality/self in psychotherapy.

23 Although these aspects of Simone de Beauvoir's writing practice might be illustrated by a close reading of all the texts under consideration, the textual strategies being present to a greater or lesser extent in *Les Belles Images,* and in the three stories in *The Woman Destroyed,* in each case I have opted to consider a particular feature in just one, two, or sometimes three, texts that best exemplify it. I do not discuss 'The Age of Discretion' here but the disruptive textual strategies in question are by no means absent from the least transgressive text of my corpus. Of course, the text does not simply present a pre-existing fixed identity but characters construct themselves/are constructed by their narratives. In 'The Woman Destroyed', Monique writes her diary precisely in order to forge an identity, to discover who she is. Aware that her diary is not a repository of absolute truth, she continues to keep it all the same: 'I have taken up my pen again not to go back over the same ground but because the emptiness within me, around me, was so vast that I needed the movement of my hand to reassure myself that I was still alive' (p. 194*; 'The Woman Destroyed', p. 223). The process of character construction is referred to explicitly in the text. Monique's psychiatrist insists that she writes her diary and she is in no doubt as to his reasoning: 'he is trying to get me interested in myself again, to give me back my identity' (p. 208*; 'The Woman Destroyed', p. 239).

24 As Jane Heath argues, Laurence's identification with Catherine heightens Laurence's desire to protect Catherine in that 'Catherine's escape is to some extent Laurence's too'. *Simone de Beauvoir* (London: Harvester Wheatsheaf, 1989), p. 133.

25 These might well, of course, be taken for first person interpolations in a third person narrative.

26 The psychological test, *le test du passeur* (the ferryman's test) is described by Elizabeth Fallaize in *The Novels,* p. 141, note 21. As she points out, the test is incomprehensibly translated by O'Brian as the test 'about the man who takes you over the frontier'.

27 Peter Brooks, 'Psychoanalytic Constructions and Narrative Meanings', *Paragraph,* 7 (1986), 53-76, pp. 53-54.

28 The distinction between dialogue and narrative is also blurred on p. 39 (French edition, p. 32) where Laurence's conversations with Lucien, her lover, have a pantomime quality.

29 Roger Fowler, *A Dictionary of Modern Critical Terms* (London: Routledge, 1987), p. 243.

30 Alice Jardine, 'Pre-texts for the Transatlantic Feminist', *Yale French Studies,* 62 (1981), 220-36, p. 234.

31 Readers attempting to read unpunctuated sections of text aloud can actually experience breathlessness, as they are deprived of the breathing space punctuation provides.

32 Note the epigraph from Flaubert: 'The monologue is her form of revenge.'

33   I am reminded of what Julia Kristeva says about Marguerite Duras in an interview with Susan Sellers: 'It's through being imperfect that Duras' sentences translate suffering rather than in the fireworks of musical and vocal pleasure we find in Joyce. For Duras, the expression of pain is painful'. *Women's Review*, 12 (1986), 19-21, p. 21.

34   An alternative analysis of such syntax is to read it as sentences that are fragmented and the fragments separated by full-stops. See Liisa Dahl's discussion of James Joyce's expressionistic sentences in 'The Attributive Sentence Structure in the Stream of Consciousness Technique with Special Reference to the Interior Monologue used by Virginia Woolf, Joyce and O'Neill', *Neuphilogische Mitteilungen*, 68 (1967), 440-54, pp. 449-50.

35   The Cinquantenaire du Deuxième Sexe in Paris in January 1999.

Bibliography

Works by Simone de Beauvoir

Le Deuxième Sexe, 2 vols., coll. folio (Paris: Gallimard, 1949); *The Second Sex*, trans. by H. M. Parshley (Harmondsworth: Penguin, 1975).

Les Mandarins, coll. folio (Paris: Gallimard, 1954); *The Mandarins*, trans. by Leonard M. Friedman (London: Fontana, 1982).

Une Mort très douce (Paris: Gallimard, 1964); *A Very Easy Death*, trans. by Patrick O'Brian (Harmondsworth: Penguin, 1969).

Les Belles Images, coll. folio (Paris: Gallimard, 1966); *Les Belles Images* trans. by Patrick O'Brian (London: Collins, 1968).

La Femme rompue, coll. folio (Paris: Gallimard, 1968); *The Woman Destroyed*, trans. by Patrick O'Brian (London: Fontana, 1971).

Tout Compte fait, coll. folio (Paris: Gallimard, 1972), *All Said and Done*, trans. by Patrick O'Brian (Harmondsworth: Penguin, 1987).

Lecture

Contribution to a 1964 debate on literature published in *Que peut la littérature?*, ed. by Yves Buin (Paris: Union Générale d'Éditions, 1965), pp. 73-92.

Interviews

'Interview with Simone de Beauvoir', Saetre, Ved Solverg, in *Vinduet*, 3 (1968), 196-201. Summary and extracts in Claude Francis and Fernande Gontier, *Les Écrits de Simone de Beauvoir: La vie – L'écriture* (Paris: Gallimard, 1979).

Francis and Gontier, *Les Écrits*, pp. 233-34.

Interview first published in *Le Nouvel Observateur*, 14 February 1972, pp. 47-54. Reprinted in Alice Schwarzer, *Simone de Beauvoir aujourd'hui: Six entretiens* (Paris: Mercure de France, 1984), pp. 27-51, trans. by Marianne Howarth in *Simone de Beauvoir Today: Conversations 1972-1982* (London: Chatto and Windus, The Hogarth Press, 1984), pp. 29-48.

Interview with Alice Jardine, *Signs*, (Winter 1979), 224-36.

Secondary sources

Brooks, Peter, 'Psychoanalytic Constructions and Narrative Meanings', *Paragraph*, 7 (1986), 53-76.

Butler, Judith, *Gender Trouble: Feminism and the Subversion of Identity* (London: Routledge, 1990).

Cardinal, Marie, *Les Mots pour le dire* (Paris: Grasset, 1975).

Chinn, Sarah E., 'Gender Performativity', in *Lesbian and Gay Studies: A Critical Introduction*, ed. by Andy Medhurst and Sally Munt (London: Cassell, 1997).

Dahl, Liisa, 'The Attributive Sentence Structure in the Stream of Consciousness Technique with Special Reference to the Interior Monologue used by Virginia Woolf, Joyce and O'Neill', *Neuphilogische Mitteilungen*, 68 (1967), 440-54.

Fallaize, Elizabeth, *The Novels of Simone de Beauvoir* (London: Routledge, 1988).

Fowler, Roger, *A Dictionary of Modern Critical Terms*, (London: Routledge, 1987).

Francis, Claude and Fernande Gontier, *Les Écrits de Simone de Beauvoir: La vie – L'écriture* (Paris: Gallimard, 1979).

Heath, Jane, *Simone de Beauvoir* (London: Harvester Wheatsheaf, 1989)

Jardine, Alice, 'Pre-texts for the Transatlantic Feminist', *Yale French Studies*, 62 (1981), 220-36.

Jeanson, Francis, *Simone de Beauvoir ou l'entreprise de vivre* (Paris: Seuil, 1966).

Kristeva, Julia, 'A Question of Subjectivity', an interview with Susan Sellers, *Women's Review*, Number 12, 19-21.

Merleau-Ponty, Maurice, *Phénoménologie de la perception* (Paris: Gallimard, 1945).

Moi, Toril, *Sexual Textual Politics: Feminist Literary Theory* (London: Methuen, 1985).

Moi, Toril, 'Intentions and Effects: Rhetoric and Identification in Simone de Beauvoir's "The Woman Destroyed"', in Toril Moi, *Feminist Theory and Simone de Beauvoir* (Oxford: Blackwell, 1990), pp. 61-93.

Moi, Toril, *Simone de Beauvoir: The Making of an Intellectual Woman* (Oxford: Blackwell, 1994).

Sartre, Jean-Paul, *What is Literature?*, trans. by Bernard Frechtman (London: Methuen, 1978).

11 Discursive Configurations of Identity in *El cuarto de atrás* and *Crónica del desamor*

Vanessa Knights

El cuarto de atrás (*The Back Room*), Carmen Martín Gaite's first post-Franco novel, was published in 1978 at a critical juncture in recent Spanish history. This was the year of the new Spanish Constitution which recognized the principle of equality for all in Article 14:

> All Spaniards are equal before the law without there prevailing any form of discrimination whatsoever for reasons of birth, race, sex, religion, opinion or any other condition or circumstance, either personal or social.[1]

A year later Rosa Montero, already acclaimed as a journalist and interviewer, published her first novel, *Crónica del desamor* (*Chronicle of Unlove*).[2] 1979 may perhaps be regarded as the key year for the development of the post-Franco feminist movement in Spain. At the mass meeting held in Granada the ever-widening schism between double and single militancy feminists appeared to have become unbreachable as the conference dissolved into an acrimonious debate. These divisions broadly correspond to older, militant, anti-Franco feminists who were linked to political parties and younger feminists, known as *independientes*, who had grown up in a more liberal Spain and tended to reject the formal political arena due to feelings of anger and disappointment with legal or juridical equality; an equality which seemed to exist more in theory than in practice. The discourse of these independent groups has tended to focus on the issues of female sexuality and the fight for reproductive rights. This reflects the influence, particularly since the early 1980s, of Italian feminists, such as Carla Lonzi, and French theorists, such as Luce Irigaray and Annie Leclerc, on difference feminism in Spain. However, the concepts of equality and difference, as promoted by double and single militancy feminists respectively, are not mutually antithetical. Being equal does not by necessity imply homogeneity or being identical and the pursuit of equality should not imply the suppression of diversity. Within feminist theory there is a need to reformulate the concepts of equality and difference in a way which does not conflate equality with identifying with the normative dominant model (in the case of a patriarchal society, the masculine) or limit difference to binary gender divisions. The recognition of differences between women, however, does not obviate the strategic need for an operative collective or generic identity as recognized in recent Spanish feminist theorizing of subjectivity and identity.[3] An operative, rather than substantive or essentializing, generic would be contingent and politically assumed in order to give agency in a particular context.

Metafiction and Writing Women

I will be arguing that both collective and personal identity are formulated as shifting discursive configurations in the highly self-referential texts, *El cuarto de atrás* and *Crónica del desamor*. Both of these texts may be inserted into the trend noted by many commentators towards metafiction – fiction about the narrative process in the post-Franco period.[4] *El cuarto de atrás* relates how through the course of a stormy night, the narrator C., who is closely identified with the author herself, converses with a stranger. As they talk, a stack of pages grows beneath his hat. At the close of the novel the narrator falls asleep and is later awoken by her daughter. The stranger has gone but before leaving he has ordered the pages which the narrator begins to read. They are marked 'El cuarto de atrás' and begin with the same phrase as the novel. *Crónica del desamor* interweaves the stories of several women all related in some manner to the principal protagonist, Ana. She works as a journalist, writing articles with a feminist slant but what she would like to do is to write a book about the everyday life of her and her friends. As we progress through the novel, we come to identify the book which we are reading with the book which Ana had thought about writing at the beginning of *Crónica del desamor*, had attempted to start, whilst on holiday with her mother and son, and finally feels ready to write by the close of the novel. Robert Spires argues that the tendency towards metafiction was a reaction against the illusion of absolute truth and authority as embodied in the monologic discourse of the Franco regime and a celebration of the creative process once censorship had been removed.[5] More specifically, metafiction has been isolated by both Concha Alborg and Phyllis Zatlin as the most important unifying thread in Spanish women's fiction of the 1980s.[6] I would argue that in the case of women writers, this was not only a reaction against the discourse of the Franco regime, but also against hegemonic patriarchal discourse in which the masculine generic is conceived of as the agentive subject/producer of discourse thereby invalidating alternative discursive practices. By empowering female protagonists/narrators through the creative process these writers subvert phallologocentric writing practices in which the masculine is privileged.

Patricia Waugh suggests that metafiction is a form of exploring social and cultural conscience when a society is going through a period of change (p. 3). Previous social and cultural formations are shown to be of a constructed rather than given, nature and narratives are written which try and make sense of the process of change. The transition period in Spain has certainly seen many significant changes in women's position in society and this is reflected in their narrative. Both of the texts I will be analysing chronicle these changes albeit with different temporal and generational emphases. *El cuarto de atrás* looks to the past and the narrator's memories invoke the norms of behaviour for women who were children during the Civil War and grew up under the Franco dictatorship. In contrast, *Crónica del desamor* focuses on the then contemporary moment of the immediate post-Franco years and documents issues important to the women's movement in that context including illegal abortion

(abortion was not legalized until 1985 and then in a limited fashion), the (un)availability of contraceptives (legalized in 1978), domestic violence, marital rape, single mothers, inequality, and sexual harassment in the workplace. The female characters portrayed are on the whole the daughters of the generation depicted in *El cuarto de atrás*.[7] These texts are valuable socio-historical documents, which can be inserted into the trend for women writers to produce testimonial literature in the late 1970s. Isabel Romero, Isabel Alberdi, Isabel Martínez and Ruth Zauner in their discussion of women's narrative and feminism in the 1970s describe the narrative of this period as an auto-analytical literature which asks the questions 'Who am I?', 'What is my role?'.[8] Both C. of *El cuarto de atrás* and Ana of *Crónica del desamor* attempt to define the female self through textual means which protest against the dominant parameters of patriarchal discourse. These novels appear to reflect a need, at that time in Spain, for women to question prevailing cultural paradigms. Thus, in these highly self-reflexive texts, identity is shown to have been constructed within a particular socio-historical moment and it can therefore be deconstructed. Consequently the key question asked in these first person narratives becomes not only 'Who am I?' but perhaps more crucially 'How am I represented?' I would argue that by foregrounding the discursive nature of these texts, Martín Gaite and Montero enter into negotiation with the realist mode to explore how experience is mediated through discursive practice to produce configurations of identity. They combine the commitment to a seemingly referential, testimonial narrative of self-discovery with an aesthetically self-conscious experimental writing which represents experience whilst interrogating the very premises of a representative fiction.

Representing Experience and Stylistic Experimentation

Many women writers gaining prominence in the 1980s were professionals in the tertiary sector and a particularly high proportion were journalists, literary critics or university lecturers.[9] They are thus highly conscious of the use and influence of language. Martín Gaite has combined her career as an author with that of literary critic and, as already noted, Montero was renowned as a journalist when she published *Crónica del desamor*. Indeed, the majority of critical reactions to *Crónica del desamor* point out its journalistic underpinning and the question has been raised as to whether it constitutes propaganda or art.[10] This debate has no doubt been fuelled by the author's own comments on the dust-jacket of the Debate edition of the novel:

> A novel? No, I don't consider my book to be a novel. I think that *Crónica del desamor* is just that, a chronicle without pretensions, a rapid look at the world around us, an approximation to the everyday problems we all confront. And I would be happy if it turned out to be suggestive in the slightest.

Eunice Myers, whilst admiring the boldness of the novel's approach to previously taboo issues, censures Montero for allowing polemics to inhibit the action (p. 112). In contrast, Catherine Davies draws a useful analogy with nineteenth-century realist narrative, which also crossed the demarcations of genre, mixing fiction and documentary, to produce a fiction of debate.[11] A prominent feature of such a fiction would be the replacement of narrative techniques such as the detailed delineation of character by the representation of issues such as the position of women within a patriarchal society. Miguel Martínez described *Crónica del desamor* as a 'vitalizing variant' within the panorama of Spanish fiction at the time, in which themes predominate over character and plot to leave a testimony of the life situation of thirtysomethings in 1978 (pp. 12-19). However, I would agree with Zatlin that *Crónica del desamor* is not a straightforward testimonial text and that it can actually be classed as experimental fiction not only for its groundbreaking content but also its form.[12] Whilst it does have features which lend themselves to the journalistic tag so often ascribed to it, such as the use of vivid description and characterization, it is a self-conscious text, which questions the relationship between fiction and reality through the use of techniques such as narrative commentary and metafictional inflections. Furthermore, through the counterposition of a plurality of female voices in a dialogic mosaic, the multiplicity of possible interpretations of any one representation of reality is emphasized.

Many of the criticisms directed at *Crónica del desamor* allude to the fact that this was Rosa Montero's first novel and therefore stylistically immature. In contrast, Martín Gaite has been publishing narrative since 1954 and *El cuarto de atrás*, which won the Premio Nacional de Literatura in 1978, is her most studied novel. It would seem to be a conscious stylistic experiment in which the fantastic is combined with semi-autobiographical narrative to produce a hybrid text, which defies generic categorizations. It is a blend of sociological document, autobiographical memoir, *novela rosa* (romantic fiction) and fantastic novel (to name but a few of the genres invoked in this highly intertextual text). During the course of the novel, the narrator comments on two projects she has which the reader recognizes as being inextricably meshed together in *El cuarto de atrás*: a social history of women in post-war Spain and a fantastic novel following on from the theoretical work of Todorov.[13] At the beginning of the novel the narrator trips over a copy of Todorov's *Introduction à la littérature fantastique*, quite literally loses her footing and stumbles into another dimension in which distinctions between the real and imaginary are suspended.[14] The fantastic mode allows Martín Gaite to examine various facets of identity, both conscious and subconscious. However, this is not only a narrative of personal identity but a work which gives insights into post-war Spanish society. A variety of discursive practices are incorporated in order to question the authority of official discourses such as history consisting of so-called facts and dates. The project of writing her own contestatory account of her childhood and youth first occurred to Martín Gaite whilst watching Franco's burial in 1975 but, bored by the proliferation of memoirs written at the time, she let the project drop.[15] In *El cuarto de atrás*, the narrator's recollections, which can clearly be identified with Martín Gaite, are merged with the fantastic narrative of the man in black who appears to listen to her. In interviews Martín Gaite remains deliberately vague as to whether or not he is real or a figment of her imagination and goes so far as to say that she still has the golden box he gave her.[16] The main protagonist of *Crónica del desamor*, Ana, has also been consistently identified with Montero herself by critics. Montero herself has stated that, in writing her early novels, she was working out her own problems and setting down her thoughts. In answer to the question of whether her first two novels were autobiographical, she has preferred to term them a biographical cocktail in which real and imaginary ingredients are mixed together until they become indistinguishable from one another.[17] Reality and fiction are thus melded together in both these texts. According to Davies, integration of the personal and the social was a feature of women's writing in Spain in the late 1970s and early 1980s in a process in which the boundaries between fiction, history, biography, and autobiography were dissolved.[18]

Memory and Self

This process is foregrounded in *El cuarto de atrás* where it is particularly easy to confuse the author, Carmen Martín Gaite, with the narrator, C., as many of the memories invoked by the latter clearly incorporate the biographical details of the former. Despite this identification, by not naming the narrator, Martín Gaite distances herself from her, thereby highlighting the fact that experience cannot be represented unproblematically. The self at the centre of autobiography is necessarily a subjective, fictive structure through which identity cannot be fixed. No autobiographical or biographical text is ever complete as experience is mediated through particular discursive practices. A selective and ordering process is applied to the chaotic mass of memories which constitute a lifetime as Martín Gaite explains in her suggestive essay *El cuento de nunca acabar* (*The Never-Ending Story*):

> Everything is definitively a matter of order, of a certain amount of disciplining intuition, of a resignation that it must be converted into something else, in exchange for saving it to a certain extent [...] A stirring from being into non-being. The text has to be a mere reflection of this hidden elaboration. Getting something out of chaos is, clearly, a betrayal of that same chaos. Darkness made light. Life made word.[19]

This transformative process invests past events with a meaning they may not necessarily have had at the time of their occurrence as they are filtered through language and retrospectively recalled from the complex perspective of the present:

> They are not really memoirs, but a reflection upon the tricks memory plays, a meditation on the passing of time and the chaos of memories.[20]

Memories thus do not assert truths but produce meaning for the remembering self. The text highlights the illusory nature of attempting to construct a coherent self as autobiography, fictional or otherwise, is demonstrated to be an act of continual self-invention in which identity is invested with meaning for a particular subject.

If this is to be considered a semi-autobiographical text, the question arises of which memories have been selected for inclusion and which have been omitted? The latter include events traditionally regarded as major passage in a woman's life, such as Martín Gaite's marriage, the birth of her daughter and subsequent separation. Whilst the text does focus primarily on the process of growing up during the Civil War and its aftermath, the memories selected for inclusion are those which are vital to her evolution as a writer. Many refer to texts read ostensibly by the narrator, written by or to be written by Martín Gaite.[21] Particular reference is made to texts written by her as a child such as the romantic novel and Bergai story written with her friend. These texts bring us to the back room of the title which was a permissive physical space in which the young Martín Gaite played before shortages caused by the war meant her parents could not keep the room as her playroom and it was converted into a larder:

> It was very big and within it disorder and freedom prevailed, you could sing at the top of your voice, move the furniture about, jump up and down on a dilapidated sofa with broken springs which we called the poor sofa, lie on the rug, spill ink on it, it was a kingdom where nothing was forbidden.
>
> (CA, p. 187)

As she could no longer physically escape to play, she turned to literature and the imagination through which she could transform reality into an extraordinary world in a 'room of her own' in her mind in which she cultivated her ability, remarked upon several times in the text to 'escape' ('*fugarse*'). Through the narrative process she was able to escape the official, restrictive codes of the regime for women: 'stay, conform and put up with it' (CA, p. 125). The back room is, therefore, also the mental space where creation takes place and memories are stored:

> [It's] a kind of attic which, I think, we all have in the mind, it's separated from the more ordered rooms of memory by a curtain which is only pulled back from time to time. The memories which may surprise us always live in 'the back room'.[22]

Who is responsible for pulling back the curtain for the narrator? None other than the mysterious man in black whose identity ultimately remains a mystery. The answer to this puzzle may perhaps be found in Martín Gaite's essay *La búsqueda del interlocutor* (*Search for an Interlocutor*) and *El cuento del nunca acabar* (*The Never-Ending Story*). He would seem to be the perfect interlocutor whom she has created in order to write. On 27 December 1975 her close friend Gustavo Fabra died; she dedicated *El cuento del nunca acabar* to him and in it recalls their conversations which served as a catalyst for her thoughts about the narrative process.[23] Through a similar dialogic process the man in black helps the narrator to transform the disorder of her memory into text. He is a very well-informed reader of her work and knows the precise question to ask in order to invoke apposite memories.

Male-Female Relationships

The relationship between the narrator and the man in black provides an interesting point of comparison with *Crónica del desamor* in which the feminist academic, Elena, feels that her relationship with Javier stifled her creativity and robbed her of her personal space, 'he burst into her house, robbing her of her space, space in the cupboards, on the desk, space in her existence' (CD, p. 58). There would seem to be a contradiction between women achieving agency and entering into a relationship with a man. As *Crónica del desamor* opens, Ana feels the need to be in a relationship despite her previous negative experiences, particularly with Juan. She admits the difficulty of knowing oneself and living alone. However, as the novel closes, she questions the validity of the conventions, which have trapped her in a series of unsatisfactory relationships culminating in the fling with Soto Amón:

> Now Ana realizes melancholically that she has spent half her life inventing nonexistent loves: and this Soto Amón of her thirties is no more than a new and sophisticated artifice.
>
> (CD, p. 216)

Both Montero and Martín Gaite have addressed the problem of learning to live with solitude. In an interview with *La mujer feminista* (*The Feminist Woman*) Montero states that the fundamental task facing women is to free themselves sentimentally, that is to say from the obligation of having a man at one's side in order to feel a complete person:

> As women we have been educated to be half-people, and that's so deep rooted! You have to work so, so, so hard with both yourself and your surroundings to manage to be a whole person by yourself.[24]

Similarly, in an interview given to Linda Chown in 1980, Martín Gaite notes the importance of solitude not as physical aloneness but as an intense awareness of one's own experience (Chown, p. 231). Whilst the narrator of *El cuarto de atrás* does occasionally resist the man in black's interpretations of her discourse, on the whole their relationship is a positive one. This is perhaps due to the fantastic nature of the encounter which meets Todorov's requirements for a fantastic text: ambiguity and hesitation. The reader is left unsure as to whether what is recounted is a dream experience or actually happened. There are a number of strange occurrences which would suggest the former, particularly the steadily increasing pages of the manuscript which at the end of the text is revealed to be the novel we have just read. However, even after the man in black has vanished, the pillbox he gave the narrator remains and there are two glasses on the table. When the narrator's daughter quizzes her as to the origin of the pillbox, the credibility of her answer, that it was given to her some time ago by a friend, is undermined by her reaction to it. She is left breathless with a buzzing in her ears. Thus the reader's hesitation is shared by the narrator.

The relationship between the narrator and the man in black is unconventional in that, despite there being a great deal of unresolved sexual tension between them, there is no typical romance ending as would be expected in one of the genres invoked in the novel, the romantic novel or *novela rosa*. There are several references to this genre, in particular to the immensely successful *Cristina Guzmán* (1936) by Carmen de Icaza and the romantic novel the narrator herself wrote with a friend at school. Both the 'handsome hero' in it and the man in black appear to be named Alejandro (CA, p. 144) and at various points the latter's relationship with the narrator is described in terms taken from the *novela rosa* with particular reference to two characters named Esperanza and Raimundo, for example when the narrator is scared by the storm (*CA*, p. 38) or just as it would seem that he is about to reveal his identity (*CA*, pp. 140-41). At this point they are interrupted by a phone call from a friend of his named Carola. The ensuing conversation between C. and Carola is of particular interest because it demonstrates how multiple readings may arise from the same text. Whilst both women refer to the popular song genre of coplas as sung by another 'C', Conchita Piquer, in the 1940s and 1950s, they have quite different interpretative strategies.[25] Although they share a common socio-historical, contextual background, Carola seems to be imprisoned by romantic conventions. For the narrator, Piquer is resignified as an emblem of those marginalized women who did not conform to the strictures of the Franco regime. Her songs valued passion in the anaesthetized world of the post-war period, for example 'Tatuaje' ('Tatoo') which:

> [...] came to represent what was most real and tangible through the broken voice of Conchita Piquer. Such a passion was forbidden for the sensible, decent girls of the new Spain.
>
> (*CA*, p. 154)

Bermúdez describes the act of listening to Piquer as an erotic, sensual encounter which can be read as a form of cultural resistance for women expected to conform to the Catholic models of marriage and motherhood.[26] Furthermore, both men and women could identify with the abandoned and betrayed women in songs such as 'Tatuaje' which eliptically evoked the betrayals and losses endured in post-war Spain.

Reader Identification

Crónica del desamor was an extremely successful best-seller which has been reprinted several times. It would seem that readers, particularly women of a similar age and professional position to Montero, certainly identified with the novel. This is borne out in Consuelo de la Gándara's article on images of women in which she describes *Crónica del desamor* as:

> A journalistic novel, written quickly and concisely, it's the typical book you read in one go in a night, but it's also much more. I have some friends of that age [between 20 and 35 years old] who tell me that they see themselves reflected from top to toe in some of the characters in that chronicle.[27]

Likewise Jesús Lucía, the director of Debate who published *Crónica del desamor*, has singled out reader identification as one of the most important factors in the success of Montero's narrative: 'Rosa Montero's success is extraordinary. It is due to the affection her readers feel for her; she has made a connection with them because of the way in which she engages with reality.'[28] Indeed, Montero told interviewer Sergio Vila San Juan that this identification had reached the extent that readers of *Crónica del desamor* wrote to her asking for advice as if she were some sort of agony aunt.[29]

The reader's identification with the characters is explicitly encouraged through the use of narrative commentary. Early on in the narrative, the narrator's sympathies with the women characters are made clear through the insertion of parenthetical commentary and the use of rhetorical questions and interjections for example when the three main characters, Ana, Elena and Candela, visit the gynaecologist together:

> 'How do you put it in? Do you stop the guy and tell him to wait?' (There is something that many gynaecologists have in common: that lack of respect for the individual, the crudeness of men in high places who-see-and-cure fannies.)
>
> (*CD*, p. 29)

> The pill, the IUD, are the woman's problem. She takes them, she suffers. However, the diaphragm is something which affects the couple: Does the man have to break off his foreplay so that she can insert the rubber disc? How awful. Does he sometimes have to use spermicide? What a disaster. The pill or IUD are so comfortable, those methods which men don't suffer...
>
> (*CD*, p. 30)

This interruption into the narrative by the narrator is one of the features that Myers dismisses as obstructing the narrative flow. However, it is used effectively as both a means to elicit the reader's empathy and to foreground issues of power and control within discursive practice. As the novel reaches its conclusion, the main character, Ana, usurps the position of the narrator through the use of similar techniques when narrating the romantic encounter with her boss, Soto Amón, about whom she has fantasized for a year. After spending the night with him, she disappointedly realizes that he is bound by stereotypical modes of behaviour. Whereas he mistakenly assumes that he knows what she wants, 'it's as if I've known you for a long time' (*CD*, p. 269), she recognizes this as nothing more than an empty cliché which she has already heard many times. The layout of this section of narrative describing what happened back at Soto Amón's 'bachelor pad', noting that he has a wife and children, is particularly interesting. Only two lines of dialogue are marked off by conventional linear separation: when they arrive, Soto Amón comments:

> Don't look too closely at the house: it's awful... well you know what I mean.
>
> (*CD*, p. 270)

and, when they leave, Ana says:

> Don't accompany me: I'll grab a cab.
>
> (*CD*, p. 271)

In the space of three paragraphs between these two parallel statements the long-awaited affair with Soto Amón occurs. In the first paragraph, the flat is described by the narrator in a concise, matter-of-fact style. Only one item of speech is included and this is enclosed in parenthesis suggesting Soto Amón's flippancy, 'Are you sure you don't want to?' (*CD*, p. 270), which could apply as much to their fling as to the glass of whisky he is proffering. In the second paragraph, which is entirely enclosed in parenthesis, Ana predicts Soto Amón's every word and move, ironically concluding that what they have done has not meant anything. Presumably it has not signified anything for Soto Amón, but for Ana it is a turning point. In the third paragraph, the narrator's description is punctuated by Ana's commentary in the form of rhetorical questions and interjections inserted parenthetically into the text, and Soto Amón's dialogue which has already been predicted by Ana:

> Well, the pantomime unfolds surprisingly much as she had predicted (what am I doing here with this stranger?), they make love silently without meaning (what an absurd situation, absurd, absurd), the air fills with silences (it's as if I were contemplating myself from outside, so far away from reality, from him, from everything), 'I'm sorry but it's very late for me, we have to go', he says finally (a whole year ending up like this, if only he knew), 'leave it Ana, leave it, the maid who comes every day will tidy it up'.
>
> (*CD*, p. 271)

Ana's first-person commentary not only challenges the narrator's authority to tell her story, but she also manages to silence Soto Amón, the main representative of patriarchal power in the novel by not behaving as he would expect and refusing his offer to accompany her home. This contrasts sharply with the many occasions where women are silenced by men during the course of the novel. Her rebuff leaves him rather perplexed and she finds herself stifling her laughter. It is this liberating step out of character due to her increased self-awareness which inspires her to write the 'chronicle of everyday disenchantment' ('*crónica de desamor cotidiano*') which is Montero's novel.

Resignifying Identity

How then do these texts address the complex issue of resignifying identity outside existing cultural paradigms? Metafiction is used in these self-reflexive texts as a means of consciousness-raising whilst these are not strictly programmatic texts, in that the characters, who are often confused and insecure, are not put forward as role models; the female narrating 'I' of the text, nevertheless, encourages a complex interplay of distanciation, identification and interaction on the part of the female reader. In these life narratives, identity is perceived to be a continual process of self-definition. By focusing on how experience is mediated through discursive practice the novels serve to suggest possible new interpretive strategies for reading not only fiction but also lives. Through techniques such as narrative commentary patriarchal codes are deconstructed and the focus on dialogic communication encourages readers to actively participate in decoding the text. They may then apply a similar deconstructive process to the cultural and social codes governing their own thoughts and behaviour. Furthermore, resistance against the fictions of dominant patriarchal discourse is encouraged by characters taking up the position of writing subject and thus breaking out of the passive silence or stifling codes which would seem to trap women.

By depicting the perspectives of several female protagonists, Montero confronts the reader with a number of fluctuating identities and diverse experiences. To a certain extent this is also the case with the multiple aspects of C. and her relationship with Carola. As a multiplicity of discourses are invoked, identity is revealed to be shifting, fragmentary and even self-contradictory. On the one hand, this would seem to reflect the uncertainty surrounding identity politics during the transition period in Spain in which women found it perhaps easier to negate role models from the past than construct new role models for the future due to the difficulty of constructing an identity for women outside patriarchal paradigms. On the other, it situates these texts as participating in the postmodern project of questioning fixed, stable identities. However, this deconstructive tendency does not exclude the proposition within these texts of provisional collective identities for women based on gender-based commonalities. Both Martín Gaite and Montero show an awareness of how the meaning of the socio-cultural category of Woman, as inscribed in the culturally dominant model of patriarchy, affects the lives of individual women. Furthermore, some sort of collective identity as women would seem enabling, through the formation of communities of mutual support such as that which is formed by Ana and her circle of friends, who frequently meet up with each other to talk, offer advice and sympathy. Despite their initial differences, C. and Carola would also seem to develop empathy for each other as their conversation progresses. It would seem that female-authored metafiction can play a part in bringing about cultural and social change. But in order for change to occur self-knowledge is necessary. It is a sense of heightened self-awareness which finally leads to Ana's decision to write the book of 'all the Anas' (*CD*, p. 9) and the man in black would seem to function as a therapist aiding C. to critically confront her past in order to better inform her writing. For both C. and Ana, the goal and conclusion of their texts are not the man and happy-ever-after marriage of romantic fiction but the impulse to create and construct one's own identity. These texts help promote an awareness of how feminine identity has been constructed in phallologocentric discourse and how it can be deconstructed. This is vital if women are to be able, like C. and Ana, to write beyond the ending of the conventional plots of hegemonic patriarchal discourse to resignify their identity. The complexity of this project continues to be the focus of much feminist debate in Spain. Recent studies focus on the divisive dichotomy drawn between equality and difference feminism, which led to the disintegration of the mass movement in the 1980s.[30] Nonetheless, it is important to state that the feminist struggle continues in Spain, despite attempts by the media to portray it as an old-fashioned anachronism in a supposedly post-feminist age. Large numbers of women still attend the general meetings called by the movement and smaller networks of groups are flourishing. The general meeting of feminists in Madrid, held on the 4-6 December 1993, was attended by some 3,000 women from groups as distinct as the Transexual Collective (*Colectivo Transexualia*) and the Christian Women of Logroño (*Mujeres Cristianas de Logroño*) whose motto was 'One for all and all for one' (*Juntas y a por todas*), implying solidarity through diversity. Their closing statement emphatically denied the collapse of feminism in Spain, 'In the light of the crowing about the crisis in feminism, we would like to state that it is not dead'.[31]

Indeed, the Belgian delegate, Françoise Collin, was astounded by the strength of the movement in Spain as compared to other European countries. The work of best-selling writers such as Martín Gaite and Montero can be seen as one of the strengths of the Spanish feminist movement. Their novels bring issues concerning identity politics to the attention of a mass readership in a country where on the one hand, relatively few women belong to feminist organizations, but on the other, they seem to positively value the achievements of the movement. The work of young women writers such as Lucía Etxebarría, who confidently proclaim their feminist stance, would suggest that the issues engaged with by Martín Gaite and Montero at the close of the 1970s remain topical as Spain moves into the new millennium. Despite legal provisions for change it would seem that the damaging substructures of patriarchy indicted in *El cuarto de atrás* and *Crónica del desamor* are still in place in the late 1990s. The promotional leaflet for Etxebarría's first novel, *Amor, curiosidad, prozac y dudas* (*Love, Curiosity, Prozac and Doubts*), published in 1997, combines synopses with three pages of statistics related to a variety of topical women's issues, including discrimination relating to literary studies and academic recognition, stereotypical portrayals of women in advertising and the mass media, sexual discrimination in the workplace, anorexia and bulimia, post-natal depression, sexual abuse and rape, under the title 'la realidad supera la ficción' (fact is stranger than fiction). Her female characters/narrators in *Amor, curiosidad, prozac y dudas* and *Beatriz y los cuerpos celestes* (*Beatrice and the Heavenly Bodies*), published in 1998, carry on the search for alternative configurations of identity through the interrogation of past and present models which continue to circumscribe women, both in the private sphere of relationships and the public sphere of work.

References

1   The Constitution has been criticized for not going far enough, because it was a text born of consensus, a consensus from which women were excluded as none were involved in elaborating the first draft, and for actually being discriminatory in some aspects such as the privileging of male accession to the throne.

2   Quotations from *El cuarto de atrás* will be denoted as *CA* and from *Crónica del desamor* by *CD*. All translations are the author's own.

3   See Amelia Valcárcel, *Sexo y filosofía: Sobre 'mujer' y 'poder'* (Barcelona: Anthropos, 1991) and *El concepto de la identidad* (Madrid: Pablo Iglesias, 1994). See also Rosa Mª Rodríguez Magda, 'De la modernidad olvidadiza a la usurpación postmoderna', *Canelobre*, 23-24 (1992), 53-63 and 'Por un feminismo transmoderno', in Federación de Organizaciones Feministas del Estado Español, *Juntas y a por Todas: Jornadas Feministas* (Madrid: Comunidad de Madrid, Dirección General de la Mujer, 1994), 303-12.

4   Phyllis Zatlin, 'The Contemporary Spanish Metanovel', *Denver Quarterly*, 17: 3 (1982), 63-73; Robert Spires, *Beyond the Metafictional Mode: Directions in the Modern Spanish Novel* (Lexington: University of Kentucky Press, 1984). The literature available on metafiction is extensive. For an overview, see Patricia Waugh, *Metafiction: The Theory and Practice of Self-Conscious Fiction* (London: Methuen, 1984) and Linda Hutcheon, *Narcissistic Narrative: The Metafictional Paradox* (London: Methuen, 1984).

5   Spires, p. 128. The stringent censorship laws of the old regime were revoked on 31 December 1978.

6   Phyllis Zatlin, 'Women Novelists in Democratic Spain: Freedom to Express the Female Perspective', *Anales de la Literatura Española Contemporánea*, 12 (1987), 29-44; Concha Alborg, 'Metaficción y feminismo en Rosa Montero', *Revista de Estudios Hispánicos*, 22 (1988), 67-76.

7   The most important exception to this is Antonia, Elena and Candela's mother. Through Candela's
      memories and daydreams (*CD*, p. 226), it becomes evident that Antonia resisted the role of dutiful wife
      and mother that was imposed upon her. For example, she secretly used contraception (*CD*, pp. 30-31).

8   Isabel Romero, Isabel Alberdi, Isabel Martínez and Ruth Zauner, 'Feminismo y literatura: la narrativa de
      los años 70', in *Literatura y vida cotidiana: Actas de las cuartas jornadas de investigación interdisciplinaria del
      Seminario de Estudios de la Mujer de la Universidad Autónoma de Madrid*, ed. by María Ángeles Durán and
      José Antonio Rey (Zaragoza: Prensas Universitarias de la Universidad Autónoma de Madrid y la
      Universidad de Zaragoza, 1987), pp. 337-57, p. 341.

9   The journalists include Neus Aguado, Lidia Falcón, Cristina Fernández Cubas, Carmen Rico Godoy and
      Montserrat Roig; the literary critics Aurora de Albornoz, Marina Mayoral, Lourdes Ortiz, Rosa María
      Pereda and Soledad Puértolas and the lecturers Albornoz, Mayoral and Carme Riera.

10   See Emilio de Miguel Martínez, *La primera narrativa de Rosa Montero* (Salamanca: Salamanca University,
      1983); Eunice D. Myers, 'The Feminist Message: Propaganda and/or Art? A Study of Two Novels by
      Rosa Montero', in *Feminine Concerns in Contemporary Spanish Fiction by Women*, ed. by Roberto Manteiga,
      Carolyn Galerstein and Kathleen McNerney (Potomac: Scripta Humanistica, 1988), pp. 99-112.

11   Catherine Davies, *Contemporary Feminist Fiction in Spain: The Work of Montserrat Roig and Rosa Montero*
      (Oxford: Berg, New Directions in European Writing, 1994), p. 101.

12   Phyllis Zatlin, 'The Novels of Rosa Montero as Experimental Fiction', *Monographic Review/Revista
      Monográfica*, 8 (1992), ['Experimental Fiction by Hispanic Women Writers'], 114-24.

13   These projects were later written by Martín Gaite as separate texts: *Usos amorosos de la postguerra española*
      (1987) and the fantastic novels *El castillo de las tres murallas* (1981) and *El pastel del diablo* (1985).

14   The novel is dedicated to Lewis Carroll. On oneiric intertextualities in *El cuarto de atrás*, see Mirella
      d'Ambrosio Servodidio in *From Fiction to Metafiction: Essays in Honour of Carmen Martín Gaite*, ed. by
      Mirella d' Ambrosio Servodidio and Marcia L. Welles (Lincoln, Nebraska: Society of Spanish and Spanish
      American Studies, 1982).

15   Kathleen M. Glenn, 'Martín Gaite, Todorov, and the Fantastic', in *The Scope of the Fantastic – Theory,
      Technique, Major Authors: Selected Essays from the First International Conference on the Fantastic in Literature
      and Film*, ed. by Robert A. Collins and Howard D. Pearce (Connecticut: Greenwood Press, 1985), pp. 165-
      72, p. 165.

16   Marie-Lise Gazarian Gautier, *Interviews with Spanish Women Writers* (Elmwood Park: Dalkey Archive
      Press, 1991), 175-81, pp. 177-78.

17   Lynn Talbot, 'Entrevista con Rosa Montero', *Letras femeninas*, 14 (1988), p. 93. Women's writing is often
      criticized as being too autobiographical. The use of this label as a derogatory accusation by male critics in
      Spain when reviewing Montero's early novels is discussed by Montserrat Roig, 'La mirada de Rosa
      Montero', *Círculo*, 2 (1988), 26-28, p. 28.

18   Catherine Davies, 'Women Writers in Spain since 1900: From Political Strategy to Personal Inquiry', in
      Textual Liberation: European Feminist Writing in the Twentieth Century, ed. by Helena Forsås-Scott (London:
      Routledge, 1991), pp. 192-226, p. 215. See also Jean Chittenden's discussion of *El cuarto de atrás* as
      fictional autobiography, '*El cuarto de atrás* as Autobiography', *Letras Femeninas*, 12 (1986), 78-84.

19   *El cuento de nunca acabar: Apuntes sobre la narración, el amor y la mentira* (Barcelona: Destinolibro, 1985), p. 26.

20   Jorge A. Marfil, 'Carmen Martín Gaite: La narración incesante', *El Viejo Topo*, 19 April 1978, pp. 62-64, p.
      64.

21   These include fairy tales such as Little Red Riding Hood, Puss in Boots, Bluebeard and Tom Thumb;
      children's literature such as Alice in Wonderland, Robinson Crusoe and the stories of Antoniorrobles; the

detective fiction of Dashiell Hammett; romantic novels by Carmen de Icaza and Elisabeth Mulder; the 'high' literary texts of Ruben Darió, Kafka and Cervantes; popular song genres such as Portuguese fados, Latin American boleros and the coplas of Conchita Piquer and Hollywood cinema, for example the films of Deanna Durbin.

22 Cited by Javier La Cruz Pardo, 'En *El cuarto de atrás* se va viendo mi concepción del amor', *Nueva*, 6 August 1978, p. 16.

23 Linda Chown, *The Teller in the Tale: The Eye's I in Four Novels by Doris Lessing and Carmen Martín Gaite* (Seattle: University of Washington, 1986), p. 41.

24 *La mujer feminista*, 'Rosa Montero. Nunca pensé casarme', 21 (1985), 7-10, p. 9.

25 On the possible subversiveness of popular romance, see Helen Graham, 'Popular Culture in the Years of Hunger', in *Spanish Cultural Studies: An Introduction*, ed. by Helen Graham and Jo Labanyi (Oxford: Oxford University Press, 1995), pp. 237-45 and Stephanie Sieburth, 'La cultura popular en la novela, de Cervantes a Puig: Ideología y recepción', in *Ensayos de literatura europea y hispanoamericana*, ed. by Félix Menchacatorre (San Sebastián: Universidad del País Vasco, 1990), pp. 543-48, p. 547.

26 Silvia Bermúdez, '"Music to My Ears": *Cuplés*, Conchita Piquer and the (Un)making of Spanish Nationalism', *SigloXX/Twentieth Century*, 15: 1-2 (1997), 33-54, p. 37.

27 Consuelo de la Gándara, 'La imagen de la mujer a través de la novela española contemporánea', in *La mujer en el mundo contemporáneo*, ed. by María Ángeles Durán (Madrid: Universidad Autónoma de Madrid, Seminario de Estudios de la Mujer, 1981), pp. 131-54, p. 152.

28 Miguel Ángel del Arco, 'Así se fabrica un best seller: Los cazatalentos de las editoras dan con un filón de novelistas rentables', *Tiempo*, 316 (1988), 156-63, p. 160.

29 Sergio Vila San-Juan, 'Rosa Montero: "No existe una *mafia violeta*"', *El Correo Catalán*, 2 April 1981, [supplied by R. Montero, no page number]).

30 Amelia Valcárcel, *Sexo y filosofía: Sobre 'mujer' y 'poder'* (Barcelona: Anthropos, 1991), pp. 52-53; Juana María Gil Ruiz, *La política de la igualdad en España: Avance y retrocesos* (Granada: Universidad de Granada, 1996), pp. 286-94.

31 Rosa Rivas, 'El nuevo feminismo salta al ruedo', *El País*, 7 December 1993, p. 24.

Bibliography

Alborg, Concha, 'Metaficción y feminismo en Rosa Montero', *Revista de Estudios Hispánicos*, 22 (1988), 67-76.

Ambrosio Servodidio, Mirella d' and Marcia L. Welles (eds), *From Fiction to Metafiction: Essays in Honour of Carmen Martín Gaite* (Lincoln, Nebraska: Society of Spanish and Spanish American Studies, 1982).

Arco, Miguel Ángel del, 'Así se fabrica un best seller: Los cazatalentos de las editoras dan con un filón de novelistas rentables', *Tiempo*, 316 (1988), 156-63.

Bermúdez, Silvia, '"Music to My Ears": *Cuplés*, Conchita Piquer and the (Un)making of Spanish Nationalism', *SigloXX/Twentieth Century*, 15: 1-2 (1997), 33-54.

Chittenden, Jean S., '*El cuarto de atrás* as Autobiography', *Letras Femeninas*, 12 (1986), 78-84.

Chown, Linda, *The Teller in the Tale: The Eye's I in Four Novels by Doris Lessing and Carmen Martín Gaite* (Seattle: University of Washington, 1986).

Davies, Catherine, 'Women Writers in Spain since 1900: From Political Strategy to Personal Inquiry', in *Textual Liberation: European Feminist Writing in the Twentieth Century*, ed. by Helena Forsås-Scott (London: Routledge, 1991), pp. 192-226.

————, *Contemporary Feminist Fiction in Spain: The Work of Montserrat Roig and Rosa Montero* (Oxford: Berg, New Directions in European Writing, 1994).

Gándara, Consuelo de la, 'La imagen de la mujer a través de la novela española contemporánea', in *La mujer en el mundo contemporáneo*, ed. by María Ángeles Durán (Madrid: Universidad Autónoma de Madrid, Seminario de Estudios de la Mujer, 1981), pp. 131-54.

Gazarian Gautier, Marie-Lise, *Interviews with Spanish Women Writers* (Elmwood Park: Dalkey Archive Press, 1991), pp. 175-81.

Gil Ruiz, Juana María, *La política de la igualdad en España: Avance y retrocesos* (Granada: Universidad de Granada, 1996).

Glenn, Kathleen M., 'Martín Gaite, Todorov, and the Fantastic', in *The Scope of the Fantastic – Theory, Technique, Major Authors: Selected Essays from the First International Conference on the Fantastic in Literature and Film*, ed. by Robert A. Collins and Howard D. Pearce (Connecticut: Greenwood Press, 1985), pp. 165-72.

Graham, Helen, 'Popular Culture in the Years of Hunger', in *Spanish Cultural Studies: An Introduction*, ed. by Helen Graham and Jo Labanyi (Oxford: Oxford University Press, 1995), pp. 237-45.

Hutcheon, Linda, *Narcissistic Narrative: The Metafictional Paradox* (London: Methuen, 1984).

La Cruz Pardo, Javier, 'En *El cuarto de atrás* se va viendo mi concepción del amor', *Nueva*, 6 August 1978, p. 16.

Marfil, Jorge A, 'Carmen Martín Gaite: La narración incesante', *El Viejo Topo*, 19 April 1978, pp. 62-64.

Martín Gaite, Carmen, *La búsqueda del interlocutor y otras búsquedas* (Barcelona: Destinolibro, 1973).

————, *El cuento de nunca acabar: Apuntes sobre la narración, el amor y la mentira* (Barcelona: Destinolibro, 1985).

————, *El cuarto de atrás* (Barcelona: Destinolibro, 1992 [1978]).

Miguel Martínez, Emilio de, *La primera narrativa de Rosa Montero* (Salamanca: Salamanca University, 1983).

Montero, Rosa, *Crónica del desamor* (Madrid: Debate, 1979).

La mujer feminista, 'Rosa Montero. Nunca pensé casarme', 21 (1985), 7-10.

Myers, Eunice D., 'The Feminist Message: Propaganda and/or Art? A Study of Two Novels by Rosa Montero', in *Feminine Concerns in Contemporary Spanish Fiction by Women*, ed. by Roberto Manteiga, Carolyn Galerstein and Kathleen McNerney (Potomac: Scripta Humanistica, 1988), pp. 99-112.

Rivas, Rosa, 'El nuevo feminismo salta al ruedo', *El País*, 7 December 1993, p. 24.

Rodríguez Magda, Rosa Mª, 'De la modernidad olvidadiza a la usurpación postmoderna', *Canelobre*, 23-24 (1992), 53-63.

————, 'Por un feminismo transmoderno', in Federación de Organizaciones Feministas del Estado Español, *Juntas y a por Todas: Jornadas Feministas* (Madrid: Comunidad de Madrid, Dirección General de la Mujer, 1994), pp. 303-12.

Roig, Montserrat, 'La mirada de Rosa Montero', *Círculo*, 2 (1988), 26-28.

Romero, Isabel, Isabel Alberdi, Isabel Martínez and Ruth Zauner, 'Feminismo y literatura: la narrativa de los años 70', in *Literatura y vida cotidiana: Actas de las cuartas jornadas de investigación interdisciplinaria del Seminario de Estudios de la Mujer de la Universidad Autónoma de Madrid*, ed. by María Ángeles Durán and José Antonio Rey (Zaragoza: Prensas Universitarias de la Universidad Autónoma de Madrid y la Universidad de Zaragoza, 1987), pp. 37-58.

Sieburth, Stephanie, 'La cultura popular en la novela, de Cervantes a Puig: Ideología y recepción', in *Ensayos de literatura europea y hispanoamericana*, ed. by Félix Menchacatorre (San Sebastián: Universidad del País Vasco, 1990), pp. 543-48.

Spires, Robert, *Beyond the Metafictional Mode: Directions in the Modern Spanish Novel* (Lexington: University of Kentucky Press, 1984).

Talbot, Lynn, 'Entrevista con Rosa Montero', *Letras Femeninas*, 14 (1988), 90-96.

Valcárcel, Amelia, *Sexo y filosofía: Sobre 'mujer' y 'poder'* (Barcelona: Anthropos, 1991).

————, *El concepto de la identidad* (Madrid: Pablo Iglesias, 1994).

Vila San-Juan, Sergio, 'Rosa Montero: «No existe una "mafia violeta"»', *El Correo Catalán*, 2 April 1981, [supplied by R. Montero, no page number]).

Waugh, Patricia, *Metafiction: The Theory and Practice of Self-Conscious Fiction* (London: Methuen, 1984).

Zatlin, Phyllis, 'The Contemporary Spanish Metanovel', *Denver Quarterly*, 17: 3 (1982), 63-73.

————, 'Women Novelists in Democratic Spain: Freedom to Express the Female Perspective', *Anales de la Literatura Española Contemporánea*, 12 (1987), 29-44.

————, 'The Novels of Rosa Montero as Experimental Fiction', *Monographic Review /Revista Monográfica*, 8 ['Experimental Fiction by Hispanic Women Writers']), (1992), 114-24.